UNSETTLING DIFFERENCE

signale
modern german letters, cultures, and thought

Series Editor: Paul Fleming, Cornell University
Peter Uwe Hohendahl, Founding Editor

Signale: Modern German Letters, Cultures, and Thought publishes new English language books in literary studies, criticism, cultural studies, and intellectual history pertaining to the German-speaking world, as well as translations of important German-language works. Signale construes "modern" in the broadest terms: the series covers topics ranging from the early modern period to the present. Signale books are published under a joint imprint of Cornell University Press and Cornell University Library. Please see http://signale.cornell.edu/.

Unsettling Difference

Music Drama, the Bible, and the Critique of German Jewish Identity

Adi Nester

A Signale Book

Cornell University Press and Cornell University Library
Ithaca and London

Cornell University Press and Cornell University Library gratefully acknowledge the College of Arts & Sciences, Cornell University, for support of the Signale series.

Copyright © 2024 by Adi Nester

All rights reserved. Except for brief quotations in a review, this book, or parts thereof, must not be reproduced in any form without permission in writing from the publisher. For information, address Cornell University Press, Sage House, 512 East State Street, Ithaca, New York 14850.

First published 2024 by Cornell University Press and Cornell University Library

Library of Congress Cataloging-in-Publication Data

Names: Nester, Adi, 1984– author.
Title: Unsettling difference : music drama, the Bible, and the critique of German Jewish identity / Adi Nester.
Description: Ithaca : Cornell University Press, 2024. | Series: Signale: modern German letters, cultures, and thought | Includes bibliographical references and index.
Identifiers: LCCN 2024020251 (print) | LCCN 2024020252 (ebook) | ISBN 9781501779671 (hardcover) | ISBN 9781501779688 (paperback) | ISBN 9781501779701 (epub) | ISBN 9781501779695 (pdf)
Subjects: LCSH: Bible—Influence. | Jews—Germany—Identity—History—20th century. | Jews—Germany—Civilization—History—20th century.
Classification: LCC DS134.25 .N47 2024 (print) | LCC DS134.25 (ebook) | DDC 943/.00492400904—dc23/eng/20240807
LC record available at https://lccn.loc.gov/2024020251
LC ebook record available at https://lccn.loc.gov/2024020252

For Michal Amir,
And the blessed memory of Tzion Amir and Esther
and Mordechai Ben Michael
My grandparents, my teachers

Contents

Acknowledgments	ix
Note on Translation	xii
Introduction: On Jewish Difference, the Bible, and the Great Artwork	1
1. Rudolf Borchardt's *Das Buch Joram* and the Restoration of a Biblical Language	35
2. Opening the Work: The German Oratorio and Paul Ben-Haim's *Joram*	76
3. Moses and Aron Representing the People	119
4. On Being Superfluous: Integration and Excess in Joseph Roth's *Hiob*	167
5. Inorganic Quotations: Revisiting Assimilation with Eric Zeisl's *Hiob*	204

Afterword: Identity and Difference beyond Dialectics   248

Bibliography   261

Index   275

Acknowledgments

Work on this book would not have been possible without the help of numerous individuals and institutions who supported me throughout the book's various stages. I would like to thank Cornell University Press and the Signale: Modern German Letters, Cultures, and Thought series for offering my book an ideal home. I am grateful to Paul Fleming, Kizer Walker, and Mahinder Kingra at Cornell for walking me through the publication process with kindness and patience, and for making this book a reality. A great thanks to Nicholas Jones for his help in preparing the final version of the manuscript for publication.

I am deeply grateful for the guidance I received from mentors and colleagues whose insightful comments helped shape the book and bring it to its present state. Thank you to my teachers, Helmut Müller-Sievers, who helped me conceptualize this book early on and continued to offer guidance and support throughout the final stages of manuscript preparation, and to Patrick Greaney, Elias Sacks,

David Shneer z"l, and Davide Stimilli for offering valuable advice during the first stages of writing. Their words still resonated in my mind as I was finalizing the book. I have greatly benefited from the advice and encouragement of Leslie Adelson, David Biale, Abigail Gillman, Olga Litvak, Ernst Osterkamp, Michael Steinberg, and Kirk Wetters. Thank you also to Ruth HaCohen, who was the first to evoke in me the passion for studying and writing about the link between music, politics, and religion.

I feel incredibly fortunate to have such generous and supportive colleagues at the University of North Carolina, Chapel Hill, and at Duke University. Thank you to my chairs, Eric Downing and Richard Langston, for their unwavering support as I was acclimating to life at UNC while working to finish the book, and to Ruth von Bernuth, for her careful reading and advice on large sections of the manuscript. A special thank-you to Kata Gellen for the wonderfully productive exchange on Joseph Roth, our mutual research interest. For their mentorship and friendship, I am also thankful to Pricilla Layne, Aleksandra Prica, Eliza Rose, and Gabriel Trop. During the work on this book, I also had the opportunity to teach a graduate seminar on Wagner's legacy in the twentieth century. I owe a special debt to my graduate students in this course for allowing me to work through some of the main theoretical questions of the book with them.

The assistance I received in libraries and archives throughout my writing process has been invaluable. I am grateful to the staff at the National Library of Israel in Jerusalem for their help in locating materials on Paul Ben-Haim, and to the staff at UCLA Special Collections Library for making available materials from the Eric Zeisl Collection. I am also grateful to Eike Fess at the Arnold Schoenberg Center in Vienna for his help in locating the most obscure sketches in Schoenberg's manuscripts, and to Lawrence Schoenberg at Belmont Music Publishers for the permission to reproduce them in this book. My deepest gratitude goes to Barbara Zeisl Schoenberg, who first introduced me to the beautiful music of her father, Eric Zeisl, many years ago, when I was still a music student at the University of Southern California. I am so grateful to Barbara and her husband, Ronald Schoenberg, for inviting me to their home in Brentwood,

California, for *Sachertorte* and *Kaffee mit Schlag*. If it were not for that visit, this book would probably never have been written. Barbara has been tremendously helpful in providing essential materials on Eric Zeisl. I also thank her for the permission to reproduce these materials in the book.

To my dear friends on three different continents and to my family: my parents, Rachel and Simoni Ben Michael, for always instilling confidence in me and providing an incredible model of hard work and dedication, I am forever grateful for your love and support on this long path. Most importantly, to Daniel Nester, my soulmate and partner in crime: for the countless hours of listening to me hashing and rehashing theories and arguments; for patiently and diligently reading every single word of this book throughout all of its iterations and for offering thoughtful comments, words of encouragements, as well as for challenging me on some of its points; for generously taking over "life chores" to allow me to stay in my chair and write; and for your unrivaled Finale skills and the time dedicated to the careful and meticulous transcription of all musical examples in this book, I am filled with love and appreciation.

Last but not least, to Nudnik Nester, resident fluffball and pup master supreme, thank you for reminding me who is really in charge and for putting everything in the right perspective. You are the bestest boy!

An earlier version of chapter 1 appeared under the title "'Eine ungeheure Epopöe unseres eigenen': Language and the Hebrew Bible in Rudolf Borchardt's *Das Buch Joram*," *The Germanic Review: Literature, Culture, Theory* 94, no.1 (2019): 16–38, Taylor & Francis Ltd, http://www.tandfonline.com. Chapter 3 updates and expands on ideas from "The End of Abstraction and the Beginning of the People: On Law and Representation in Arnold Schoenberg's Moses und Aron," *The German Quarterly* 93, no.1 (2020): 19–36. Copyright © 2020, American Association of Teachers of German.

Note on Translation

Where known English translations were available, I provided them without the German source (with few exceptions, including literary texts and libretti). Otherwise, translations from the German are my own and appear alongside the German source.

Unsettling Difference

Introduction

On Jewish Difference, the Bible, and the Great Artwork

The artistic and intellectual output of modern German-speaking Jewry confronts its scholarship with an intricate conundrum. As Scott Spector observes, it is, on the one hand, impossible to deny the vast and profound impact that German Jewish art and thought had on modern European culture. On the other hand, scholars who come to study this impact often "encounter a stumbling block when seeking to discuss these creative contributions as manifestations of European Jewish culture."[1] An unequivocal answer to the question "what distinguishes a German work as Jewish?" demands a clear notion of the difference between these two categories, "German" and "Jewish," one which proves to be difficult to pinpoint. The distinguishing problematic of German Jewish culture relies on an equally elusive notion of German Jewish identity, which, although

---

1. Scott Spector, *Modernism without Jews? German-Jewish Subjects and Histories* (Bloomington: Indiana University Press, 2017), ix.

increasingly attracting more and more criticism for its limitations and obfuscations, refuses to vacate the landscapes of German Jewish scholarship altogether.

This book contemplates the compound "German Jewish identity" and its underlying conception of difference between the categories "German" and "Jewish" after Wagner. The coordinates "after Wagner" here are first and foremost an indication of the undeniable aesthetic nature this conception of difference acquired in the twentieth century alongside its racialized and ultimately destructive manifestations. For the phrase German Jewish identity to have the coherence that the word "identity" commands, a stable and clearcut difference would need to exist between its two terms.[2] Yet this book argues that the difference between the German and the Jewish (henceforth Jewish difference) is unsettled; it is simultaneously present and absent, or rather, a difference set in motion. While the polarized use of the categories German and Jewish may have been radicalized after Wagner, responses to this radicalization from the first decades of the twentieth century often emphasized the ambiguity and fluidity of Jewish difference, especially in light of repeated attempts to dominate, contain, and disambiguate it. It is this insistence upon the ambiguous and unstable nature of Jewish difference that this book places at the forefront as it argues for an unsettled difference that makes conceptualizing a "German Jewish identity" all but impossible.

Unsettling Difference probes the question of Jewish difference by examining three biblical-themed musical dramas and the literary texts they are based on, all written and composed during the first half of the twentieth century. The book leans on two fields of discourse that have historically shaped conceptions of Jewish difference in the German-speaking space: the first discourse concerns the role of the Bible in modernity, while the second concerns the political implications of what many cultural theorists in the early twentieth

---

2. See border and hyphen theories elaborated in diaspora studies, for example, Avtar Brah, *Cartographies of Diaspora: Contesting Identities* (New York: Routledge, 1996); and Sudesh Mishra, *Diaspora Criticism* (Edinburgh: Edinburgh University Press, 2006).

century termed "the great artwork," a concept that after Richard Wagner's intervention in the history of opera became inextricably bound up with the issue of drama set to music.

Modernity and Jewish difference—two terms whose use I limit in this book to the confines of German-speaking Europe—emerged as intertwined problems through a discourse on Bible translation and interpretation that became prominent during the eighteenth century, a time where conversations about Jewish integration within German-speaking lands began to take place. The Bible discourse outlined the parameters for inclusion and exclusion in modernity while serving as the foundation upon which the "German" and the "Jewish" consolidated as two mutually defining categories. It thereby ensured that modernity's own fundamental problematic, namely, the tension between values of newness, progress, and universality on one hand and the continued engagement with what was deemed historical, archaic, and superseded on the other, would characterize the question of Jewish difference as well. Through a Christian-tinted lens, Jewish difference appeared as a persistent anachronism that was nevertheless indispensable to modernity. Many of the debates about the status of the Hebrew Bible and its rendering in German are troubled and traversed by this tension. It is no coincidence, then, that discussions about Jewish integration into German-speaking society emerged concomitantly with debates about Bible translation and interpretation. The problems that defined both areas were similar. As one ventured to convey the significance of a theologically laden, archaic document such as the Hebrew Bible to a European modernity that at least outwardly presented itself as secular and new, having superseded its oriental past, so did the other endeavor to articulate the place of a "superseded" people in that same modernity, whose claim to universality was perpetually challenged by the persistence of Jewish difference.

It was only in post-Wagnerian modernism, however, that conscious critical reflection on the inner tension defining both modernity and its accompanying "problem" of Jewish difference gained significant traction. To better understand this tension, *Unsettling Difference* turns its attention to modernist works and their surrounding critical debates that offer insight into the intricacies of

Jewish difference and its embeddedness in the problem of modernity.[3] This book positions more familiar modernist works such as Arnold Schoenberg's unfinished opera *Moses und Aron* (*Moses and Aaron*, 1932–1951) and Joseph Roth's novel *Hiob* (*Job*, 1930) next to works whose critical contribution has been previously understudied. These include Rudolf Borchardt's epic poem *Das Buch Joram* (*The Book of Joram*, 1905) and its musical rendition, the oratorio *Joram* (1932) by the composer Paul Ben-Haim, as well as the operatic rendition of Roth's *Hiob* (1939–1957) by the composer Eric Zeisl.

This book does not aim to map an entire field or present a comprehensive examination of the modernist use of biblical materials in literary and musical works; rather, it offers intellectually and historically contextualized readings of select works that demonstrate the aesthetic and theoretical concerns entangled within the question of Jewish difference in German-speaking Europe. The works selected for this study allow us to trace the confluence of the two discourses on the roles of the Bible and the "great artwork" (read: music drama) in modernity and see how they guided modernist debates that link the "problems" of Jewish difference and modernity. Tracing this confluence emphasizes the shared problematic of all such debates, which takes the shape of contending with what has been rendered historically superseded and its stubborn persistence within the foundational structures of an only seemingly homogeneous and universal modernity.

In his book *Judaism Musical and Unmusical*, Michael Steinberg considers the musical inflection of Jewishness in the central European context. For Steinberg, music's repute as a nonsignifying art carries a suspicion of representation and image making. Music's implicit critique of representation is, as he notes, a critique of "old-regime

---

3. My understanding of this internal conflict in modernity leans on the secularization debate involving figures like Max Weber, Carl Schmitt, Karl Löwith, and Hans Blumenberg. The debate posited the persistence of sacral elements in the "secularized" structures of modernity and was therefore bound to a troubled assessment of the status and legitimacy of the modern age. For an insightful discussion of this debate and its coalescence with the "Jewish question" see Spector, *Modernism without Jews?*, 40–51.

power," of the visual, idolatrous power of images.[4] With its suspicion of representation, music is likewise poised to serve as a means toward a critique of identity since identity equally postulates a capacity to be *rendered*, that is, substituted by an image or sign.

Understanding the musicality of Jewishness as a critical rebuttal of the totalities of identity, Steinberg is careful not to identify Jewishness with a position of minority and renunciation of sovereignty, for such unequivocal confinement of Jewishness or music to marginality would itself be an absolute rejoinder to the absolutism of identity. The musicality of Jewishness indeed responds to studies that propose considering the German Jewish condition through the prism of diaspora studies and argue that the German Jewish experience presents a model form of marginality that resists easy categorization or reduction to a single principle.[5] Yet it is exactly the assumption that such fluidity has a model—exactly the understanding of the German Jewish condition as a source for the diasporic paradigm—that negates its own efforts to remain untethered to rigid categorization.[6]

By associating Jewishness with musicality, Steinberg acknowledges that positioning Jewish marginality as the total opposite of identity reintroduces the rigid categorization a critique of identity is meant to dismantle. Steinberg accordingly observes that musicality itself implies the power of self-critique. It contains an "unmusical" element within, which calls attention to music's own complicity with and susceptibility to the lures of representation. Though he does not state so explicitly, Steinberg approximates the philosopher Theodor W. Adorno's view on music and representation here by theorizing the musical, which is also partly unmusical, as an impure category. Musicality is both a critique of and a partaking in representation and identity.

---

4. Michael P. Steinberg, *Judaism Musical and Unmusical* (Chicago: University of Chicago Press, 2007), 8. See also Steinberg, *Listening to Reason: Culture, Subjectivity and Nineteenth-Century Music* (Princeton, NJ: Princeton University Press, 2004).

5. See for example Samuel Moyn, "German Jewry and the Question of Identity: Historiography and Theory," *The Leo Baeck Institute Yearbook* 41, no. 1 (1994): 291–308.

6. On the problem of associating Jewishness with an "ideal experience" of diaspora, see James Clifford, "Diasporas," *Cultural Anthropology* 9, no. 3 (1994): 302–38.

Steinberg's understanding of musicality and Jewishness invites us to contemplate the expressions of an impure, irrepresentable, and unsettled Jewish difference, which is partnered in this book with an equally impure and irrepresentable notion of "Germanness." But alongside the abstractions of aesthetics, music also plays a specific and concrete role in the present study. It is through musical-dramatic forms like the opera and the oratorio that these discussions acquire additional heft. For if we understand modernity as a vexed relationship between newness and an undeniable entanglement with the historical and superseded "old," then the drama set to music becomes the definitive aesthetic form embodying this relationship.

The birth of opera at the turn of the seventeenth century is often associated with the advent of modern music. It marked the transition from austere, convoluted, archaic polyphony into a new, monodic style replacing the multiple voices of counterpoint with a single melodic singing line. This transition complemented epochal changes like the emergence of modern science and the rise of modern subjectivity. Yet opera's vaunted novelty was never pure. Its "modern" attribute was facilitated by a speculative act of *re*composition. While it opened the gates of modernity in the musical realm, opera also first came about as an attempt to reconstruct the musical-dramatic art form of antiquity, Greek tragedy. The operas and oratorios I discuss in this book are caught in this predicament of a musical modernity that emerged through a reconstruction of an archaic art form. Each of the works I explore prompts a conscious deliberation on its own historical situatedness as a drama set to music and on its imputed political power as a modern rendering of Greek tragedy, the great *collective* artwork of antiquity.

After Wagner, the problem of opera and modernity became explicitly tied to the issue of Jewish difference as the German composer tethered his own revival of the Greek collective artwork to a German collective that was defined against a Jewish foil. In works like Schoenberg's *Moses und Aron*, the political nature of the collective artwork is revisited through the opera's link between questions of aesthetic and political representation, as chapter 3 in this book illustrates. These are brought to bear on Wagnerian claims concerning Jewish difference and the collective artwork not only through Schoenberg's self-imagining as Wagner's successor but also through the opera's return to the founding moment of the Jewish people. But even works that do not explicitly respond to Wagner, like Ben-Haim's oratorio *Joram*, can be read as intervening in the debate concerning Jewish difference and collective artworks, as chapter 2 demonstrates. Evoking the history of the oratorio in this chapter as a musical-dramatic form bent on unsettling boundaries between different communities of faith undermines the clear boundaries that Wagner's music drama sought to delineate around the category "German." The focus on musical-dramatic works in this book, then, emphasizes both a continued engagement with aesthetic considerations of a musical genre whose form and history embody the problem of modernity as well as a reflection on each work's position as a musical drama after Wagner.

Philosophy and (Jewish) Difference: Heine as a Paradigmatic Example

Critical negotiations with modernity and its relation to difference were primarily the domain of various projects of Critical Theory in the twentieth century. These projects, appearing in the thought of theorists like Adorno and Walter Benjamin, who responded to a tradition of German idealist philosophy from Kant to Hegel, form the theoretical foundation of this book. Yet, as Willi Goetschel argued, the constitutive presence of Jewish difference in modernity was already asserted a century earlier by the German Jewish poet and critic Heinrich Heine.

Heine's insistence on the irreducible nature of Jewish difference in the face of a philosophical tradition oriented toward universalism was formative for the critical endeavors that followed in the twentieth century. It allowed him to articulate a "modernity that no longer required the erasure of the particular,"[7] to quote Goetschel, and thereby prefigure the negative dialectics of Benjamin and Adorno that similarly resisted an "equalizing universalism that can accommodate for

---

7. Willi Goetschel, *Heine and Critical Theory* (New York: Bloomsbury, 2019), 4.

difference only as a form of failure or aberration."[8] Although Heine is not this book's primary object of study, lingering on his emancipatory understanding of Jewish difference will help elucidate the philosophical underpinnings of the term "difference" that *Unsettling Difference* engages.[9]

Out of the numerous examples of Heine's emancipatory view of Jewish difference permeating his entire oeuvre, it would be helpful to focus here on one instance from his three-part essay *Zur Geschichte der Religion und Philosophie in Deutschland* (*On the History of Religion and Philosophy in Germany*). Writing the essay in Paris in the 1830s, Heine declared its aim was to impart a popularized account of German intellectual history to make accessible knowledge that the "doorkeepers" of German philosophy kept restricted from the broad public. But beneath the popular veneer of Heine's narrative lay a profound critical provocation to the main tenets of Hegel's philosophy. Heine's attack was carried out through an application of Hegel's model of philosophy of history that challenged its fundamental assumptions from within while offering an alternative scheme of German intellectual history.[10]

Of particular interest is Heine's account of Luther's Bible translation as the decisive event that paved Germany's way into modernity. It was Luther's rendering of the Bible in the German vernacular, Heine observed, that granted human reason the authority of interpreter and arbiter in religious controversies. In the accepted narrative of German intellectual genealogy that Heine cites, the Reformation loomed large for introducing a freedom of thought that was essential

---

8. Goetschel, *Heine and Critical Theory*, 10.

9. For another attempt to theorize Jewish difference according to the model of gender difference, see Lisa Silverman, "Rethinking Jews, Antisemitism, and Jewish Difference in Postwar Germany," in *The Future of the German-Jewish Past: Memory and the Question of Antisemitism*, ed. Gideon Reuveni and Diana Franklin (West Lafayette, IN: Purdue University Press, 2021), 135–45.

10. Briefly put, Heine contested Hegel's view of history as the teleological unfolding of absolute spirit by presenting an alternative genealogy of German thought guided by a continuous reciprocation between spiritualism and sensualism. See also Willi Goetschel, *Spinoza's Modernity: Mendelssohn, Lessing, and Heine* (Madison: University of Wisconsin Press, 2004), 253–65.

Jewish Difference, the Bible, and the Artwork 9

to the later development of modern German philosophy and literature. What Heine finds most noteworthy about this mythologized achievement is the fact that the entrance into modernity was made possible through the act of Bible *translation*: "Martin Luther gave us not only freedom of movement, but also the means for this movement: he gave the spirit a body. He provided thought with the word. He created the German language. This he did by translating the Bible."[11]

The attribution of Germany's launch into modernity to an act of translation is Heine's subtle but pointed subversion of any claims to a self-contained, "pure" notion of German modernity. Luther's modern German was not created ex nihilo but rather translated from Hebrew, Aramaic, and Greek. For Heine, who was interested in the Jewish claim to German modernity, it was specifically the reliance on Hebrew that was noteworthy, as he writes:

> It is true that people had the Vulgate, which they understood, as well as the Septuagint, which they were capable of understanding. But the knowledge of the Hebrew had vanished from the Christian world. Only the Jews, who kept themselves hidden here and there in odd corners of this world, still maintained the traditions of the language. Like a ghost guarding a treasure that was entrusted to him during his life, this murdered nation, this ghost nation, sat in its dark ghettos and preserved the Hebrew Bible; and German scholars could be seen secretly descending into these disreputable dens in order to uncover the treasure, to acquire knowledge of the Hebrew language.[12]

With this image, Heine confronts a key assumption regarding Jewish difference as it is most prominently captured in Hegel's philosophy of history. Heine's insistence on the indispensable role of Jewish knowledge in Germany's advance into modernity challenges idealist philosophy's removal of Judaism from modernity and most notoriously Hegel's consignment of Judaism to a superseded past. For Hegel, the persistence of Judaism in modernity posed the utmost problem of

---

11. Heinrich Heine, *The Harz Journey and Selected Prose*, trans. Ritchie Robertson (London: Penguin, 1993), 229.
12. Heine, *Harz Journey and Selected Prose*, 230.

difference, namely, the existence of an "anachronism" stubbornly lodged within a historical epoch he understood to have contained, incorporated, and transcended it.[13]

Hegel's philosophical system did allow for difference but only as an internal tension within identity. This dialectical scheme that hinged on the containment of difference as a model for historical progress had immediate implications for the understanding of Jewish difference, which it perceived in similar terms. Unable to exist on its own, Jewish difference required contextualization, its perception against a background. This background was the notion of a German modernity that established itself as simultaneously opposed to and as the integrative telos of such difference.[14] In other words, Hegel's model allowed for Jewish difference or particularity only insofar as it depended on the stability of a German position presented as its universal horizon.

Heine's subversion lies in obstructing this configuration. He grants the Jewish position agency as the custodian of a knowledge that had opened the gates of modernity. The "ghost nation"—Heine teasingly applies Hegel's terminology—refuses to remain superseded and instead lays claim to the very horizon against which it is perceived. Heine rejects the passivity ascribed to the Jewish position in the familiar narrative of German Jewish emancipation by implying that German modernity arrived with Jewish "assistance" and not the other way around. Heine's counternarrative deliberately obfuscates who introduced whom into modernity, who is the facilitator guiding the other.[15]

Heine's critique employs a role reversal that unsettles the stability of the Jewish and the German as mutually defining minority and

---

13. On the "Jewish problem" in Hegel's philosophy, see also Yirmiyahu Yovel, *Dark Riddle: Hegel, Nietzsche, and the Jews* (Cambridge, UK: Polity Press, 1998).

14. The same problem of Jewish difference is further demonstrated in Heine's discussion of Spinoza in the same essay. See further Goetschel, *Spinoza's Modernity*, 261–64.

15. Goetschel similarly observes that Heine "challenges the terms that define the claims and counterclaims of the discourse of modernity by comically upstaging the hegemonic assumptions of a Hellenocentric discourse that puts Jewish and other differences under categorical erasure." Goetschel, *Heine and Critical Theory*, 10.

majority positions, as well as their respective philosophical counterparts, particularity and universality. This unsettling gesture also complicates the historical conception that accompanies these positions. As Heine shows, it is impossible to relegate the Jewish position to a superseded past just as it is impossible to affiliate modernity with a homogeneous, universal German position. Heine's critical vision of modernity as an open-ended conflict between old and new, a movement without a telos, corresponds with the notion of Jewish difference that achieves freedom from containment through a constant play with role reversal, confusion, and ambiguation. This play contests the relational structure underlying the hybrid "German Jewish" condition, the coherence of its two underlying categories, as well as its accompanying notion of difference shaped by Hegelian dialectics. Unsettling difference, as Heine shows us, does not mean abolishing difference but rather setting it in motion by removing it from confinement within a major-minor dialectic.

Heine's example opens an alternative perspective on the German and Jewish positions, one that suspends their coherence by exposing them in moments of confusion and interchangeability. His subverting gesture of confusion guides this book's exploration of similar moments of ambiguation a century later. Heine's decision to approach the problem of Jewish difference and German modernity through the issue of Bible translation is especially significant to the present study. It prompts a reflection not only on Luther's Bible and the Jewish claim that Heine recognized in it but also on later German engagements with the Hebrew Bible, which yielded similar moments of confusion and ambiguation between the German and the Jewish. The eighteenth century, which saw a proliferation of conversations on Jewish integration in German-speaking society, was also a period of heightened scholarly interest in the Hebrew Bible—as part of Enlightenment debates on the nature of emerging modern institutions like the nation and the state—that played an important role in further ambiguating Jewish difference. Since these debates continued to reverberate in the renewed critical reflections on the same topics in the twentieth century, it is important to give them brief consideration here.

Jewish Difference and the Bible Discourse

Eighteenth-century formulations of German modernity through questions of Bible interpretation and translation aligned Jewish difference with a perceived rupture between the modern and its historically superseded other. And yet, such discussions eventually yielded more ambivalence than clarity regarding the boundaries of modernity and those delineating the Jewish and German positions. According to Jonathan Hess, this ambivalence played out in debates concerning Enlightenment values in the eighteenth century. Rather than demarcating Judaism as nonmodern and expecting its incorporation into a homogeneous, non-Jewish German modernity, such debates revealed competing Jewish claims to the same values. Hess shows how these claims contested modernity's imputed drive toward homogeneity as well as its depiction as the obverse of the Jewish position.[16]

The burgeoning discipline of Bible scholarship in eighteenth-century Germany served as the arena for discussions about Jewish difference largely due to the emergence of what Jonathan Sheehan termed the "Cultural Bible." In line with the Enlightenment's ongoing project of secularization, new readings of the Hebrew Bible diffused its formerly centralized authority as a source of revealed theological truth. The Bible's authority was, as Sheehan indicates, not nullified but rather spread across "a diverse set of domains and disciplines."[17] No longer the sole wellspring of revealed truth, the Bible became an authoritative source in modern aesthetic and literary discussions, debates about law and modern political order, as well as in questions of translation that emphasized the practice of translation as a bridge between the modern and nonmodern. This shift expanded debates about Jewish difference beyond the confines of religious difference. Yet, as both Sheehan and Hess observe, theology was never entirely removed from the equation.

---

16. Jonathan Hess, *Germans, Jews, and the Claims of Modernity* (New Haven, CT: Yale University Press, 2002), 8.

17. Jonathan Sheehan, *The Enlightenment Bible: Translation, Scholarship, Culture* (Princeton, NJ: Princeton University Press, 2005), 91.

Much of the biblical discourse, Hess remarks, was still guided by Protestant theological arguments as it began to develop historical forms of biblical and textual criticism. German Protestant scholars like Johann David Michaelis (1717–1791) and Johann Gottfried Herder (1744–1803) approached the Hebrew Bible "as an artifact that reflected its time and place of origin" and aspired to set it apart from Christianity as the religion of the modern world.[18] Hess notes that in their readings, "Judaism came to be viewed not just as the antiquated religion long since superseded by Christianity, but as an essentially 'Oriental' legal system," which was radically out of sync with the spirit of both Christianity and modernity.[19]

Such readings were not restricted to views of the ancient Israelites but were also applied to contemporaneous Jews. They informed debates on Jewish integration, as Hess shows for example in the case of Michaelis's study of Mosaic law. Michaelis used his biblical study *Mosaisches Recht* (Mosaic Law, 1771) to support his argument against Jewish integration, claiming that "Jewish law was designed to preserve separatism and would thus stand in the way of integrating the Jews in a modern, secular state."[20] Yet even Michaelis's intervention was not free from ambiguities. As Hess continues, although *Mosaisches Recht* served its author in arguing for an unbridgeable difference between modern Germans and their Jewish counterparts, it also earned him the sharp critique of his contemporary Herder, who complained that Michaelis's biblical study presented Mosaic law as a modern product that evinces "good European *common sense*."[21]

Ambiguity concerning the role of the Hebrew Bible vis-à-vis German modernity was prevalent in the Bible discourse of the eighteenth century, something that Ofri Ilany's work on the Bible and modern conceptions of the nation in German Enlightenment demonstrates. Ilany takes Hess's line of argument further by showing how eighteenth-century Hebrew Bible scholarship in Germany was

---

18. Hess, *Germans, Jews*, 11.
19. Hess, *Germans, Jews*, 11.
20. Hess, *Germans, Jews*, 52.
21. Hess, *Germans, Jews*, 58.

guided by a tension between relegating the Bible and its inhabitants, the biblical Hebrews, to a distant past, while simultaneously elevating them as a model for modern German national and political identification.[22] He points out that Herder's own study of biblical poetry, *Vom Geist der Ebräischen Poesie* (The Spirit of Hebrew Poetry, 1782), insisted on historical distance yet simultaneously praised this Hebraic national poetry and deemed it exemplary for the nascent modern German nation.[23] This tension affected the way in which Jewish difference continued to be perceived in contradictory terms, with Ilany remarking that eighteenth-century German Bible scholars did not always distinguish between biblical Hebrews and present-day Jews.[24] Thus, on the one hand, Judaism as the lingering tradition of the biblical Hebrews was considered a historical relic in modernity, yet on the other, the persistence of Hebrew "origins" in the fundamental political structures of German modernity created spaces for mutual identification between Germanness and Jewishness.

Importantly, as both Ilany and Hess emphasize, the eighteenth-century Bible discourse was not determined solely by the contributions of German Christian scholars. The discourse was accessible to Jews, Ilany stresses, and facilitated various kinds of interactions between Christian and Jewish writers. Furthermore, according to Hess, Jewish participation in this discourse could not be reduced to minoritarian apologetics. In his reading of Moses Mendelssohn's *Jerusalem* (1783), Hess identifies a subversion of Christian dominance in the field of Bible interpretation and of Christianity's exclusive claim to universal, modern Enlightenment values. In Mendelssohn's contention that Judaism, being the more rational religion, is better suited to exist in accordance with a modern secular political order, Hess

---

22. Ofri Ilany, *In Search of the Hebrew People: Bible and Nation in the German Enlightenment* (Bloomington: Indiana University Press, 2018). See also Anthony D. Smith, *Chosen Peoples: Sacred Sources of National Identity* (Oxford: Oxford University Press, 2003).

23. Ilany, *In Search of the Hebrew People*, 97. See also Frederick M. Barnard, *Herder on Nationality, Humanity, and History* (Montreal: McGill University Press, 2003), 18–19.

24. Ilany, *In Search of the Hebrew People*, 134.

reads a response to Michaelis's challenge to Mosaic and Jewish law's compatibility with modernity.[25]

Yael Almog uses the term "situated universalism" to describe Mendelssohn's appropriation of modern universal values through their presentation as inherently Jewish.[26] This strategy of simultaneously laying claim to the dominant narrative of universal modernity while still insisting on an irreducible Jewish particularity is not altogether different from Heine's later tactics, as we have seen. In Mendelssohn's work we can similarly recognize a notion of Jewish difference that can neither be confined to a minority position nor dissolved into a homogeneous universalism. Almog finds Mendelssohn's situated universalism in both the biblical interpretive debate on Mosaic law and Mendelssohn's own aesthetic considerations of biblical poetry. As she notes, Mendelssohn responded to Herder's notion of poetry as a bearer of national spirit by promoting the universality of biblical poetry while at the same time emphasizing the Bible's relevance as the cultural asset of the Jewish people.[27]

Unsettling Difference explores the complex dynamics of Jewish difference that the eighteenth-century Bible discourse articulated as they are revisited in modernist debates about the Bible. Modernist considerations of the Bible recognize the entanglement of categories like "old" and "new," "religious" and "secular," among others, as the foundational structure of modernity just as they continue to pursue a corresponding notion of Jewish difference attuned to the same complexities that emerged in the original discourse. The modernist Bible discourse similarly accentuates the ambiguity that accompanied the erection of the German and Jewish categories in the eighteenth century and thus continues to convey an unsettled vision of Jewish difference that refuses to coagulate.

Contemplating the ambiguities of modernity and Jewish difference in the first decades of the twentieth century naturally carries different undertones. In response to a social and political climate

---

25. Hess, *Germans, Jews*, 97.
26. Yael Almog, *Secularism and Hermeneutics* (Philadelphia: University of Pennsylvania Press, 2019), 91.
27. Almog, *Secularism and Hermeneutics*, 94.

aiming to reify Jewish difference, the modernist perspective offers a more conscious critique of the unsettled conditions under which Jews first entered German society. This return to engagement in the biblical discourse, then, uses the "problem" of modernity's porous boundaries to critique rigid categorization, including the increasingly rigid categories of the Jewish and the German.

Aesthetic and scholarly engagements with the Bible in the twentieth century approach scripture as a vehicle for deliberations on law, national poetry, language, and translation, as well as theology in a manner similar to the eighteenth century. These areas, for which the eighteenth century first established the authority of the Bible, continue to operate as the main scenes for contemplating Jewish difference. This book's first chapter, for example, foregrounds the role of the Bible as national poetry in Borchardt's attempt to revive Luther's biblical German in his poem *Das Buch Joram*. Borchardt's project reanimates questions of Jewish difference and its porosity by designating his pseudobiblical poem an exemplary instance of German national poetry. Borchardt's direct references to Herder's study of biblical poetry are not limited to his own efforts to assert the parameters of German national poetry. Herder's views on translation, specifically his notion of translation's dual task of bridging over while maintaining boundaries between different peoples and epochs—a view born of his encounter with biblical poetry—echo in the debate on Bible translation between Borchardt and Martin Buber that the first chapter examines.[28]

Eighteenth-century debates on Mosaic law continue to resonate in the third chapter's exploration of Schoenberg's opera *Moses und Aron*. Moses's law and its ability to create distinctions between peoples stand at the center of this chapter as it investigates how the issues of law and difference directed the principles of Schoenberg's compositional technique. And lastly, theological considerations are never entirely absent from the modernist Bible discourse as we can

---

28. Herder's remarks, which begin to articulate a theory of translation, are found in his fragment collection *Letters Concerning the Latest Literature* (*Briefe, die neueste Litteratur betreffend*, 1767). Translations for Herder were meant to set boundaries between peoples and assert historical distance yet at the same time render the foreign familiar and accessible. See also Sheehan, *Enlightenment Bible*, 171.

see, for example, through the continuous fascination with the figure of Job and the question of theodicy inhabiting both Borchardt's *Das Buch Joram* and Roth's and Zeisl's works, both titled *Hiob*. Roth's novel and Zeisl's opera offer modernized retellings of the Book of Job that stress the universality of Job's story and its relevance to modernity while still insisting on the particularity of Jewish suffering that the story conveys.

The Aesthetics of Jewish Difference: Tragedy and Music Drama

Alongside the Bible discourse and its expression of Jewish difference as a porous and ambiguous term through its association with the problem of modernity, another discourse contributed to the perception of difference between Germanness and Jewishness from a specifically aesthetic angle. The philosophical and aesthetic deliberations on Greek tragedy that prevailed particularly within the German idealist tradition came to supplant the Bible discourse in the nineteenth century as German thinkers increasingly conceptualized Germanness through a philhellenic lens that excluded Jewishness.[29]

It is as an extension of this German tradition and its reflections on Greek tragedy that *Unsettling Difference* considers Wagner's music dramas, theoretical writings, and the composer's infamous comments on Judaism and German culture. Wagner's work represents an intensified point of intersection between the question of Jewish difference and that of tragedy and drama set to music. *Unsettling Difference* reads all the musical dramatic works it explores in the twentieth century as responding in some way to Wagner's work and claims. Yet Wagner was not a phenomenon born out of thin air. He was rather the product of the long-lasting German obsession with Greek tragedy that shaped his work just as it informed

---

29. Among German-speaking Jews, however, German translations of the Bible continued to facilitate participation in German culture. See Abigail Gillman, *A History of German-Jewish Bible Translation* (Chicago: University of Chicago Press, 2018).

further philosophical and theoretical deliberations on tragedy by later figures responding to Wagner, from Friedrich Nietzsche to Walter Benjamin.[30] Seeing therefore how Wagner fits within this German philhellenic tradition will help elucidate both the importance of investigating Jewish difference through the medium of musical drama and the relevance of the German philosophical engagement with tragedy to such an investigation.

A great deal of the German philosophy of the tragic revolved around the question of tragedy's relevance beyond the historical confines of Greek antiquity. In its search for tragedy's place in modernity, the philosophy of the tragic took a similar shape to the Bible discourse and its inquiry into the Bible's role in modernity. Both cases emphasized modernity's indebtedness to "nonmodern" texts. As Miriam Leonard notes, the philosophy of the tragic was itself a thoroughly modern phenomenon.[31] Its objective was to locate Greek tragedy's universalist aspects. Yet, as Peter Szondi commented in his *Essay on the Tragic*, while the philosophy of the tragic knew "neither national nor epochal borders," it was at the same time "fundamentally German."[32] This paradox of the "fundamentally German" universality of the philosophy of the tragic points to how Jewish difference troubled German attempts to render the tragic wholly universal. George Steiner's polemic observation that "tragedy is alien to the Judaic sense of the world" reiterated the questioned universality of an aesthetic genre and form, which German idealists like Hegel defined simultaneously as both universal and the opposite of "Jewish."[33]

Hegel's philosophical treatment of Greek tragedy is important to understanding the relation between tragedy and Jewish difference. Taking the shape of his dialects, Hegel's tragic philosophy was defined as a reconciling and sublating movement from difference as a conflict between two ethical forces to identity. Szondi's analysis of Hegel's

---

30. Nietzsche's and Benjamin's writings on tragedy are thoroughly discussed in chapter 2 of this book.
31. Miriam Leonard, *Tragic Modernities* (Cambridge, MA: Harvard University Press, 2015).
32. Peter Szondi, *An Essay on the Tragic*, trans. Paul Fleming (Stanford, CA: Stanford University Press, 2002), 2.
33. George Steiner, *The Death of Tragedy* (New York: Alfred Knopf, 1963), 4.

evolving work on the subject of tragedy stresses that reconciling and sublating Jewish difference in particular was at stake in the reconciliation motion that Hegel identified in tragedy. Hegel's early reflections on the tragic in the 1798 essay "The Spirit of Christianity and Its Fate" separated Judaism and its perceived indebtedness to a posited law from the continuity of tragic fate that Hegel saw originating in Greek paganism and continuing in Christianity.[34] Locating the continuity of tragic fate within Christianity, Hegel secured the tragic as universal while opposing it to the historically superseded spirit of Judaism and its law. Yet, as Szondi points out, Hegel could not leave this plain opposition with Judaism unresolved. In the later reflections on Greek tragedy and Sophocles's *Antigone* in *The Phenomenology of Spirit*, Szondi reads Hegel's treatment of the conflict and reconciliation between Creon's law and Antigone's love as a reconciliation of the respective conflict between Judaism and Christianity.[35]

Szondi's analysis shows how Jewish difference perturbed Hegel's conception of the tragic to the point where its containment and sublation became an imperative. We find a similar gesture of intolerance to plain, uncontained difference also in Wagner's dealings with the Greek tragic form and his notion of the total work of art.

There are many aspects in Wagner's treatment of Greek tragedy that extend from the idealist philosophy of the tragic and especially, as Philippe Lacoue-Labarthe observed, from Hegel's work.[36] Although the explicit stakes for Wagner were not purely philosophical but rather aesthetic-political—his goal was in fact to (re)create an artform that would serve Germans the way he believed Greek tragedy had served the ancient Greeks—his efforts were similarly motivated by the desire to recover suprahistorical, universal elements from the historically contingent coordinates of Greek tragedy.

Furthermore, in Wagner's work the question of tragedy's relevance to modernity and the "problem" of Jewish difference are

---

34. See Georg Friedrich Hegel, "The Spirit of Christianity and Its Fate," in *Early Theological Writings*, trans. T. M. Knox (Chicago: Chicago University Press, 1948), 182–301.
35. Szondi, *Essay on the Tragic*, 21.
36. See Philippe Lacoue-Labarthe, *Musica Ficta: Figures of Wagner*, trans. Felicia McCarren (Stanford, CA: Stanford University Press, 1994).

also entwined, although, interestingly, in essays like "Das Kunstwerk der Zukunft" ("The Artwork of the Future," 1849) and "Das Judentum in der Musik" ("Judaism in Music," 1850), Wagner flipped the script on the relationship between modernity and the Jewish position. Unlike for Hegel, Jewishness for Wagner was not restricted to a superseded past but rather associated with modernity. However, contrasted with Wagner's timeless vision of tragedy that was now perpetuated in the German total work of art, the modern itself became a historically contingent category awaiting supersession.

The drive toward containment and reconciliation of Jewish difference present in Hegel's dialectics and his philosophy of the tragic has parallels in Wagner's ideas on aesthetic form. As the successor of the Greek drama, Wagner's German Gesamtkunstwerk, or total artwork, was conceived as an organic, well-integrated, and complete art form. For Wagner, organicism was one of the enduring traits of the Greek drama. In "Das Kunstwerk der Zukunft," he derived his vision of an organic artwork from the perception prevalent in German intellectual circles at the time of the organic life of the ancient Greeks. This prompted Wagner to seek a similarly organic vision of the German people that would correspond to the German total artwork: as Greek tragedy reflected the organic structure of the Greek polis, so Wagner's total artwork was meant to reflect the organic, homogeneous, and closed notion of the German art-*Volk*. This vision afforded no room for Jewish difference.

Wagner's notion of the "complete" or "closed" artwork speaks to formal-theoretical debates that accompanied the operatic genre since its inception as a modern revival of Greek tragedy. Spurred by Aristotle's indication in the *Poetics* that Greek tragedy was sung, speculations about the function of the singing tragic chorus and the organic union between poetry and music in Greek tragedy became the core of the project of opera in Italy around 1600.[37]

Italian opera placed weight on the chorus's capacity for punctuation and division. From the reflective, punctuating interjections of

---

37. On the early history of opera, see Donald Jay Grout and Hermine Weigel Williams, *A Short History of Opera* (New York: Columbia University Press, 2003), 11–38.

the Greek chorus, it derived its own division into sections of dramatic action that were recited rather than fully sung (the opera's recitative or *stile rappresentativo*) and lyrical scenes (the opera's arias, choruses, and ballets).[38] This division was targeted by Wagner in his attack on opera in "Das Kunstwerk der Zukunft" and his longer essay *Oper und Drama* (*Opera and Drama*, 1851). Instead of opera's mechanical and artificial association with individual arts—music, poetry, and dance, once blissfully united in the Greek drama and now unnaturally separated in modern opera—Wagner offered his vision of an organic, well-integrated, and hermetically sealed total artwork that claimed to realize the proper union between the arts that opera as the Italian revival of Greek tragedy failed to accomplish.[39]

Opposing closedness and completion to punctuation and division distinguished a specific German approach to tragedy and its modern re-creation as drama set to music. Although Wagner was arguably the most vocal about the fundamental distinction between the German and the Italian approaches to the modern musical-dramatic rendering of Greek tragedy, his views resonated with those of other German thinkers like Friedrich Schiller and Nietzsche. In their respective essays on tragedy, both understood the function of the chorus as creating a closed-off arena in which the artwork could be conjured.[40] In Wagner's understanding, this sealed aesthetic arena that delineated the total artwork was coterminous with sealing off German art in its entirety to foreign Jewish infiltration. Wagner's notorious essay "Judaism in Music" rejected any form of Jewish participation in German art as inauthentic and inorganic.

---

38. See Grout and Weigel Williams, *A Short History of Opera*, 10–11.
39. Michal Ben-Horin sees something similar in the compulsion toward redemption in Wagner's music dramas. She likewise reads various Jewish modernist gestures as resisting Wagnerian redemption. Michal Ben-Horin, *Reading the Voices: Musical Poetics between German and Hebrew* (Jerusalem: Bialik Publishing, 2022).
40. See Friedrich Schiller, "Über den Gebrauch des Chors in der Tragödie," accessed October 11, 2023, https://www.friedrich-schiller-archiv.de/die-braut-von-messina-oder-die-feindlichen-brueder/ueber-den-gebrauch-des-chors-in-der-tragoedie/2/; Friedrich Nietzsche, "The Birth of Tragedy out of the Spirit of Music," in *The Basic Writings of Nietzsche*, trans. Walter Kaufmann (New York: Modern Library, 2000), 58.

While the philosophical engagement with Greek tragedy as it appeared in Hegel's work was primarily concerned with the containment and sublation of Jewish difference, Wagner's work took Greek tragedy and its attendant organic vision of the Greeks to be the foundation of an organic notion of Germanness that was entirely intolerant to Jewish difference. Nonetheless, in reflecting on the joined questions of Jewish difference and the problem of modernity that his rendering of Greek tragedy encompassed, Wagner continued the same German philhellenic tradition that perceived Jewish difference in aesthetic terms as it strove to conceptualize the German people aesthetically as the modern heirs to the ancient Greeks.

While it seems that the borders between Germanness and Jewishness that the aesthetic expressions of Jewish difference drew were stricter than the ones formulated by the more ambiguous Bible discourse, it is important to note that ambiguity also invaded Wagner's treatment of Jewish difference. For all the vitriol he directed at Judaism in German art and culture and despite his trenchant efforts to assert a notion of Germanness that excluded Jewishness unambiguously, even Wagner could not help but admit that he must hold himself unqualified to fully define "what is German?" in the 1878 essay bearing the same question as its title. Jewishness proved a fickle foil. Designating it an "imputed likeness" (*Zerrbild*) of Germanness, Wagner betrayed a latent fear of the identical. As "Judaism in Music" already indicated fifteen years earlier, it was the "cultivated Jew" (*der gebildete Jude*), the one who could not be distinguished from other fellow Germans, that Wagner found most threatening. And while "Judaism in Music" rebuked the Jewish imitation of German culture as an inauthentic gesture of appropriation, "Was ist Deutsch?" admitted that there is in fact no authentic content to German culture. The German is praised there for the very same thing for which the Jew was rebuked earlier, namely, for adopting the cultural products of other peoples, Romanic, Gaelic, French, and making it his own.[41] Ultimately, Wagner's resolve to distinguish between Germanness and Jewishness still amounts to

---

41. Richard Wagner, "What Is German?," in *Prose Works*, vol. 4, *Art and Politics*, trans. William Ashton Ellis (London: Paul, Trench, Trübner, 1895), 160.

admitting the difficulty of doing precisely that. And in that, even Wagner takes on a shade of ambiguity that prevents us from considering him in absolute opposition to Jewishness.[42]

Artworks, Boundaries, after Wagner

In the preface to his collection of essays on Wagner's philosophical legacy, the French philosopher Philippe Lacoue-Labarthe reflects on the birth of modern opera as the rebirth of ancient Greek tragedy:

> The largest part of musical or poetico-musical research conducted in the last years of the cinquecento is ordered, as is well known, by the dream of reestablishing tragedy. On the basis of a sort of *ut musica poesis* ... one sought a renaissance of what one imagined to have been a total art. (A "renaissance" of tragedy is also the key word of the propaganda of Bayreuth, as we see in *The Birth of Tragedy*.) From the *Camerata fiorentina* ... to Mantua and to Venice, in all of erudite Italy, an intense study of Aristotle's *Poetics* was undertaken, practically the only document that classical antiquity had left us on Athenian theater. It was translated and commentated, in an attempt ... to draw from it the principles and rules for a practice of *dramma per musica*, which was thus, by an obvious necessity, first an affair of music or musical invention. This is why the renaissance of tragedy, which is really the only birth of it that we know (this renaissance being a birth of something other than what tragedy had been, which remains forever lost), destined the new art ... to represent by predilection the birth of music, and to "sing" its incomparable power.[43]

With this opening gambit Lacoue-Labarthe indicates that the question of reconstructing a great collective artwork in the sense imputed to Greek tragedy is ultimately a question of music. Lacoue-Labarthe focuses on the reverberating effect Wagner's legacy had on modernist figures from Charles Baudelaire to Adorno. What Wagner realized, as Lacoue-Labarthe specifies, was nothing short of the (in)

---

42. On the many ambiguities that Wagner's figure acquired through its reception, see also Alex Ross, *Wagnerism: Art and Politics in the Shadow of Music* (New York: Farrar, Straus and Giroux, 2020).
43. Lacoue-Labarthe, *Musica Ficta*, xviii.

famous Hegelian "end of art," the establishment of a limit, a completion of the artwork and of the historical project of art itself within music. In alignment with contemporaneous views that raised music above other, mimetic arts, Wagner and his Gesamtkunstwerk presented this completion as a sublation of all representational arts into the sensuous homogeneity of music.

"The dialectical confrontation of the individual arts in the 'total work of art,'" Lacoue-Labarthe continues, "is consequently a means of containing excess.... It is, like all dialectical operations, a strictly economic measure."[44] Lacoue-Labarthe observes that the total artwork's gesture of containment and closure was both diachronic and synchronic. Wagner accomplished the "end of art" diachronically by composing opera to completion. This meant that anyone composing an opera after Wagner had to be conscious of a certain untimeliness of writing operas after Wagner allegedly redeemed and reconciled all arts in the music drama and thus also "completed" the project of opera. But this "closure" also meant a completion of the artwork at any given moment. Here, we can distinguish between Hegel's and Wagner's gestures of containment and totality. Totality in Wagner's idea of the artwork was not a capacity to absorb all excess in a gesture of continuous expansion. Unlike later interpretations of the Gesamtkunstwerk, which expanded the boundaries of the artwork to include practically all aspects of life and were therefore closer to the Hegelian model, for Wagner, not everything could be absorbed into the artwork.[45] Rather, closure and totality in Wagner's work were simply the intolerance of excess. The political ramifications of Wagner's aesthetic legacy came to light in the twentieth century as the "*figuration* of the political."[46] Lacoue-Labarthe's insistence on this phrasing, which denotes the literal embodiment of the political in Wagner's notion of the artwork, confirms that the composer's greatest political achievement was turning the German people

---

44. Lacoue-Labarthe, *Musica Ficta*, 12.
45. For the development of the Gesamtkunstwerk in the twentieth century see Matthew Wilson Smith, *The Total Work of Art: From Bayreuth to Cyberspace* (New York: Routledge, 2007).
46. Lacoue-Labarthe, *Musica Ficta*, xv.

itself into a total artwork. The culmination of this condition, as Eric Michaud observed, was the molding of this "artwork" by an artist-dictator.[47]

The term "after Wagner," marking a notable trend in the study of modernist operas in the twentieth century, is perhaps the best illustration of the historico-philosophical problem that Wagner's work evokes.[48] "After Wagner" denotes a kind of rupture in the history of opera to the extent that for some composers and scholars of twentieth-century dramas set to music, the word "opera" itself has become suspect.[49] After Wagner, a conscious reconsideration of the timeliness and untimeliness of specific art forms and the validity of Wagner's own claim to restore the idea of a collective artwork from the distant realm of Greek antiquity took center stage. It was, for example, Wagner's disregard for *Geschichtsphilosophie*—specifically his refusal to recognize the irretrievability of collective art forms in a radically atomized bourgeois era—that stood at the center of Adorno's critique in his essay *In Search of Wagner*.[50]

A similar perspective guides this book's focus on modernist works and their historical embeddedness after Wagner. In its exploration of both literary biblical adaptations and their musical-dramatic renderings (the individual chapters will stick to the traditional titles "operas" and "oratorios," as their composers did), *Unsettling Difference* centers around questions of the restoration and completion of artworks and their implication for our understanding of the boundaries between Jewishness and Germanness. It is not by coincidence, for example, that two of the works this book discusses, Schoenberg's *Moses* and Zeisl's *Hiob*, are opera *fragments* whose unfinished status poses a challenge to Wagner's aesthetic ideals of

---

47. Michaud's astute analysis shows how Hitler later fashioned himself as an artist who shapes the German *Volk* as his artwork. See Eric Michaud, *The Cult of Art in Nazi Germany*, trans. Janet Lloyd (Stanford, CA: Stanford University Press, 2004).

48. See, for example, Mark Berry, *After Wagner: Histories of Modernist Music Drama from Parsifal to Nono* (Woodbridge, UK: Boydell Press, 2014); Juliet Koss, *Modernism after Wagner* (Minneapolis: University of Minnesota Press, 2009).

49. See Berry, *After Wagner*, 4.

50. Theodor W. Adorno, *In Search of Wagner*, trans. Rodney Livingstone (New York: Verso, 2005). See especially chapter 7, Music Drama.

completion and organicism. Other works, as we will see, present their own challenging response to the conception of the complete, organic, and total artwork and its attendant vision of a homogeneous and impermeable German people.

Before grouping all musical and literary works here under the umbrella of "modernism," it is important to first clarify how this book employs the term. *Unsettling Difference* understands modernism as a mode of self-criticism and continuous questioning of seemingly natural procedures. This understanding bypasses the plurality of definitions and subdefinitions that have been appended to modernism's numerous manifestations in various disciplines. Modernism as self-criticism is especially helpful in thinking about the different responses to Wagner in this book, since it allows us to see that the movement bearing this title undertakes a continued engagement with the underlying questions of previous centuries, including the revival or reconstruction of archaic art forms.

Without conflating the two terms "modern" and "modernism," I would like to point out an affinity between them, namely, the way in which both refute the assumption of complete novelty, though it is only after Wagner that consciousness of this condition openly directs deliberations on the nature of modernity. To demonstrate this, no example is more fitting than Lacoue-Labarthe's above observation that the emergence of *modern* music, the monody of the *seconda pratica* around 1600,[51] was nothing but a gesture of restoration: "Modern music was discovered as the recomposition of ancient music."[52] This becomes further instructive when we consider the indispensable place of tradition and conservatism in the modernist program. Not only are we unable to associate modernism itself with a clear divide between "old" and "new," it is also impossible to

---

51. The *seconda pratica* or "second practice," also known as *stile moderno*, denoted the rise of monody (single melody and accompaniment) and a freer treatment of dissonance in contrast to the *prima pratica*, which was associated with the rigorously restricted polyphony of composers like Giovanni da Palestrina (1525–1594).

52. Lacoue-Labarthe, *Musica Ficta*, xvii.

separate the modernist fascination with technology and industrialization from an equally strong impulse toward archaism.[53]

Unsettling Difference locates this impulse in the renewed interest in the Bible during the first decades of the twentieth century. This interest spans aesthetics and *Kulturkritik*, as well as philosophical and theological debates. It involves composers like Schoenberg, Hanns Eisler, and Kurt Weill, authors such as Roth, Franz Werfel, Thomas Mann, Lion Feuchtwanger, Stefan Zweig, Richard Beer-Hofmann, and Bertolt Brecht, as well as critics and philosophers from Benjamin, Gershom Scholem, and Adorno to Martin Buber, Franz Rosenzweig, and Siegfried Kracauer.[54]

The word "renewed" here is key. It emphasizes that modernism was itself a repetition (or a sort of radical revisiting) of the same complex engagement with questions of revival and the condition of being universal or historically contingent that initially allowed modernity to set its own parameters of inclusion and exclusion in the eighteenth century. Biblical discourse provided the settings for such debates then. It is no surprise, therefore, that many figures engaged in the modernist biblical discourse were Jewish. In essence, the biblical discourse, like that of opera and tragedy, was grounded in questions of restoration, of a troubled relationship between a-historical universality and historical particularity. And so was the question of Jewish difference, which German-speaking Europe had originally formulated as a historico-philosophical problem.

There is, however, a fundamental difference between the biblical discourse of the eighteenth century and that of the twentieth century. Resuming a conversation about Jewish difference that is rooted in practices of biblical scholarship and translation in the first half of

---

53. See for example Jeffrey Herf, *Reactionary Modernism: Technology, Culture, and Politics in Weimar and the Third Reich* (Cambridge: Cambridge University Press, 1984).

54. See also Caroline A. Kita, *Jewish Difference and the Arts in Vienna: Composing Compassion in Music and Biblical Theater* (Bloomington: Indiana University Press, 2019). With her focus on the concept of compassion and its implication for the understanding of Jewish difference, Kita also investigates a response to Wagner in turn-of-the-century, biblical-themed Viennese works.

the twentieth century is inevitably, whether explicitly stated or not, a gesture that opposes the racially defined discourse of Jewish difference that started dominating German-speaking Europe in the late nineteenth century. Wagner may have striven to present the clash between *Deutschtum* and *Judentum* in absolute terms, but it was in the writings of his disciples like Houston Stewart Chamberlain that this clash was explicitly expressed as that of "two pure races."[55]

In the pseudoscientific language of racial antisemitism, Jewish difference became immutable. Unlike cultural inclusion or exclusion by modernity, bloodlines left little room for interpretation. Scholars have shown that racial antisemitism was not a new, secular phenomenon, and that it had been underlying theologically driven debates on Jewish difference well before the nineteenth century.[56] There is no doubt that German Christian participants in the theological discourse of Jewish difference, whether they were eighteenth-century Protestant Bible scholars or nineteenth-century idealist philosophers and their intellectual descendants, did not always distinguish between their perception of Jewish individuals as racially distinct and the relegation of Judaism to a superseded historical period. But these perspectives represent only one voice and one part of the German conversation on Jewish difference, the Christian part. To say that it defines it as a whole would be again to marginalize the Jewish side of the same conversation as mere apologetics.

In the twentieth century it became even more apparent that Jewish voices resumed this same German conversation about Jewish difference not from a marginalized Jewish position but as Germans, plain and simple. To understand responses by figures like Benjamin, Adorno, or Schoenberg (who could be more suitable intellectual and artistic heirs to figures like Hegel and Wagner?) as anything but German and accordingly to render the modernist conversation on Jewish difference an internal Jewish affair amounts to perpetuating a limited and limiting sense of Jewish difference and to upholding the

---

55. See Saul Friedländer, *Nazi Germany and the Jews*, vol. 1, *The Years of Persecution* (New York: Harper, 1997), 89.

56. See for example Yosef Hayim Yerushalmi, *Assimilation and Racial Anti-Semitism: The Iberian and German Models*, Leo Baeck Memorial Lecture (New York: Leo Baeck Institute, 1982).

habitual major-minor dialectic relation between the Jewish and the German positions that this book sets out to dissolve. *Unsettling Difference* is accordingly a call to move away from the view of German Jewish marginality and imagine an alternative relation between the German and the Jewish positions. It is a call to account for moments that unsettle the boundaries between them through ambiguity, role reversal, and a constant shift of perspectives.

Translation, Critique, and Afterlife: The Incomplete Artwork

The modernist biblical discourse references much of the earlier conversations on Bible translation and its simultaneous setting of boundaries and channels of exchange between different peoples and different epochs. In the twentieth century, however, references to translation involve a more direct commentary on the underlying philosophy of history that designated Judaism an original that had been translated and therefore "outgrown" by Christianity. Naomi Seidman's study of translation as a site for Jewish-Christian encounter insists on the dynamic nature of this translative relation which is guided by the deconstructive insight that "the original is always already a translation" and that "a translation is itself another original."[57]

This is also the insight of modernist deliberations on the issue of Bible translation that are characterized by a free bidirectional movement between Judaism and Christianity, as well as between Jewishness and Germanness.[58] Walter Benjamin's theory of translation offers an additional dimension to this book's understanding of translation. Benjamin's view abolishes translative hierarchies altogether. For him, translations complement one another; there is in fact no "original" but only the infinite aspiration of all languages and all renditions toward one ever-elusive pure language.

---

57. Naomi Seidman, *Faithful Renderings: Jewish-Christian Difference and the Politics of Translation* (Chicago: University of Chicago Press, 2006), 32.

58. See also Jacques Derrida, "What Is a 'Relevant' Translation?," trans. Lawrence Venuti, *Critical Inquiry* 27, no. 2 (2001): 174–200.

Translation, then, has a specific aesthetic import in *Unsettling Difference*. Benjamin's observation in his essay "The Task of the Translator" that translations have a bearing on the afterlife of works indicates a challenge to the Wagnerian impulse toward closure and completion of artworks. If the existence of numerous translations in Benjamin's theory implies a certain collective aspiration toward an infinite goal, then the idea of the "work" itself receives a certain openness. For Benjamin, translations, like interpretations (a term that encompasses works of criticism as well as renditions in this book), are equally of the order of an artwork. The capacity of every artwork to be further interpreted or rendered ensures that limits and boundaries in art will never be accomplished. This understanding guides the study of the musical renditions of literary works as in the case of Rudolf Borchardt's narrative poem *Das Buch Joram* and Joseph Roth's novel *Hiob*. But it also includes discussions of renditions in the sense of performances. Such considerations in the second and third chapters on Ben-Haim's *Joram* and Schoenberg's *Moses* highlight the transience and variability of the never-truly-complete artwork even further.

After Wagner, challenging the notion of a closed, organic artwork is tantamount to resisting the corresponding notion of a complete, organic, and homogeneous German collective. This defiance operates above all as a statement against social and political conditions in German-speaking Europe of the 1930s, when all three musical renditions were conceived. But more profoundly, this is a statement against the remainderless, all-subsuming, collective structures that restrict the German and Jewish positions to the fixed dialectical roles of dominance and subservience since the early debates on Jewish emancipation. Thus, each chapter in this book merges an aesthetic problem concerning the "completion" of the work with a corresponding political question concerning the clear delineation and figuration of collective categories.

At the center of the first chapter stands Borchardt's pseudobiblical poem *Das Buch Joram* and its accompanying theory of translation. Written with the declared objective of restoring Luther's German, Borchardt's work is an example of the poet's aesthetic program of Creative Restoration that envisioned a reconstruction of archaic forms as part of a German national poetic project. This chapter traces the tension between Borchardt's aesthetic program and his own Jewish ancestry. It pays close attention to Borchardt's view of translation as one of the main vehicles for restoration and revival of art forms. With its focus on the correspondence between Borchardt and Buber concerning the place of biblical language in modernity and the purpose of Bible translations, the first chapter situates the poem amid a debate on two competing language and translation theories that Borchardt and Buber defined as "German" and "Jewish" respectively. While Borchardt and Buber present seemingly irreconcilable views on biblical language and translation, the chapter identifies in their debate numerous moments of crossing where a purportedly "Jewish" argument would serve Borchardt's adherence to Luther's Bible and its poetic and theological legacy, while a "German" perspective would guide Buber and Rosenzweig's wish to create a new German Bible translation.

Chapter 2 examines the composition of Borchardt's poem as an oratorio and the translation of the poem's accompanying debates into the realms of music and theater. This chapter studies the oratorio *Joram* by the composer Paul Ben-Haim (born Paul Frankenburger) against the tradition of the oratorio in Germany using the passions of Johann Sebastian Bach as the genre's exemplary model. My reading of *Joram* unfolds on two fronts: The first involves outlining the oratorio's affinities with the German *Trauerspiel* following Benjamin's understanding of the form. Like the *Trauerspiel*, the German oratorio encapsulates the condition of modernity expressed through the absence of a firm notion of collectivity and a fragmented, open-ended view of the "work" itself. Having established the oratorio as a musical-dramatic—and, indeed, *theatrical*—form that undermines the Wagnerian view of the artwork, I proceed to examine how this opposition operates more specifically with regard to the question of Jewish difference. I do so by showing how *Joram* is embedded in and responds to a German oratorical tradition that boasts a history of confounding the identities of various religious and national communities and specifically the difference between German Christian and Jewish collectives.

Chapter 3 reads Arnold Schoenberg's opera-fragment *Moses und Aron* as another response to the political-aesthetic thrust of Wagner's work by focusing on the concept of the law and its ability to create both unity and distinction between peoples. From an exploration of Schoenberg's twelve-tone method as an aesthetic law, I proceed to examine the reference to Moses's law in the opera and its interaction with a series of reflections on Moses, law, and Jewish difference by twentieth-century thinkers and writers from Sigmund Freud and Thomas Mann to Jacob Taubes. While Wagner's aesthetic program strove to see its people as a homogeneous entity established against a fixed Jewish other, Schoenberg's opera lends its fragmentariness also to the notion of the people it evokes, whose volatile heterogeneity poses a challenge for representation. The mutability of the people in *Moses* calls for an extended reflection on the question of political representation since the critique of fixed collective identities inevitably raises the problem of representing any collective through stable, concrete means. Guided by Schoenberg's political drafts and with an emphasis on his critical view of democracy as a representation of the general will, this chapter introduces *Moses* to a much broader politico-theoretical debate on the nature of representation, both as *Darstellung* of the law and *Vertretung* of the people, that has enticed prominent political thinkers from Thomas Hobbes and Jean-Jacques Rousseau to Schoenberg's contemporary Carl Schmitt.

The term German Jewish identity relies both on a clear distinction between its two opposing ends, the "German" and the "Jewish," as well as on an underlying principle of integration which operates as a kind of horizon even where rejected. While the first three chapters challenged the opposition between the two ends, the final two question the validity of the integrative paradigm underlying the term. Chapters 4 and 5 are dedicated to Joseph Roth's novel *Hiob* and its unfinished operatic rendition respectively. The modernist impulse of both novel and opera conveys a concentrated aesthetic instance of the tension between the old and the new.

In Roth's case, the tension between old and new is evident in the contrast between a retelling of a biblical story that evokes premodern literary forms like the *Legende* and the novel's critical capacity to expose the entanglement of a modern, fragmented society with an incompatible principle of integration. Reading Roth's *Hiob* alongside his and Hannah Arendt's respective writings on immigrant Jews in the interwar period, this chapter shows how both authors challenged the integrative model of the nation-state by focusing on those who were bound to remain superfluous exceptions to this model. The chapter theorizes the position of Eastern European immigrant Jews in Roth's and Arendt's writings as "superfluous" or "uncontained exceptions." Rather than exemplifying any innate Jewish resistance to integration (which perpetuates the antisemitic view of the "unintegrated Jew"), the possibility of being superfluous allows both writers to challenge the validity of a model that assumes integration and homogeneity as its highest ideal. This chapter further traces the aesthetic implication of such observations by showing how the novel *Hiob* relates to the tradition of the German-language novel. Whereas this tradition is predicated upon a similar integrative paradigm, Roth's superfluous protagonist and the exceptional role that the miracle plays in the novel allow it to transcend the ideals of integration and organicism.

The final chapter shows how *Hiob*, the opera by the Viennese-born composer Eric Zeisl, continues to address the critical potential of being superfluous by centering around the question of assimilation. The chapter addresses the criticism of the term "assimilation" in the context of German Jewish studies as part of an effort to preserve and highlight a particular (minor) sense of Jewish difference that persisted against a dominant German culture. Focusing on Zeisl's opera, this chapter recovers the critical capacity of the concept of assimilation and exposes the challenge it raises to the view of a German Jewish minority culture and its dialectical underpinnings. Chapter 5 highlights the affinities between the gestures of assimilation and quotation as two forms of repetition and traces the practice of musical quotation in Zeisl's opera. Looking at the Viennese Jewish composer Gustav Mahler as a model and precursor of Zeisl's quotational practice, the chapter shows how repetition as both quotation and assimilation undermines the originary status of the so-called quoted or assimilated original and thereby turns on its head the Wagnerian accusation of Jewish imitation (*Nachsprechen*—a literal repetition) of German culture. Like the superfluous, inorganic nature of quotation as repetition, the corresponding act of assimilation as repetition offers an alternative view of Jewish difference that exceeds the contained economy of a "German Jewish identity."

If Heine's provocation at the opening of this introduction allowed us to recognize the limitations involved in conceptualizing Jewish difference within a dialectical framework, he has also given us another way to conceive of such difference beyond the contained systems of dominance and subservience, majority and minority, universality and particularity. Abandoning the economy of German Jewish identity entails accepting a notion of Jewish difference that is both there and not there, that may surface for a moment only to disappear again and repeatedly bring us to question its very essence. It is to such moments of uncertainty that this book calls attention. Through instances of confusion, ambiguity, radical heterogeneity, excess, and repetition, it aims to continue Heine's gesture and offer an alternative view of the relation between Germanness and Jewishness.

1

Rudolf Borchardt's *Das Buch Joram* and the Restoration of a Biblical Language

Those who approach Rudolf Borchardt's narrative poem *Das Buch Joram* (The Book of Joram) without previous knowledge of the poet or his creative program might initially mistake the work for a lost apocryphal text.[1] With chapter and verse numbers, Borchardt's poem exhibits an astounding command of Martin Luther's biblical German. Only a more attentive reading reveals certain stylistic features that situate the work in the early twentieth century. The first edition of *Das Buch Joram* appeared in private print in 1905. The poem is loosely modeled on the Book of Job and relates the trials and tribulations of a fictive biblical figure, Joram, who is exiled to Chaldea from his home in Judea and sold as a slave. Joram returns

---

1. An earlier version of this chapter was published as Adi Nester, "Eine ungeheure Epopöe unseres eigenen: Language and the Hebrew Bible in Rudolf Borchardt's *Das Buch Joram*," *The Germanic Review: Literature, Culture, Theory* 94, no. 1 (2019): 16–38.

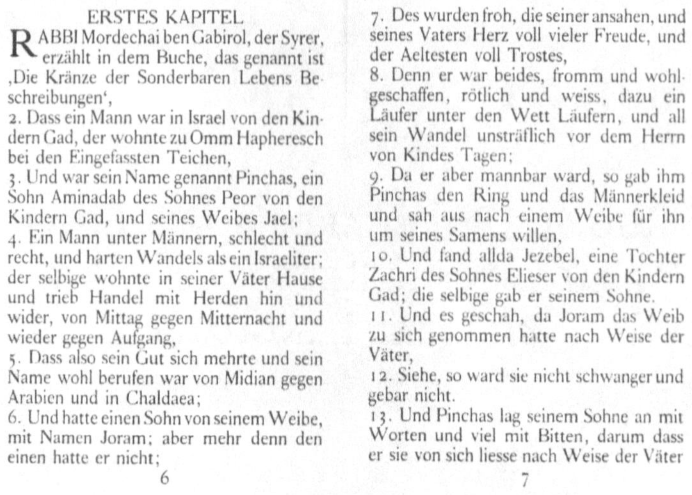

ERSTES KAPITEL

R ABBI Mordechai ben Gabirol, der Syrer, erzählt in dem Buche, das genannt ist ‚Die Kränze der Sonderbaren Lebens Beschreibungen',

2. Dass ein Mann war in Israel von den Kindern Gad, der wohnte zu Omm Hapheresch bei den Eingefassten Teichen;

3. Und war sein Name genannt Pinchas, ein Sohn Aminadab des Sohnes Peor von den Kindern Gad, und seines Weibes Jael;

4. Ein Mann unter Männern, schlecht und recht, und harten Wandels als ein Israeliter; der selbige wohnte in seiner Väter Hause und trieb Handel mit Herden hin und wider, von Mittag gegen Mitternacht und wieder gegen Aufgang,

5. Dass also sein Gut sich mehrte und sein Name wohl berufen war von Midian gegen Arabien und in Chaldaea;

6. Und hatte einen Sohn von seinem Weibe, mit Namen Joram; aber mehr denn den einen hatte er nicht;

7. Des wurden froh, die seiner ansahen, und seines Vaters Herz voll vieler Freude, und der Aeltesten voll Trostes;

8. Denn er war beides, fromm und wohlgeschaffen, rötlich und weiss, dazu ein Läufer unter den Wett Läufern, und all sein Wandel unsträflich vor dem Herrn von Kindes Tagen;

9. Da er aber mannbar ward, so gab ihm Pinchas den Ring und das Männerkleid und sah aus nach einem Weibe für ihn um seines Samens willen,

10. Und fand allda Jezebel, eine Tochter Zachri des Sohnes Elieser von den Kindern Gad; die selbige gab er seinem Sohne.

11. Und es geschah, da Joram das Weib zu sich genommen hatte nach Weise der Väter,

12. Siehe, so ward sie nicht schwanger und gebar nicht.

13. Und Pinchas lag seinem Sohne an mit Worten und viel mit Bitten, darum dass er sie von sich liesse nach Weise der Väter

Figure 1.1. Rudolf Borchardt, *Das Buch Joram*. First two pages of chapter 1 from the 1907 edition published in Leipzig by Insel Verlag.

home years later and discovers that in his absence, his wife and all his possessions were lost.

The various elements of the poem, from language to subject matter, give the first impression of a text that might have been written a few millennia ago and translated into German by Luther. Even the aesthetic presentation of the physical booklet, which was published in a second edition in 1907 by Insel Verlag in Leipzig, aspires to emulate the scriptures, as an image of the first pages from this edition demonstrates (see figure 1.1).

Borchardt does not simply settle for organizing his work in chapters and verses, mimicking a division that was added to both the Hebrew Bible and the New Testament around the thirteenth century and has since become characteristic of scriptural texts in both Jewish and Christian traditions.[2] He also makes use of specific idioms as well as syntactical and grammatical structures that are typical of

---

2. See G. F. Moore, "The Vulgate Chapters and Numbered Verses in the Hebrew Bible," *Journal of Biblical Literature* 12, no. 1 (1893): 73–78.

Luther's language. These include, for example, the use of the genitive as direct object with certain verbs—as in the verse: "Joram aber achtete *ihrer* nicht noch *des* Kindes, das sie geboren hatte" (But Joram paid no heed to her nor to the child that she bore)[3] —or the use of the old *Bindevokal* letter *e* in past tense verbs, as in the following: "Aber der Herr hat sie ausgetilg*e*t um ihrer Wollüste willen" (But the Lord blotted them out because of their lust).[4] Such choices were considered archaic even in Luther's time but are nonetheless characteristic of his language.[5]

Yet despite its overt biblical language and settings, *Das Buch Joram* is in fact undeniably modern. Joram's strife with God after returning home marks the poem's climax and is perhaps the most obvious element setting the text apart from its biblical model. With the defiant tone of Joram's plea and the absence of a proper rejoinder from God, this episode indicates that Borchardt's poem bears a decidedly contemporary meaning and speaks to a modern reality that has indeed been forsaken by God.

Das Buch Joram carries a specific poetic message for the twentieth century. Behind its unusual style stands Borchardt's desire to restore the German of Luther's Bible as part of a call to the German nation to return to its poetic heritage and draw its defining features from this tradition.[6] Borchardt's conservative aesthetic program

---

3. Rudolf Borchardt, *Gesammelte Werke in Einzelbänden: Gedichte*, ed. Marie Luise Borchardt (Stuttgart: Klett-Cotta, 2004), 378; *Gesammelte Werke in Einzelbänden*; hereafter abbreviated as *GW*.

4. *GW: Gedichte*, 381.

5. See further Erwin Arndt und Gisela Brandt, *Luther und die deutsche Sprache* (Leipzig: VEB Bibliographisches Institut, 1983), 160, 175.

6. Luther's German translation of the Bible is in many ways a historical construct. Not only did Luther have collaborators who worked on the translation with him (especially on the Old Testament), the translation itself has been reprinted and revised repeatedly since it first appeared in 1534, continuing long after Luther's death. Nevertheless, some canonic status is attributed to the 1545 edition of the full Bible translation, the last edition printed in Wittenberg during Luther's lifetime. This version later allowed future generations to mythologize Luther's German as a single entity of unrivaled cultural and historical significance and idealize it as the first unified German *Schriftsprache* (literary language). See Werner Besch, *Luther und die deutsche Sprache: 500 Jahre deutsche Sprachgeschichte im Lichte der neueren Forschung* (Berlin: Erich Schmitt, 2014).

sought to move away from the modern, political conception of a German state and return to the romantic idea of a German *Kulturnation*.⁷ However, the particular dynamics of *Joram* often appear to clash with its avowed national program. The poem's evocation of Luther's Bible translation presents an ambiguous national image that suspends Borchardt's work between national German poetry and translated world literature. In fact, this is only one in a series of apparent conflicts that distinguish the national aspirations of the poet, whose output Adorno once designated "inherently lyrical" or "speaking into a darkness."⁸ Another one is Borchardt's troubled Jewish background and the fact that he remains to this day primarily associated with the German Conservative Revolution movement.

In his retrospective address "Germans and Jews" from 1966, Gershom Scholem identified this ambivalence in Borchardt as a sign of German Jewry's failed assimilation project. As Scholem wrote, "the exorbitantly talented Rudolf Borchardt, convinced he had annihilated everything Jewish within himself, became the most eloquent spokesman of a culturally conservative German traditionalism. He himself was the only person to read his work who was not alarmed by the paradox."⁹ For Scholem, Jewishness and German traditionalism were mutually exclusive. The paradox he saw in Borchardt's work and person followed this view as well as the conviction that no degree of assimilation, not even the earlier conversion of Borchardt's family, could eliminate Borchardt's Jewishness. Yet as I argue, rather than demonstrating the irreconcilability of an ineradicable Jewishness and a conservative, national Germanness, the ambiguities surrounding Borchardt and his work complicate both categories. They

---

7. See also Daniela Graetz, "Ästhetische Selbstmächtigung im Namen der Nation: Rudolf Borchardt als Nationalpädagoge und Anthologe," in *Die Souveränität der Literatur: Zum Totalitären der Klassischen Moderne 1900–1933*, ed. Uwe Hebekus und Ingo Stöckmann (München: Wilhelm Fink, 2008); and Kai Kaufmann, *Rudolf Borchardt und "der Untergang der deutschen Nation": Selbstinszenierung als Geschichtskonstruktion im essayistischen Werk* (Tübingen: Niemeyer, 2003).
8. Theodor W. Adorno, *Notes to Literature*, vol. 2, ed. Rolf Tiedemann, trans. Shierry Weber Nicholsen (New York: Columbia University Press, 2019), 457.
9. Gershom Scholem, "Jews and Germans," in *On Jews and Judaism in Crisis* (Philadelphia: Paul Dry Books, 2012), 85.

reveal both Jewishness and Germanness as simultaneously distinct and permeable, different but still interchangeable in certain moments.

Although *Das Buch Joram* was one of Borchardt's earlier works, it accompanied Borchardt throughout his life and resurfaced in key moments as the poet repeatedly confronted questions concerning the poetic and linguistic makeup of the German nation and its relation to Jewish difference. It is not insignificant that these moments all revolved around the issue of translation. Beyond the fraught matter of Bible translation, which, through Luther, tied the fate of modern German with Hebrew, translation was the primary principle of Borchardt's program of Creative Restoration (*Schöpferische Restauration*).[10] Translation expanded the boundaries of his notion of national German poetry while pointing to the historico-philosophical problem called forth by his wish to restore archaic poetic forms in modernity.

Borchardt's Creative Restoration program blurred the lines between a "national" German poetic tradition and a general Western tradition, which reached back to the classic works of Greek and Latin literature and advanced through the medieval *Minnesinger* to the romantic English poets of the nineteenth century. A significant part of his program relied on translating various European masterworks into German and counting them as part of the German national canon. Borchardt's translations form a notable portion of his oeuvre and include Pindaric odes, Platonic dialogues, works by Horace and Virgil, Dante's *Vita Nova* and *The Divine Comedy*, as well as the poetry of Walter Savage Landor, Lord Byron, and Algernon Charles Swinburne, who was known for his own archaistic style.[11] Constituting a kind of canonical anthology, these translations fulfilled a dual purpose. They were meant both to ensure the continued revival and circulation of historical poetic forms in modernity and to compensate for what Borchardt perceived as lacks in the existing canon of German poetry.

---

10. See also Borchardt's 1927 address "Schöpferische Restauration," in *GW: Reden*, 230–53.

11. On the direct influence of Swinburne's poetry on *Das Buch Joram*, see Markus Neumann, *Die "englische Komponente"* (Göttingen: Vandenhoeck & Ruprecht, 2007), 114.

Although, strictly speaking, *Das Buch Joram* is not a work of translation, its affinity with Borchardt's translation project was elucidated in the afterword that was appended to the poem's 1907 edition. Like his translations, Borchardt's *Joram* was intended as a creative gesture toward a German archaic poetic form: Luther's Bible. For Borchardt, Luther's own Bible translation occupied a revered place in the pantheon of German poetry. Borchardt compared its national import to other monumental works in English and Italian, which, as he stressed, were similarly the respective pillars of each nation's poetic language and character:

> Denn in höherem Grade als von der English Bible das Englische, so ausschließlich wie von der Commedia das Italienische, stammt das Deutsch, als Dichtersprache und als Idiom, von Luthers Bibel. Man gewöhne sich nun daran, sie endlich wieder als das anzusehen, was sie in unserer gesamten älteren Literatur gewesen ist, als wirkliches Gegenbild der [sic] homerischen Tones bei den Griechen, als eine ungeheure Epopöe unseres eigenen, keines orientalischen, geschichtlichen Daseins.[12]
>
> [For to a higher degree than English from the English Bible, and so exclusively as Italian from [Dante's] Commedia, the German, as poetic language and idiom, is descended from Luther's Bible. One now finally grows accustomed to viewing it again as that which it had been throughout our entire older literature, as a veritable counterimage of [what] the Homeric tone [was] for the Greeks, as a tremendous epopoeia of our own and not of any oriental, historical existence.]

The fact that *Joram* was modeled after a translation is important. Understanding the creative element of translations to be on par with that of original poetry, Borchardt did not hesitate to include not only Luther's Bible but also Schlegel's translation of Shakespeare in a poetic canon he now perpetuated, conjured, and revived in his own creative-restorative poem.[13] By including translated masterpieces as essential exemplars of German poetry and treating *Joram* as an extension of this translative practice, Borchardt complicated the boundaries of the German canon and, with it, the German category itself. However, this complication was not a simple subversive act.

---

12. Borchardt, *Das Buch Joram* (Leipzig: Insel Verlag), 48.
13. See Borchardt, *Das Buch Joram*, 48.

Joram *and the Restoration of a Biblical Language* 41

What makes Borchardt's work stand out is exactly his refusal to relinquish the notion of a national, dominant German category.

In the afterword to *Joram*, Borchardt explained the aim of his restorative project and noted that Luther's Bible, despite being translated from Hebrew among other languages, was strictly a German work, "our own tremendous epos." His insistence that Luther's translation was "no oriental, historical being" indicates a strategy that aims to define his project as German by contrasting it with its historical Hebrew source. It is this insistence and the strategy of occupying a German dominant position that makes Borchardt an important figure to explore as an example of unsettling Jewish difference. In attempting to maintain a distinct German position while participating in the broader contemporaneous debate on translation, Borchardt nonetheless disrupted the category he wished to uphold. However, his disruption of "Germanness" and, subsequently, of Jewish difference operated subtly by creating ambiguities between the dominant and marginalized positions rather than defying the former from the position of the latter.

Borchardt and Judaism

Das Buch Joram offers the most concise expression of Borchardt's attitude toward Judaism. The poem's overall adherence to the narrative style of the Hebrew Bible makes its final chapters stand out with their depiction of the birth of a Messiah as a redemptive, New Testament conclusion. The calamities that befall Joram are all meant to amplify the main predicament of the poem: Joram and his wife Jezebel are barren. Their *Unfruchtbarkeit* has often been interpreted as Borchardt's critique of what he considered the poetic barrenness that marked his time.[14] In his numerous addresses, he frequently deplored the linguistic poverty of modern poetry, describing it as

---

14. See Hildegard Hummel, *Rudolf Borchardt: Interpretationen zu seiner Lyrik* (Frankfurt am Main: Peter Lang, 1983), 117–26; and Markus Bernauer, "Das Zentrum der Poesie: Rudolf Borchardts Gartenidee," in *Rudolf Borchardt und seine Zeitgenossen,* ed. Ernst Osterkamp (Berlin: De Gruyter, 1997), 258–61.

"ein fruchtloses und wertloses Wortwesen ... taub und krank im Kerne"[15] (a barren and worthless word-being ... deaf and sick to the core). Similar language depicts the foreboding vision of barrenness and extinction that appears to Joram's father at the beginning of the poem:

4. Und sah allda einen Feigenbaum von den Bäumen seines Frucht Gartens, ohne Blätter noch Frucht und schütterer Wurzel; darauf stand geschrieben "Unfruchtbar,"
5. Und hatte ein Gesicht zum andern; und sahe den selbigen Baum in einem Donner und Gewalt des Regens, und alle seine Wurzeln wüst und nackt, und hielt sich nicht an seiner Stätte, da er stand.[16]

[4. And there he saw a fig tree from the trees of his fruit garden, with no leaves nor fruit and of sparse root; on it was written "barren,"
5. And he had a second vision; and saw the same tree under thunder and violent rain, and all its roots desolate and naked, and held itself not on the site where it stood.]

Read with an eye to the poem's unusual pseudobiblical language, it is difficult to ignore how this reference to one of the more common themes of the Hebrew Bible, barrenness, produces an additional level of commentary. This one specifically targets the *Unfruchtbarkeit* of Judaism, as Borchardt saw it. Joram's condition stands for a Jewish sterility, which in Borchardt's view could only be redeemed through its complete dissolution into Christianity. In the poem's final verses, this dissolution occurs when Joram and his wife are finally granted offspring. The son is designated simply as *ein Heiland* (a Messiah or Redeemer) and his birth is followed by the death of his Hebrew parents:

---

15. *GW: Reden*, 49.
16. *GW: Gedichte*, 378–79.

8. Und es geschah, da die Amme das Kind tränkte in des Chaldäers Hause Nächtens, so fiel ein Feuer Gottes vom Himmel in den Pfahl von Jorams Zelte, daß er auf dem selbigen Feuer zu Gott ging, sich zu stillen, er und sein Weib; aber die Knechte blieben verschont.
9. Und sie zogen das Kind auf im Lande Chaldäa und fürchteten Gott.
10. Es ist aber dies Kind der Meister gewesen, dessen Namen man nicht kennt, sondern es ist genannt "ein Heiland,"
11. Und sind viele unter uns, die wissen, dass Gott seiner ansahe, und zu ihm sprach wie ein Bruder spricht zu einem Bruder.[17]

[8. And it came to pass, as the wet nurse nursed the child in the Chaldee's house by night, so God's fire fell from heaven onto Joram's tent, and he went to God to be appeased on that same fire, he and his wife; but the slaves were spared.
9. And they raised the child in the land of Chaldea and feared God.
10. This child became a Master, whose name is not known, but he is called a "Redeemer,"
11. And there are many among us, who know that God looked upon him, and spoke to him as a brother speaks to a brother.]

By concealing his name and leaving for Chaldea, his father's place of exile, Borchardt's Redeemer is redeemed from his Hebrew past. However, the severance of all past ties through the death of his progenitors and the move to Chaldea are not enough to set him apart. His depiction as the one who speaks with God "as a brother" is his true validation. This insistence on a communicative ability is noteworthy. It indicates that the redemption in question is not only historical but also linguistic. Joram's ineptitude was ultimately revealed within

---

17. *GW: Gedichte*, 396–97. Borchardt's choice of the ambiguous phrase "sich zu stillen" (to appease, or to nurse) creates a parallel between Joram's relation to God and the child's relationship to his nurse in the previous verse, which is not fully transferred in the translation.

language. Unlike his son, the Messiah, Joram was unable to elicit a verbal response from God despite desperate attempts to do so in his strife.

This image serves Borchardt's depiction of Judaism's redemption as a linguistic event and ties it to the discourse on Bible translation. Just as Borchardt's new Messiah transcends his Hebrew origins, the biblical language that Borchardt uses in his poem declares itself liberated from its original "oriental" origins. *Das Buch Joram* invokes a long-standing claim concerning the Christian "translation" of Judaism, which manifests quite literally in Borchardt's view of Luther's Bible and its replacement of Hebrew scripture with an unequivocally "German work." Borchardt's assertion of this replacement implies a similarly unequivocal difference between the Jewish position of the Hebrew Bible and the purely German status of Luther's Bible. Yet, his declarations notwithstanding, the evocation of an ultimately ambiguous translative discourse reveals that the role Judaism played in Borchardt's work was far from unequivocal.

The poet's letters and autobiographical writings reveal an ambivalent relation to Judaism. In his autobiography *Rudolf Borchardts Leben von ihm selbst erzählt* (Rudolf Borchardt's Life Told by Himself), he returns to the vision of Judaism's ultimate subsumption under Christianity and German *Geist*. Borchardt's account centers around what he defines as "the East Prussian process" undergone by Jews in his ancestral city of Königsberg.[18] He presents the conversion of many distinguished Jewish families in Königsberg as a model for Jewish assimilation in Germany or, more accurately, as the only possible answer he saw to "the most hopeless of all societal problems which threaten[ed] to bring our poor nation to despair, the Jewish question."[19] Borchardt deemed Moses Mendelssohn's idea of cultural assimilation lacking. He rejected Mendelssohn's separation between German language and culture and the Christian religion, referring to it as "the Berlin half solution."[20] In contrast, the poet

---

18. *GW: Prosa VI*, 82.
19. *GW: Prosa VI*, 79.
20. *GW: Prosa VI*, 80.

Joram *and the Restoration of a Biblical Language* 45

noted conversion to Protestantism and "surpassing Hebrew law" as necessary conditions for being German.[21]

Although he discusses the conversion of Königsberg's Jews quite extensively, Borchardt refrains from linking his own background directly to any of the Jewish families mentioned in his autobiography. The objectivity with which he reflects on the "Jewish question" and its proposed solution seems to imply that the account has no immediate bearing on him personally. The autobiography does not make explicit the fact that Borchardt's ancestors on both his maternal and paternal sides converted to Protestantism during the first half of the nineteenth century.[22] It is unclear whether this omission betrays an attempt to conceal his own background for fear it might undermine his self-portrayal as a German poet. In his private correspondence, however, Borchardt had no qualms about disclosing his Jewish lineage. To Wilhelm Ruer, whose daughter he once courted, he wrote that his mother, "born Bernstein, came from a Jewish family."[23]

Whether Borchardt expressly acknowledged his Jewish background or not, the fact remains that in his eyes, the earlier conversion qualified him to participate as a German poet in the German cultural and spiritual world. He viewed this world as inherently Christian. "The spirit of German poetry is Christian," he wrote elsewhere, "since Christianity is the spirit of German history."[24]

Yet as decisive as Borchardt's assertions about severing all ties with a Jewish past may sound, the reception of his work indicates a much more complex involvement with Judaism. Commentaries on the "Jewish" aspects of his poetry did not emanate solely from anti-semitic readers for whom no conversion could erase Borchardt's

---

21. See *GW: Prosa VI*, 81.
22. On Borchardt's family's conversion, see Alexander Kissler, *Wo bin ich denn behaust? Rudolf Borchardt und die Erfindung des Ichs* (Göttingen: Wallstein, 2003), 78–89.
23. Letter to Wilhelm Ruer, April 11, 1902, in Rudolf Borchardt, *Gesammelte Briefe I*, ed. Gerhard Schuster und Hans Zimmermann (München: Carl Hanser, 1994), 186.
24. *GW: Prosa IV*, 205. Importantly, for Borchardt, Christianity meant Protestantism above all. The poet tended to write Catholicism out of his conception of Germanness.

Jewishness. "Jewish readings" of *Joram* came in large measure from Jewish figures. The conclusion of Borchardt's biblical poem did not escape the critic Werner Kraft, for example. In his monograph on Borchardt, Kraft referred to *Joram* as a "Jewish poem that aspires towards a Christian resolution."[25] Many others of Borchardt's contemporaries chose to focus on what they took to be the Jewish nature of the poem. In a letter to his brother Ernst, Borchardt in fact complained about his poem's reception as the "German poetry of a Jewish poet."[26] Georg Hecht's 1909 review in the *Jüdische Rundschau* concluded its praising of Borchardt's poem with the words: "Wie lange werden sich jüdische Dichter solche Stoffe entgehen lassen?"[27] (How long will Jewish poets let such material slip away?), indicating that while Hecht did not consider Borchardt a Jewish poet, the poem was certainly befitting of one.

Martin Buber, who initially also understood the poem as an example of modern Jewish poetry based on traditional motifs, wrote the following in 1907:

> Besprechen will ich dieses Buch, das ich schon, als es ein Privatdruck war, gekannt und geliebt habe, nicht. Es erscheint mir als aller Analyse entrückt. Man berührt sein Wesen nicht, wenn man es ein Meisterwerk an Bewältigung des Archaischen nennt. Denn es wiederholt nicht, paßt nicht an, ist ganz und gar aus der Gnade geboren, einmalig, notwendig, unbegrenzbar. Es hat den Herzschlag des Gewaltigen. Der Hiobmythus ist hier in die Erde unseres Traumes gepflanzt.... Das Gedicht vom heimgekehrten Joram hat Unendlichkeit und Reinheit, Geheimnis und Gestalt, Stille und Pathos zugleich.[28]
>
> [I do not wish to discuss this book, which I have already known and loved as a private print. It seems removed from all analysis. One does not grasp its essence by calling it a masterpiece of conquering the archaic.

---

25. Werner Kraft, *Rudolf Borchardt: Welt aus Poesie und Geschichte* (Hamburg: Claassen, 1961), 62.

26. Rudolf Borchardt to Ernst Borchardt, October 2, 1907, Borchardt Papers, Deutsches Literaturarchiv (DLA), Marbach am Neckar.

27. Georg Hecht, "Das Buch Joram," *Jüdische Rundschau* 33, August 13, 1909, Borchardt Papers, DLA.

28. Martin Buber, "Das Buch Joram," *Die Zukunft*, 1907. Cited in Kraft, *Rudolf Borchardt*, 64.

For it does not repeat, does not adapt; it is entirely born of grace, singular, essential, limitless. It has a mighty heartbeat. The Job myth is planted here in the soil of our dream.... The poem of the homecoming Joram has infinity and purity, mystery and form, silence and pathos all at once.]

In a letter to Kraft ten years after the publication of this review, Buber recalled his first personal encounter with Borchardt on March 18, 1908, during which the latter "corrected" Buber's first impression of the poem's Jewish character. As Buber later wrote to Kraft, "Borchardt belongs to the Jewish people neither in person, since he is—as he himself expressly stated to me several years ago at our first conversation contrary to my earlier assumption—of no Jewish blood, nor in disposition."[29]

To Borchardt's dissatisfaction, he continued to be identified as a Jewish poet by Jews and non-Jews alike. References to his Jewish origins varied from antisemitic remarks by members of the George circle to the inclusion of his name in Theodor Lessing's *Jüdischer Selbsthaß* (*Jewish Self-Hate*) and the aforementioned address "Jews and Germans" by Scholem.[30] Adorno was another figure to join the list of critics by noting a messianic Jewish voice that emanates from Borchardt's German poetry.[31]

Among the reviews published during Borchardt's lifetime, Willy Haas's contribution to Gustav Krojanker's 1922 collection *Juden in der deutschen Dichtung* (Jews in German Poetry) is of particular interest. Haas's essay, bearing the scathing title "Der Fall Rudolf Borchardt. Zur Morphologie des dichterischen Selbsthasses" (The Case of Rudolf Borchardt: Towards a Morphology of a Poet's Self-Hatred) derided Borchardt's self-appointment as the preserver and advocate of the German poetic tradition. In an address delivered as an introduction to a reading of *Joram* from 1911, Borchardt described the poet's duty to remember what the rest of the world

---

29. Buber, letter to Werner Kraft, March 15, 1917. Cited in Gerhard Schuster, ed., *Rudolf Borchardt, Martin Buber: Briefe, Dokumente, Gespräche 1907–1964* (Ebersberg: Rudolf Borchardt-Gesellschaft, 1991), 77.
30. See Theodor Lessing, *Jüdischer Selbsthaß* (Berlin: Jüdischer Verlag, 1930).
31. Adorno, *Notes to Literature*, 465.

might forget: "Es ist das Recht der Welt, zu vergessen, aber die Pflicht der Dichter zu gedenken" (It is the world's right to forget but the poet's duty to remember).[32] Finding Borchardt's "duty to remember" fairly selective, Haas added sardonically: "Nun, dieser jüdische Dichter hat das Recht der Welt, zu vergessen, für sich und sein Judentum in einem nicht unerheblichen Maße als sein eigenes Recht in Anspruch genommen. Dieser Bewahrer des Hergekommenen hat sein Hergekommenes zu allerletzt bewahrt."[33] (Now, this Jewish poet has claimed the world's right to forget for himself and his own Judaism to a not inconsiderable degree. This keeper of tradition has kept his own tradition away from all.)

Haas's critique charged *Joram* with linking Judaism to a debased Orientalism.[34] After elaborating on what he called Borchardt's "apostate psychology," Haas proceeded to examine another aspect of the poet's work that he found representatively "Jewish," namely, Borchardt's relation to language. Haas emphasized Borchardt's dedication to a pan-European poetic tradition, which, in his eyes, contrasted with Borchardt's professed role as a conservative German poet. He noted Borchardt's numerous translations of great European works and declared him one of the best translators the German language had known since August Wilhelm and Friedrich Schlegel, Ludwig Tieck, and Friedrich Hölderlin. Such sensitivity to a "general European style" that united an array of works in various languages, Haas concluded, could only live in one who never felt entirely at home in any one language and always remained an immigrant:

> Allgemein europäisch; international also—wie das Judentum. Das ist nicht als bloßer Einfall hingeschrieben. Die psychologische Situation des Juden in der Diaspora begünstigt die Apperzeption eines Sprachtraditionalismus, der erst durch das philologische Experiment hindurch zu sich selbst kommt, weil er eben nicht der *Nation* angehört, sondern der

---

32. *GW: Reden*, 177.
33. Willy Haas, "Der Fall Rudolf Borchardt," in *Juden in der deutschen Literatur: Essays über zeitgenössische Schriftsteller*, ed. Gustav Krojanker (Berlin: Weltverlag, 1922), 232. For Borchardt's dismissal of Haas's critique, see Peter Sprengel, *Rudolf Borchardt, der Herr der Worte: Eine Biographie* (München: C. H. Beck, 2015), 297.
34. See Haas, "Der Fall Rudolf Borchardt," 234.

"Weltliteratur" (dieses Wort in seinem humanistisch-kosmopolitischen Sinne, so, wie es etwa Herder oder die deutsche Romantik angewendet hat): denn das Judentum der Diaspora ahnt in der seelischen Voraussetzung eines solchen Experimentativ-Traditionalismus etwas verwandtes; sich selbst; seine eigene zerbrochene, ewig schmerzlich aktuelle, ewig problematische Seelentradition. . . . Die nationale Sehnsucht dessen, der seine Nation verloren hat, wird zum traditionalistischen Ressentiment. Kurz: der internationale Archaismus ist die typische Theorie des Immigranten mit einem tiefen und unglücklichen Heimatsgefühl für das nationale Immigrationsgebiet.[35]

[Generally European; international, then, like Judaism. This is not written down as a mere idea. The psychological situation of the Jew in the diaspora favors the apperception of a linguistic traditionalism, which only comes to itself through philological experimentation, because it does not belong to the *nation*, but to "World Literature" (in the humanistic-cosmopolitan sense of the word, applied by Herder or German Romanticism): for diaspora Jewry intuits in the mental presupposition of such an experimental-traditionalism something akin to itself; its own broken, eternally painfully current, eternally problematic soul-tradition. . . . The national longing of one who has lost his nation turns to a traditionalist ressentiment. In short, international archaism is the typical theory of the immigrant and his deep and unhappy sense of belonging to the national territory [to which he immigrated].]

The description in Borchardt's autobiography supports Haas's verdict. Reflecting on his early childhood years in Moscow and the family's subsequent return to Berlin, Borchardt recalled how he had to forget the Russian and French languages he already had command of in order to acquire German.[36] Whether intentionally or not, the autobiography acknowledged not only the fact that German was not Borchardt's first spoken language but also that his strong connection to Königsberg, his ancestral city with whose monarchic spirit he deeply identified, was mediated through the stories he was told by his grandmother, as he himself spent his early childhood elsewhere. This preference for the verbally mediated over the factual and lived experience accompanied Borchardt throughout his entire life, most of which he spent not in Germany but rather in a self-imposed Italian exile.

---

35. Haas, "Der Fall Rudolf Borchardt," 236.
36. See *GW: Prosa VI*, 65.

50   Chapter 1

The spectral presence of Judaism in Borchardt's work allows us to see just how subversive the conservative poet's definition of Germanness ultimately was. Alongside his translative engagement with *Weltliteratur*, which Haas understood to betray a Jewish cosmopolitan rather than German national stance, Borchardt's ambivalence toward German soil also contributed to the ambiguity of his German national project. Contrary to views that developed only a few years later in Germany, Borchardt's project emphasized a poetic and linguistic notion of Germanness independent of material ties to blood or soil.

This ambiguity was also manifest in anthologies like *Der Deutsche in der Landschaft* (The German in the Landscape, 1927), which Borchardt compiled as another alternative canon of German writing.[37] The anthology comprises a collection of essays and segments from larger works by various German writers featuring depictions of landscapes in foreign lands. In its afterword, Borchardt declared: "Der Deutsche ist überall zu Haus und nicht zu Haus, ist zu Haus wo er eben steht.... Er ist der alte Wanderer seiner Geschichte, der Gast auf Erden."[38] (The German is everywhere at home and not at home, he is at home where he stands.... He is the old wanderer of his history, the guest upon the earth.) As he noted, the tradition of *Reise- und Landschaftsbeschreibungen* (travel and landscape depictions) was a specifically German one, and his book was therefore "ein nur innerhalb der deutschen geistigen Geschichte und Charakterwelt, nur deutsch mögliches Buch"[39] (a book possible only within the German intellectual history and character-world). The same assertion was reaffirmed by Walter Benjamin in his own review of Borchardt's anthology.[40] Yet neither the decision to compile a German anthology of impressions from foreign lands nor the explicit reference to wanderers who were nowhere and everywhere

---

37. See also Stefan Knödler, *Rudolf Borchardt Anthologien* (Berlin: de Gruyter, 2010).

38. Rudolf Borchardt, *Der Deutsche in der Landschaft besorgt von Rudolf Borchardt* (München: Bremer Presse, 1927), 489.

39. Borchardt, *Der Deutsche in der Landschaft*, 489.

40. See Walter Benjamin, "Landschaft und Reisen," in *Gesammelte Schriften III/1: Kritiken und Rezensionen* (Frankfurt am Main: Suhrkamp, 1980), 88–94.

at home could avoid conflating the romantic image of the German wanderer with the iconic one of the wandering Jew.

Contrary to arguments by some of Borchardt's critics, this conflation does not expose Borchardt as more of a Jewish poet than a German one. Borchardt's example neutralizes the distinction altogether. It is exactly his designation of what some may consider Jewish as the utmost German characteristic that leads one to reflect on the coherence of the German character and see that it too cannot be discussed in uniform terms. Though it was not his intention, Borchardt's case exemplifies the inseparability of Jewishness from the constitution of the German character. His work demonstrates the intertwinement of the two to such a degree that one cannot identify specific, individual elements within his notion of Germanness that can be considered "Jewish." Being able to do so would still uphold the misconception that there is a coherent notion of the German out of which one can winnow foreign Jewish elements. Borchardt's work instead offers us a poetic and linguistic project that is simultaneously entirely Jewish and entirely German.

Borchardt on Language and Translation

Adorno was one of the first to recognize just how subversive Borchardt's German conservatism was. This was the focus of his essay "Die beschworene Sprache" ("Charmed Language"), which was written as an introduction to a volume of Borchardt's selected poems Adorno edited in 1968.[41] The modernist image of Borchardt that emerges from this essay begins to explain why an ostensibly reactionary poet was able to occupy the minds of critics like Benjamin and even Adorno himself, who sought to defend him in 1968 amid the student movement protests in Germany. For Adorno, Borchardt was far from a straightforward reactionary. Though the critic does not fail to condemn the poet's problematically abiding

---

41. Rudolf Borchardt, *Ausgewählte Gedichte: Auswahl und Einleitung von Theodor W. Adorno* (Frankfurt am Main: Suhrkamp, 1968). The essay is reprinted in Adorno's *Notes to Literature*.

loyalty to the idea of the German nation and the "shrill passages in which [Borchardt] proclaimed himself and himself alone not only the spokesperson of that nation but even its very embodiment," he still attributes a critical capacity to Borchardt's work, one that rises precisely from the work's retrospective posture.[42]

According to Adorno, Borchardt's forceful evocation of concepts like the "nation" and "tradition" ultimately undermined rather than confirmed these same concepts. In Borchardt's "sympathy with power and established tradition," Adorno recognized a subconscious awareness that a coherent notion of collectivity was in fact no longer possible. This brought Borchardt to seek refuge exactly in the thing he knew was unavailable. Borchardt's "spellbinding gesture swung so far beyond anything cozy and homegrown," Adorno summarized, "that the conservatives found him just as objectionable as the Left and the literary avant-garde found his conservatism."[43]

Importantly, it was again through language that the ambiguously conservative gesture of Borchardt's poetry manifested. Adorno recognized in Borchardt an uneasiness that compelled the poet to renounce the German of his time, a "language devastated by commerce and communication, by the ignominy of exchange,"[44] as the critic put it, and resort to a different, conjured language in which "substance crystalizes . . . as though it were the authentic language Jewish mysticism speaks of."[45] For Adorno, Borchardt's work exhibited an aspiration toward what Benjamin, inspired in part by Jewish mystical teachings, called "pure language," an idealized language that transcends the need to communicate a meaning external to itself.

This reference hinted further at what Adorno's predecessors, like Haas, understood as a connection between Jewishness and a certain linguistic homelessness that prevents one from feeling rooted in any single empirical language. Nonetheless, Adorno's recurrent references to Borchardt's "Jewishness" do not follow Haas's argument. Haas

---

42. Adorno, *Notes to Literature*, 464.
43. Adorno, *Notes to Literature*, 458.
44. Adorno, *Notes to Literature*, 452.
45. Adorno, *Notes to Literature*, 451.

Joram *and the Restoration of a Biblical Language* 53

took Borchardt's uneasiness with language as a marker of a Jewish essence that the poet could not shed, try as he may. But for Adorno, the term "Jewishness" indicated a modernist stance that could be assumed by any artist whose work exhibits a certain critical rejection of the status quo during his or her own time and throughout history. Indeed, in Adorno's analysis, Borchardt's retrospection did not prevent him from being a modernist alongside figures like T. S. Eliot and Samuel Beckett. For although he claimed to reach back to the past with his work, Borchardt never truly recovered anything that was previously in existence.

As Adorno insisted, Borchardt "would hardly have had anything but contempt for the notion of a linguistic *renewal.* . . . Instead, he want[ed] a radical *reconstruction.*"[46] The difference between renewal and reconstruction is key to understanding Borchardt's modernism, according to Adorno. Since language confronted Borchardt "as something that was a failure historically,"[47] the poet relentlessly sought to compensate for what he perceived as its unfulfilled potential at various historical moments. He did so not by renewing—that is, by replicating previous manifestations of language—but by means of reconstruction, which was in fact, as Adorno points out, a whole new construction.

This distinction was expressed by Borchardt himself, notably, in his responses to criticism that *Joram* evinced a strikingly contemporary style despite its evocation of Luther's language. In a letter to the essayist and critic Josef Hofmiller from February 1911, Borchardt contrasted his notion of "genuine archaism" to a deficiently regressive "hybrid archaism," in a manner that corresponds to Adorno's distinction between reconstruction and renewal:

> Der hybride Archaismus also will die Illusion, indem er sie doch unwissentlich unaufhörlich zerstört,–der genuine will sie nie und muss sie mindestens ein oder zwei Male an Stellen stärksten Accentes wissentlich zerstören, um seine Signatur zu zeigen; (dies bezieht sich auf die lange Rede Jorams an sein Weib, deren "Modernität" die Kurzsichtigkeit der Ganzgescheiten mir vorgeworfen hat; sie *sollte* modern sein. . . . Ich

---

46. Adorno, *Notes to Literature*, 452. My italics.
47. Adorno, *Notes to Literature*, 452.

handle nicht mit gefälschten Altertümern); der hybride Archaismus . . . glaubt der Geschichte zu dienen, indem er sie "zurückruft," verneint die Gegenwart, die er nicht einen Moment lang verleugnen kann; der genuine Archaismus greift in die Geschichte nachträglich ein, zwingt sie für die ganze Dauer des Kunstwerks nach seinem Willen um, wirft von Vergangenen weg was ihm nicht passt, und surrogiert ihr schöpferisch aus seinem Gegenwartsgefühl, was er braucht.[48]

[The hybrid archaism thus seeks the illusion, which it nevertheless unknowingly and incessantly destroys. The genuine [archaism] never seeks [the illusion] and must knowingly destroy it at least once or twice where the strongest accents are so as to show its own signature; (this refers to Joram's long speech to his wife, whose "modernity" won me the reproach of those shortsighted "clever folk"; it *should* be modern. . . . I do not deal in fake antiquities). The hybrid archaism . . . believes it serves history by "recalling" it, [it] denies the present, which it cannot deny for one moment. Genuine archaism intervenes in history retrospectively, forces it to its own will for the whole duration of the artwork, discards from the past what does not suit it, and supplements creatively with what it needs from its [own] sense of the present.]

Borchardt's notion of Creative Restoration emphasized the need to create something new out of the engagement with historical forms. This view guided projects like *Das Buch Joram*, but nowhere was it more pronounced than in Borchardt's translations. To shed more light on the role that *Joram* played in Borchardt's conception of language, we should study the poem in relation to Borchardt's translation of Dante's *Divine Comedy* and the afterword he included in the translation's publication in 1930.[49] *Das Buch Joram* and *Dante Deutsch*, the title Borchardt chose for his translation, were written around the same time.[50] Borchardt conceived the translation in 1904, just a year before the first edition of *Joram* appeared. But the two works share more than mere temporal proximity; they also relate to one another by offering two different responses to Luther's German Bible.[51]

---

48. Borchardt, *Briefe III*, 355–56.
49. See "Epilegomena zu Dante," in *GW: Prosa II*, 472–531.
50. Rudolf Borchardt, *Dante Deutsch* (München: Bremer Presse, 1930). The translation is also included as a separate volume in Borchardt's collected works.
51. With the undeniable similarity between the title Borchardt chose for his translation, *Dante Deutsch*, and the title Martin Luther gave his own Bible transla-

Though celebrated in *Das Buch Joram*, Luther's language was treated much more ambivalently twenty-five years later in the "Epilegomena zu Dante." As Borchardt explained, *Dante Deutsch* was an attempt to compensate for a certain historical lack: "die durchgeführte Anspielung auf ein ideell denkbares und geschichtlich fehlendes Werk, das Werk, das unser nationales Schicksal uns nicht gegönnt hat"[52] (the implemented allusion to an ideally conceivable and historically absent work, the work which our national destiny failed to grant us). According to Borchardt, this "historical lack" referred to a "*Gewaltprozess*" attributed to Luther's language: a process of consolidation that suppressed the German linguistic plurality—the ubiquity of different dialects—of the Middle Ages. Wishing to compensate for this linguistic loss, Borchardt submitted a hypothetical version of Dante's masterpiece the way it *could have been*, had it been written in German in the fourteenth century.

Borchardt's interest in Luther's German during that time—as reflected by his study of the critical edition of Luther's Bible that later also yielded *Das Buch Joram*—involved simultaneous fascination with the formation of a national literary language and acknowledgment of the loss this process entailed. In the "Epilegomena," Borchardt returned to *Joram* and stressed that his pseudobiblical poem and its afterword were meant to bring out a certain longing for the past through Luther's language rather than looking forward toward the continued ossification of the German language:

> Ich hatte 1905 im "Buch Joram" die vorläufige Summe aus dieser Bescheidung gezogen und meinen Meßpfahl bei der Lutherbibel eingeschlagen. . . . Meinem Gedichte aber ließ ich in der öffentlichen Ausgabe von 1906 [sic] ein Nachwort folgen, das doch wieder eine halbe Palinodie war und hinter den wiedereroberten Formen von 1500 den Sehnsuchtsblick weiter rückwärts lenkte: Denn inzwischen war von der unerwartetsten Seite ein Lichtstrahl in mein geschichtliches Gefängnis gefallen: ich hatte eben doch noch einmal deutsch gelernt, von Grund auf.[53]

---

tion, *Biblia Deutsch*, one should also note how Borchardt tends to turn even the Italian—that is, Catholic—Dante into a Protestant.

52. *GW: Prosa II*, 472.
53. *GW: Prosa II*, 507.

[In 1905, I had drawn the provisional conclusion in the "Book of Joram" and set the Luther Bible as my measuring stick.... But in the public edition of 1906 [sic] I appended the poem with an epilogue, which was a palinode of sorts that directed the longing view further backwards, behind the reconquered forms of 1500. For in the meantime a ray of light had penetrated my historical prison from the most unexpected side: I had just learned German once again from the ground up.]

The story of Borchardt's "relearning" of German is related in the "Epilegomena" in detail. Borchardt was sojourning in Arlesheim, a small village near Basel, when he studied the critical edition of Luther's Bible.[54] In Arlesheim, he was exposed to the pre-Lutheran *Oberdeutsch* dialect that had been preserved and was still spoken in the area. His study of Luther's German was originally intended as a way to devise an alternative to the corrupted German of his own time. However, while pursuing it, Borchardt came to regard Luther's German as itself corrupt. In his eyes, the mythologization of Luther's German as the first unified German *Schriftsprache* inevitably associated Luther's German with a process of linguistic contraction. Its elevation came at the expense of the unfulfilled literary potential of other dialects. The preserved medieval German dialect Borchardt encountered in Arlesheim offered him a glimpse into a moment in history in which certain linguistic possibilities were still available.

Yet, despite this consequential discovery and Borchardt's subsequent wish to fulfill the dialect's literary potential by "resounding" it,[55] the poet did not apply his meticulous study of *Oberdeutsch* in his translation. The ubiquity of neologisms such as *Herzengnucht* for the Italian *letizia* (joy), *Zagemut* for *viltà* (cowardice), and *funkelröten* for *rosseggiare* (to redden) reveals instead that Borchardt ultimately chose to employ a partially invented language, one that

---

54. Borchardt most likely consulted the following edition of Luther's Bible, Heinrich Erich Bindseil, Verzeichnis der Original-Ausgaben der Lutherischen Uebersetzung sowohl der ganzen Bibel, als auch größere und kleinere Theile und einzelne Stellen derselben, in systemischer Ordnung, als Festschrift zur dreihundert-jährigen evangelischen Jubelfeier der Stadt Halle (Halle: Canstein'sche Bibelanstalt, 1841).

55. See *GW: Prosa II*, 526.

boasted an archaistic tonality but was in fact the product of his own mind.[56]

In his quest for an ideal language, Borchardt positioned himself next to figures like Benjamin, whose opening words from the famous 1923 essay "The Task of the Translator," "No poem is intended for the reader," reappear almost verbatim in Borchardt's own essay on translation "Das Gespräch über Formen" (The Dialogue on Forms). The essay, published first in 1904 as a preface to his translation of Plato's dialogue *Lysis*, is likewise written as a dialogue. In Borchardt's creative-restorative gesture toward the Socratic dialogue form, two interlocutors converse about the true task of translation. "The Dialogue" provides a more explicit discussion of themes that appeared previously in *Joram* and *Dante Deutsch*. It promotes the thesis that the creative restoration of historical forms—translations being the most obvious and ubiquitous instance thereof—ought to defamiliarize language and ultimately dismiss the reader as the work's addressee. As one of the interlocutors in "The Dialogue" declares, translations were not meant for those who simply could not access the work in the original language: "Wer ein griechisches Buch lesen will und nicht Griechisch kann, soll Griechisch lernen."[57] (Whoever wants to read a Greek book and does not know Greek, should learn Greek.)

Since Borchardt considered translations poetic works of art by their own merit, he rejected the assumption that they were intended to service the reader. In an argument that closely aligns with Benjamin's view, Borchardt insisted that a translation should not be evaluated by its public reception.[58] The task of the translator, according

---

56. For further discussion of Borchardt's German neologisms in *Dante Deutsch*, see Hans-Georg Dewitz, *Dante Deutsch: Studien zu Rudolf Borchardts Übertragung der Divina Comedia* (Göppingen: Verlag Alfred Kümmerle, 1971), 216–23. Dewitz considers the effect Borchardt's fictitious German has on the interaction and reciprocity between the poet and his public by citing Borchardt's indifference to his readership and concluding that translations were meant to occupy a place in a national biography regardless of their accessibility.

57. *GW: Prosa I*, 336.

58. The similarities between the theory of translation in Borchardt's "Dialogue" and Benjamin's essay "The Task of the Translator" have been noted in a number of

to Borchardt, was not to convey the meaning of the original in a different language but rather to carry over a certain incommensurability that inheres within the original's form.[59] Borchardt's claim specifically targeted the translations of his contemporary, the classical philologist Ulrich von Wilamowitz-Moellendorff, which were known for their public accessibility. According to Borchardt, accessible translations masked the true essence of their archaic sources, which were anything but well balanced, harmonious, and easy to digest. What Borchardt sought to translate instead was a certain inadequacy that confronted readers when they encountered what he called "form." Form, for Borchardt, was a complete sensual experience that obscured as much as it revealed in the work. To accomplish this, a translation had to convey the foreignness of the original work and be, at least to some degree, inaccessible.

Das Buch Joram, *Dante Deutsch*, and "Das Gespräch über Formen" reveal much not only about Borchardt's relation to language but also about the aesthetic character of his "German nation." Just as language appeared to him inadequate throughout history, so too was the idea of the "German nation," which Borchardt associated with a certain linguistic and poetic attitude. Luther's language serves as the most compelling example here. In *Joram*, the refusal to produce an archaistic replica of Luther's Bible by obscuring the work's twentieth-century provenance was an acknowledgment that even Luther's German had not reached the state of an ideal language. Strikingly, the reservations Borchardt expressed toward the actual historical manifestation of Luther's language also encompassed the unifying act that was attributed to Luther's German. For, as Borchardt admitted in the "Epilegomena," it was not a linguistically coherent idea of the German nation he was after but rather the lost potential of a linguistically and poetically plural notion of Germanness.

Borchardt's nation ultimately proved just as elusive as the ideal language that undergirded it. This was a direct result of his rejection

---

studies. See, for example, Ernst Osterkamp, "Näherungen: Rudolf Borchardt im Werk Walter Benjamins," *Germanisch-Romanische Monatsschrift* 31, no. 2 (1981): 203–33; and Wolfgang Matz, *Eine Kugel im Leibe: Walter Benjamin und Rudolf Borchardt: Judentum und deutsche Poesie* (Göttingen: Wallstein, 2011).

59. See *GW: Prosa I*, 343.

of previously existing instances of language. What disturbed Borchardt in each historical instance was the fact that language had an empirical and practical existence: it was spoken and used as a conveyor of meaning to an awaiting addressee. Borchardt's ideal language, on the other hand, like his translations, dismissed communication as an object. However, in doing so, it also dismissed the collectivity that such communication could call into being.

Borchardt and Buber on Bible Translation

Translation stood at the heart of the debate between Borchardt and Buber, which was instigated by the publication of the first volumes of Buber and Franz Rosenzweig's German Bible translation between 1925 and 1929. A revised single-volume edition containing the five books of the Torah (*Die fünf Bücher der Weisung*) appeared in 1930 together with an appendix that laid out the theoretical framework for the project.[60] The appendix included Buber's essay "On Word Choice in Translating the Bible," which, alongside the translation itself, prompted Borchardt to resume correspondence with Buber after almost twenty years of silence since their last exchange.

We can ascertain that the issue of translation had again been on Borchardt's mind from the fact that the same year, 1930, saw the appearance of his "Epilegomena." The afterword to his Dante translation allowed Borchardt to return to his theory of translation, which he first formulated when *Dante Deutsch* was in its early stages. It also, as we saw, allowed him to revisit his earlier work, *Das Buch Joram*. The Bible in German had in fact continued to occupy Borchardt over the years. In 1926, he was engaged in negotiations with the Bremer Presse Verlag over the publication of a revised

---

60. Martin Buber and Franz Rosenzweig, *Die fünf Bücher der Weisung: Verdeutscht von Martin Buber gemeinsam mit Franz Rosenzweig* (Berlin: Lambert Schneider, 1930). The appendix and additional essays by Martin Buber and Franz Rosenzweig were later published as one collection titled *Die Schrift und ihre Verdeutschung* (Berlin: Schocken Verlag, 1936). See also Martin Buber and Franz Rosenzweig, *Scripture and Translation*, trans. Lawrence Rosenwald and Everett Fox (Bloomington: Indiana University Press, 1994).

edition of Luther's Bible. The project did not come to fruition, but two years later, Borchardt was approached by the scholar and book collector Martin Bodmer, who proposed that the former present his own Bible translation to complement his *Dante Deutsch*.[61] This continued engagement led Borchardt to conclude his first letter to Buber on the matter with the words: "An den Dingen, die ich erörtert habe, hängt *mein Leben*."[62] (*My life* hangs on the things I have discussed.) At stake for Borchardt was not simply the task of the translator but also the role of Scripture in relation to his aesthetic-national program and his view of language.

The Buber-Rosenzweig Bible was supported by a specific philosophy of language that seemed to contrast with Borchardt's ideas. Though their opinions on other matters may have differed, Buber and Rosenzweig united in the belief that language—particularly the language of the Hebrew Bible—was a spoken one in essence. This was the import of Rosenzweig's 1925 essay "Scripture and Word."[63] The aim of the new Bible translation, according to Rosenzweig, was to reverse the process through which the Bible turned from a book originally intended to serve the spoken word into *Schrifttum*, or literature, a silent, written language that is detached from human communication.

Similar tones arise in Buber's essay "On Word Choice." According to Buber, the Hebrew Bible was originally meant to be read aloud. The auditory aspect of the original Hebrew was inalienable from the text. Its preservation in the German translation was paramount, as Buber remarked: "The auditory patterns of German can never *reproduce* the auditory forms of Hebrew; but they can, in growing from an analogous impulse and in exercising an analogous effect, *correspond to* them Germanically, can *Germanize* them. To meet the demands of such a task, the translator must elicit from the letter of the Hebrew

---

61. See Schuster, *Rudolf Borchardt, Martin Buber*, 28, 83–86.
62. Borchardt's letter to Buber, November 10, 1930, in Schuster, *Rudolf Borchardt, Martin Buber*, 60.
63. Franz Rosenzweig, "Die Schrift und das Wort: Zur neuen Bibelübersetzung," in *Kleinere Schriften* (Berlin: Schocken, 1937). Republished in Buber and Rosenzweig, *Scripture and Translation*, 40–46.

text its actual auditory form; he must understand the writtenness of Scripture as for the most part the record of its spokenness."⁶⁴

For Borchardt, this attempt to imitate the spoken patterns of Hebrew in the German language betrayed a problematic reluctance to emancipate oneself from the grip of the original text. He criticized what he took to be a subjugation of the German that denied the language its place as the creative medium for a new German work, and he felt compelled to inform Buber that the translation could not in good faith be called a German Bible since it was not presented as an autonomous German work but rather as a mere commentary on the Hebrew scripture: "Es will mir scheinen ... dass Sie zwischen den Aufgaben der Interpretation und denen der durch Übersetzung bewirkten Erneuerung eines Altlebendigen in einem Neulebendigen die Grenze nicht statuieren.... Sie interpretieren. Die deutsche Sprache ist für Sie weder ein Material noch ein Ziel, sondern ein reiner Behelf zu *Bezeichnungs*- nicht zu *Ausdrucks*zwecken."⁶⁵ (It seems to me ... that you do not draw the line between the tasks of interpretation and those of the renewal of an old living [being] in a new living [one] brought into effect through translation.... You interpret. The German language is for you neither material nor goal, but a pure auxiliary for purposes of designation, not for expression.)

Borchardt also rejected Rosenzweig's "Scripture and Word," which contested Johann Gottfried Herder's view of the Hebrew Bible. In 1924, a year prior to the publication of Rosenzweig's essay, Borchardt discussed the immense influence Herder's work had on his own understanding of the Bible.⁶⁶ Recalling his first encounter with Herder's *Älteste Urkunde des Menschengeschlechts* (Oldest Document of the Human Race, 1774) as a student, Borchardt praised the poetic image that rose from its discussion of the biblical account of creation. He was taken by Herder's understanding of the

---

64. Buber and Rosenzweig, *Scripture and Translation*, 75. Italics in the original.
65. Schuster, *Rudolf Borchardt, Martin Buber*, 45–47.
66. See Borchardt, "Eranos-Brief," in *Handlungen und Abhandlungen* (Berlin-Grunewald: Horen, 1928). The fifty-page-long letter was dedicated to Hugo von Hofmannsthal on his fiftieth birthday. It is, however, focused primarily on Borchardt's own intellectual and bibliographical biography.

Hebrew Bible as the sublime poetry of an ancient Hebraic people. For Herder, the Hebrew Bible exemplified an early historical moment in the development of humanity, where poetry was the most natural and immediate form of human expression. This intuitive notion of poetry captivated Borchardt, as he marveled: "Der Dichter war Dichter nicht durch Kunst—es gab keine Dichtkunst. Er war es als Mensch, durch Menschheit. Sprache war Dichtung."[67] (The poet was poet not through art—there was no art of poetry. He was that as a human being, through humanity. Language was poetry.)

As Borchardt adopted Herder's view of biblical poetry, he also shared the latter's ambivalence toward it and the people to whom it belonged. Biblical poetry inspired Herder's wonder for a people whose national and political character could serve as a model for the nascent modern German nation.[68] Yet while he was outlining affinities between biblical Hebrews and modern Germans, Herder also insisted on an insurmountable historical gap between them.[69] With his own view of translation, Herder captured the tension that rose from his historicist approach to the Hebrew Bible. Translations, for Herder, provided modern Germans with access to the remote world of the Bible and its inhabitants. This understanding stood behind Herder's own translations of biblical texts like the Song of Songs.[70] But Herder believed that as it was bridging over historical gaps and cultural divides, a translation ultimately established firm boundaries between the historical and the modern, affirming the foreignness of the former and separating it from the latter. Herder's view of Luther's Bible leaned on this assumption. The Luther translation was,

---

67. Borchardt, "Eranos-Brief," 157–58.
68. See for example, Barnard, *Herder on Nationality*, 18–27.
69. Herder's relation to modern Jews in Germany was even more ambivalent. Liliane Weissberg has argued that Herder refused to see modern Jews as the successors of the ancient Hebrews he praised in his writings. However, some scholars have shown that Herder did associate modern Jews with biblical Hebrews on numerous occasions. See Liliane Weissberg, "Juden oder Hebräer? Religiöse und politische Bekehrung bei Herder," in *Johann Gottfried Herder: Geschichte und Kultur*, ed. Martin Bollacher (Würzburg: Königshausen & Neumann, 1994), 191–211; Ilany, *In Search of the Hebrew People*, 134.
70. See Sheehan, *The Enlightenment Bible*, 175.

in his eyes, a quintessentially German literary monument. By being translated, it rendered the foreignness of the Hebrew Bible distinct from itself.

A similar perspective guided Borchardt, in whose eyes Luther's translation wrested the Bible from its historical and "oriental" trappings and planted it at the doorstep of German modernity. In this, Borchardt's relation to biblical poetry was no less ambivalent than Herder's. Like Herder, Borchardt allowed himself to be moved by the instinctually poetic expression of the Hebrew Bible. Biblical poetry brought Borchardt simultaneously to seek to retrieve its natural spontaneity and reject its historical surroundings. Thus, for Borchardt, Luther's Bible also had an inherently poetic import. But this import fundamentally differed from the poetry of the Hebrew Bible.

Rosenzweig's understanding of the Hebrew Bible as "unpoetry" (*Nichtpoesie*) indicated a wholly other conception. "Poetry is indeed the mother tongue of the human race," Rosenzweig conceded; "we need not reject here the insights of [Johann Georg] Hamann and Herder."[71] But the Bible's language was spoken prose, delivered from meter and rhyme. For this reason, it could not be historicized and rendered an archaic and surpassed *Ursprache* (primal language). Its spokenness rendered it ahistorical. This contention raised Borchardt's objection. Buber and Rosenzweig's translation disregarded a process Borchardt deemed irreversibly momentous, namely, the embedding of the Bible in literature, in writtenness. In Borchardt's view, this was one of the most significant accomplishments of Luther's translation: the transformation of biblical poetry from an inherently oral language into a literary *Schriftsprache*. Furthermore, any attempt to ground the biblical language in the speech of a living community would only corrupt it since, for Borchardt, only *Schrifttum* could manifest the condition of an ideal language situated beyond communication.

---

71. Buber and Rosenzweig, *Scripture and Translation*, 45.

Between Dialogue, Spoken Language, and Written Language

The exchange between Borchardt and Buber about Bible translation was a debate about the nature of language. Could language be conceived independently of its addressee like the *Schrifttum* that both Rosenzweig and Borchardt saw as the outcome of Luther's translation? Or did language, by the simple fact of its existence, always entail being received by someone? Did it always presuppose dialogue?

Buber and Rosenzweig's project pushed against what they saw as the aestheticization of the Bible—its becoming literature—insofar as this process involved a certain distance and independence from the reader. As Rosenzweig wrote:

> [The Bible] must not, even *qua* book, enter entirely into *Schrifttum*, into literature.... It cannot attain the autonomous, aesthetic value of *Schrift* because it cannot attain the distance that is the precondition of this value. Its content... refuses displacement into the objectivity, the separatedness, the *madeness* that characterize all that becomes literature.... [T]he essential content is precisely what escapes the specifying and distancing power of *Schrift*: the word of God to man, the word of man to God, the word of men before God.[72]

For Buber as for Rosenzweig, the biblical account of creation embedded man within language and language itself within dialogue. The Bible, as Buber argued, is a record of a dialogue between heaven and earth: "All its stories and songs, all its sayings and prophecies are united by one fundamental theme: the encounter of a group of people with the Nameless Being whom they, hearing his speech and speaking to him in turn, ventured to name."[73] The spokenness of the biblical language that Buber and Rosenzweig wished to stress with their new translation reflected the belief that from the moment

---

72. Buber and Rosenzweig, *Scripture and Translation*, 41. Rosenzweig is playing with the dual meaning of the word *Schrift*, as both script or writing and scripture (*die heilige Schrift*).

73. Buber and Rosenzweig, *Scripture and Translation*, 4.

of creation, language was used in conversation between God and humanity.

This is exactly what is denied in Borchardt's creative gesture toward Luther's German. *Das Buch Joram* is in many ways a tribute to Luther's Bible because it promotes a view of language that not only aspires to remain written but also denies its being part of a dialogue. The distance that *Joram*'s idiom created from its potential twentieth-century readership is one way in which the poem's language renders itself incommunicable. Contrasting even more directly with Buber and Rosenzweig's position regarding the encounter between God and humanity, however, is the description of a failed dialogue between man and God in the two chapters constituting the poem's apotheosis.

The absence of dialogue In *Joram* becomes even more palpable when compared to the corresponding passages in its model text, the Book of Job. Job's lament, "Let the day perish wherein I was born" (Job 3:3) is a self-negating utterance that is directed inward. Refusing to address God directly, Job's plaint has no intention to venture beyond the sorrowful expression of acceptance. Nevertheless, it is still able to elicit a direct response from God (See Job 38). Joram's plaint, on the other hand, is the exact opposite. From the start, it addresses God directly, asserts Joram's innocence, and demands justification for his suffering:

8. Welches ist meine Übertretung und was mein Vergehen, daß du mich heimgesuchet hast und ausgetilget?
9. So ich aber untadelig bin vor dir und hast doch den Bund gemacht mit Mose,
10. Wahrlich ich sage dir, so magst du mir nicht entlaufen, so du Flügel der Morgenröte an dich nähmest, du reinigtest dich denn.[74]

[8. Which is my transgression and what is my offence that thou hast afflicted me and blotted me out?
9. But if I am blameless before thee, and thou hast made the covenant with Moses,

---

74. *GW: Gedichte*, 392.

10. Verily I say unto thee, thou mayest not escape me, if thou takest to thyself wings of dawn, thou wilt not cleanse thyself.]

Despite the direct and assertive address, Joram's plaint is never properly answered. The poem emphasizes the absence of a rejoinder by having Joram repeat his request three times, each demand more urgent than the one before, all unsuccessful. At its most intense, Joram's plaint exceeds that of Job. While Job refuses to follow his wife's suggestion to "curse God and die" (Job 2:9), Joram is not deterred from doing exactly that:

13. So du aber der Hund bist, der sein Geschlungenes von ihm speit, so will ich dich zum Hunde machen, der wieder einschlingt sein Ausgespienes.
14. Denn du bist mir verhaftet durch dich selber, daß die Welt nicht untergehe zum zweiten Male an Joram,
15. Den du dir verhaftet hast mit Gesetz und einem Bunde des Regenbogens; den du auf und nieder gehst vor mir und meinem Volke auf sieben Farben mit sieben Heeren deiner Engel, und bist gereinigt.
16. So du aber nicht gereinigt bist und zerreißest dein Gesetz und hast mir gelogen,
17. So will ich deinen Regenbogen zerbrechen mit meinen Augen und ihn auslöschen mit meinen Gedanken und sieben Heere Engel fortblasen wie sieben Flaum Federn mit meinem Munde, daß du aufgehen müßtest und untergehen wie ein Götze auf Sieben Lügen durch ein wenig Wasser.[75]

[13. And if thou art like the dog who speweth out his meal, so will I make of thee a dog, who swalloweth his spit again.
14. For thou art beholden to me through thy promise, that the world not perish a second time unto Joram,
15. Whom thou hast bound with law and a rainbow covenant that thou raisest and lettest fall before me and my people

---

75. GW: *Gedichte*, 393.

with seven colors and with thy seven armies of angels, and art pure.
16. But if thou art not pure, and hast broken thy law, and lied unto me,
17. So will I break thy rainbow with mine eyes and wipe it from my heart, and with my mouth blow away thy seven armies of angels like feathers, that thou must perish by small deluge for thy lies as a false idol.]

If God is a dog in this inverted image, Joram wishes to be the axis upon which this inversion occurs. Joram wishes to take or perhaps embody *das Ausgespiene*, that which has been "spouted out" by God, utterances—empty, meaningless ones in Joram's eyes—like the covenants with Moses or Noah, and return them to God's mouth. He will make God recommit to these utterances, make these utterances have meaning, reconstitute the conversation between God and man. But Joram doesn't seem to recall the actual nature of God's promise to Moses and Noah. These were not pledges made to individual subjects but to peoples, or even to the entirety of humanity. They differ radically from what Joram deems them to be. The destruction Joram experiences is not a collective but a private one. There is no collective forsaken by God here, only individual suffering. Interestingly, Borchardt restricts the direct biblical references in this chapter to the covenants with Moses and Noah. There is no explicit mention here of the private calamities of Job despite the more obvious affinity between Job and Joram.

In Joram's admittedly modernist reality, however, this private perspective is all that exists. Private downfall is experienced as the world's *Untergang* since there is no concrete "people" beyond the lyrical subject. What Joram ultimately inverts is precisely the dialogue between God and humanity, out of which nothing is left but the soliloquizing subject. The more strident Joram's accusations grow, the clearer it becomes that they will not be answered, for the language in which they are embedded is not that of a dialogue between man and God but rather the monologizing language of literature. It is a language that has no intention of crossing the threshold of communication.

The absence of dialogue In *Joram* is a poignant reminder of the transition from spoken language to literature that Luther's translation prompted. This literary conception of the biblical language guaranteed that in *Joram*, any address or plaint will be presented as a monologue. The creation of a literary German attributed to Luther's translation shaped Borchardt's view of a language that no longer serves as a means for communication. Man's plaints are ossified into writing, into a literature that does not anticipate response. With the understanding that this notion of language persisted since Luther, Borchardt could present *Das Buch Joram* as a work that is both biblical and modern. As he declared in an address prefacing a public reading of the poem, "[*Joram*] handelt von seinen Gestalten und ihrem Schicksal überhaupt nur insofern, als es von Ihnen und mir handelt. Es handelt von seinem Gotte und seinem Heiland nur insofern, als es von Ihrem und meinem Gotte handelt, als es Ihren und meinen Gott im Aufbruche zu seiner Offenbarung zeigt.... Und doch ist die Geschichte... eine feste biblische Geschichte."[76] (*Joram* relates to its characters and their fate only insofar as it relates to you and me. It relates to its God and Messiah only insofar as it relates to my God and yours, as it shows [our] God departing from revelation.... And yet, this is firmly a biblical story.)

In addition to indicating contrasting conceptions of language, God's departure in *Joram* hints at a theological aspect of the debate between Borchardt and Buber. Buber's and Rosenzweig's dialogic view of language guided their wish to render the God of the Hebrew Bible present. According to Buber, Luther's translation was stamped by a Marcionite separation between the Old Testament God of creation and the world.[77] For Buber and Rosenzweig, the stakes of placing God in direct conversation with man and of rendering language the vessel of spokenness and dialogue were similar.[78] The theological stakes of the debate assigned the two views of language and translation with the designations "Jewish" and

---

76. Borchardt, "Erbrechte der Dichtung," in *GW: Reden*, 176.
77. See Buber and Rosenzweig, *Scripture and Translation*, 212.
78. In this context, see also Rosenzweig's essay "Der Ewige: Mendelssohn und der Gottesname." As Rosenzweig observes, Mendelssohn's discussion of the translation of God's name revealed the stakes involved in Bible translation, namely,

"German" respectively. Insofar as it provided a theological retort to the Christian historicization of the Hebrew Bible and its God, Buber and Rosenzweig's view emerged as "Jewish," and it seemed to contrast with what Borchardt understood as a specifically "German" relation to language and translation. This relation was facilitated by Luther's induction of the Bible into the halls of literature, an induction that was inscribed with a Christian theological claim.

Biblical Language and Aesthetic Distance

In some respects, the debate between Borchardt and Buber on Bible translation appears to endorse a contrast between "German" and "Jewish" views of language and translation. In his last communication to Buber from November 1930, Borchardt admitted that, as a "Jewish" Bible, the former's project did not concern him since his own Jewish ancestors had converted long ago. Identifying Borchardt's advocacy of Luther's translation as a wish to renounce Judaism, Buber replied: "Würden Sie jedoch auch an all dem Einzelnen berechtigte Kritik üben, der Auftrag selber und seine Art blieben Ihr unzugänglich, denn der biblische Bericht ist Ihnen offenbar fremd, Sie kennen die Bibel nur als ein Schrifttum, nicht als die Schrift."[79] (Even if you were to make just criticism of all of the project's individual details, the actual assignment and its nature would remain inaccessible to you, since the biblical account is obviously foreign to you; you know the Bible only as literature, not as Scripture.)

Borchardt's renunciation of Buber and Rosenzweig's "Jewish" Bible came in response to Buber's insistence that the project was not to be conceived aesthetically but rather theologically in the broad sense, as a work meant to correspond to a certain life practice. From this perspective, Borchardt could accommodate the notion of two contrasting "German" and "Jewish" views of language and translation. But the correspondence, like the further reception of the

---

the unity of God and his ahistorical presence as the personal God of immediate experience. Rosenzweig, *Kleinere Schriften*, 191–92.

79. See Schuster, *Rudolf Borchardt, Martin Buber*, 64.

Buber-Rosenzweig Bible, raised the question of whether aesthetic considerations of their work could indeed be staved off. As Borchardt stressed to Buber, "Ich kann an ein deutsches Buch keine andern als deutsche Kriterien anlegen."[80] (To a German book I cannot apply anything but German criteria.) By asking how the Buber-Rosenzweig Bible could enter the canon of German-language works while still demanding to be evaluated by separate criteria, Borchardt indicated that in his view aesthetic considerations could not be so easily set aside.

Borchardt was not alone in insisting that the aesthetic element was inseparable from deliberations on language and Bible translation in the twentieth century. Another prominent figure to argue in a similar vein, albeit from an altogether different political position, was the cultural critic Siegfried Kracauer. Kracauer's polemic "Die Bibel auf Deutsch" ("The Bible in German") was published in the *Frankfurter Zeitung* in April 1926, shortly after the appearance of the first volume of the Buber-Rosenzweig Bible. Its main point of contention was the translators' wish to locate in the biblical text a certain truth content that is pertinent and essential to modern life. For Kracauer, such truth content was available in modernity only within the realm of the profane, that is, through expressions of modern culture like art and film.

The Buber-Rosenzweig Bible offered Kracauer a compounded problem since its authors denied its condition as an aesthetic work. His first task was to show how, contrary to the translators' claim, their German Bible could not elude aesthetic consideration. Like Borchardt, Kracauer opened his critique by stating that a German work should be evaluated on its own terms and not in relation to another work.[81] Surveying the translators' word choices as well as their decision to present the Bible without commentary "in order to present the truth of scripture without any intervention," as he put it, he concluded that the work's disposition and language were ultimately

---

80. Schuster, *Rudolf Borchardt, Martin Buber*, 60.
81. Siegfried Kracauer, "The Bible in German," in *The Mass Ornament*, trans. Thomas Y. Levin (Cambridge, MA: Harvard University Press, 1995), 190.

Joram *and the Restoration of a Biblical Language* 71

determined by an aesthetic end.[82] As an aesthetic work, however, it was reactionary. Its idiosyncratic language appeared to him not biblical but rather reminiscent of Wagner's archaistic alliterations. Kracauer admittedly lacked knowledge of Hebrew and was therefore unable to evaluate the translation in full, as Buber and Rosenzweig pointed out in their response.[83] Yet his insistence on the aesthetic nature of the translation was shared by figures like Scholem, who knew Hebrew and even worked on his own translation of segments from the Hebrew Bible. In a letter to Buber from April 27, 1926, Scholem wrote: "What fills me with doubt is the excessive tonality of this prose.... To the extent that I can speak from experience, in the case of such translations one cannot avoid deciding whether one is translating revelation or a 'work of art,' and I believe that the translation of biblical *prose* and the extent to which singing is included in it are, *nolens volens*, shaped by this determination."[84]

For Kracauer, the Buber-Rosenzweig Bible steered away from the public sphere by removing itself from the quotidian. From its removed pedestal, the translation could not disrupt modern life; it had no other choice but to retreat into the private. This understanding allowed Kracauer finally to compare rather than contrast Buber and Rosenzweig's project to Borchardt's restorative work, which likewise, as Kracauer noted, created an aesthetic distance from the profanely modern.[85]

Regardless of whether the Buber-Rosenzweig Bible can indeed be compared with Borchardt's work or discussed in terms of a romanticist archaizing gesture, the ensuing debate on the translation makes

---

82. Kracauer, "The Bible in German," 197–98.
83. Buber and Rosenzweig published their response in May 1926 in the *Frankfurter Zeitung*. For an account of the ensuing controversy, see Martin Jay, *Permanent Exiles: Essays on the Intellectual Migration from Germany to America* (New York: Columbia University Press, 1985), 206–11.
84. Nahum Glatzer and Paul Mendes-Flohr, eds., *The Letters of Martin Buber*, trans. Richard Winston, Clara Winston, and Harry Zohn (New York: Schocken, 1991), 338–39. For Scholem's German translations of sections from Job and Ezekiel, see Ilit Ferber and Paula Schwebel, eds., *Lament in Jewish Thought: Philosophical, Theological, and Literary Perspectives* (Berlin: De Gruyter, 2014).
85. Kracauer, "The Bible in German," 191, 198.

clear that aesthetic deliberations were indispensable to it. What also becomes clear is that such deliberations worked to obscure the boundaries between the profane and the sacred, the modern and the archaic, the public and the private, as well as between the "German" and the "Jewish" as opposing positions concerning language and translation.[86] Kracauer's critique was driven by a comparison between the Buber-Rosenzweig translation and the Luther Bible. According to Kracauer, the Luther Bible intervened in a particular historical constellation by instigating a socioeconomic revolution against the Catholic Church. Such an act of protest tore Scripture from its theological heights and brought it down to the worldly life of the people. This led Kracauer to surmise that for a work to bear relevance to modern times, it would have to create an effect of equal magnitude. However, since Luther's translation already facilitated the process of emancipation that led from theological to profane thought, a similarly revolutionary effect could not be attained by another Bible translation.

By holding the Buber-Rosenzweig Bible to such standards, Kracauer indicated he did not consider the work exclusively Jewish. Its revolutionary claims had to be scrutinized in relation to its intervention into German society as a whole. But in this, Kracauer was in fact not so far off from Buber's and Rosenzweig's own views. For although they understood the dialogic language conception that guided their translation to emerge from traditional Jewish sources, their project aimed to replace Luther's Bible not just for German-speaking Jews but for all German speakers. As Naomi Seidman points out, even in his rejection of Herder's view of the poetic nature of biblical language, Rosenzweig was careful to emphasize that "the Bible was the prosaic breath of the human being qua human being," and not "the song of a race."[87] There were no separate stakes for a sectarian "Jewish" Bible. Whatever claims Buber and Rosenzweig made

---

86. See also Brian Britt, "The Romantic Roots of the Debate on the Buber-Rosenzweig Bible," *Prooftexts* 20, no. 3 (2000): 262–89. Britt shows the common romantic roots of the language philosophy of both Buber and Rosenzweig as well as their critics, Benjamin and Kracauer.

87. Seidman, *Faithful Renderings*, 184; Buber and Rosenzweig, *Scripture and Translation*, 45.

regarding the essence of biblical language, they were relevant to all human beings.[88] As Seidman emphasizes, the Buber-Rosenzweig Bible "was not a *Jewish* Bible ... but *the* Bible." It made its claim "not from the confines of the Jewish tradition but from outside and 'above' the Jewish-Christian divide that is history itself."[89]

Buber and Rosenzweig did not dispute the revolutionary status of Luther's Bible. Yet, contrary to Kracauer, they believed that Luther's Bible itself needed to be modernized as its revolutionary effect had worn off. They responded to criticism of the alienating nature of their language by striving to create the same effect that Luther's German initially had before it became overfamiliar. At stake, however, was not merely the re-creation of the faded revolutionary moment that was encapsulated in Luther's Bible but rather the fulfillment of its ultimately missed potential. As Rosenzweig wrote, Luther's revolutionary intervention consisted in bringing the words of the Bible to the vernacular—to be spoken by the people. But this accomplishment could not be sustained for very long before Luther's German solidified into a *Schriftsprache*.[90] In bringing biblical language back to spokenness, Rosenzweig hoped to realize what Luther's translation sought to do but ultimately could not.

Kracauer's critique demonstrates how the debate around the Buber-Rosenzweig Bible and its accompanying deliberations on translation and the restoration of biblical language did not in fact fall neatly along clear lines of division. For although their perspectives differed on some matters, in identifying a concomitance of revolutionary potential and the instigation of a process of loss in Luther's Bible, Rosenzweig and Borchardt, for example, were united. The exchange between Borchardt and Buber foregrounded a theologically conceived Jewish difference in relation to theoretical conceptions of language and translation. But the broader surrounding

---

88. A similar sentiment is found in Buber's essay "People Today and the Jewish Bible," where the "people today," whom Buber envisions as the readership of this "Jewish Bible," are modern German-speaking intellectuals both Jewish and non-Jewish.
89. Seidman, *Faithful Renderings*, 181.
90. Buber and Rosenzweig, *Scripture and Translation*, 57.

discourse on the aesthetic and potentially revolutionary nature of a twentieth-century German Bible translation revealed the difficulty of establishing clear categories for a "Jewish" Bible that is unambiguously separated from a non-Jewish, "German" one.

The same critical considerations also made it difficult to posit unambiguous "German" and "Jewish" approaches to language and translation despite the claims of some participants in the debate. In the case of Borchardt and Buber, even the difference between the lyrical language of *Das Buch Joram* and the aspirational, dialogic-collective language of the Buber-Rosenzweig Bible becomes unsettled when one considers that both works were fated to remain audienceless. To this day, Borchardt's *Joram* remains for the most part an obscure work; when Buber finally completed the Bible translation in Israel in 1961, more than thirty years after Rosenzweig's death, Scholem publicly wondered whether this monumental project would simply go unread after the destruction of German Jewry by the Nazis.[91] Kracauer's critique anticipated this connection in comparing the Buber-Rosenzweig Bible to Borchardt's work. But Kracauer's own distinction between an archaistic retreat into the private sphere and a revolutionary, modernist intervention in the public sphere was itself undermined, as we have seen, by critics like Adorno, who made a case for the irreplaceable revolutionary potential of lyrical, archaistic works like Borchardt's. "Audienceless" works eventually had their own unique way of intimating an alternative to the status quo.

Situating Borchardt's *Joram* amid these broader debates on the reconstruction of biblical language reveals an intricate relation between questions of Jewish difference and the persistence of archaistic gestures in the modernist discourse. In the nineteenth century, engagement with German Bible translations and biblical subject matter came largely to be recognized as an exclusively Jewish marker.[92] Yet Borchardt's case demonstrates how the return of such themes in the first decades of the twentieth century unsettled this previous

---

91. See Gershom Scholem, "At the Completion of Buber's Translation of the Bible," in *The Messianic Idea in Judaism* (New York: Schocken, 1971), 318.

92. See, for example, Ilany, *In Search of the Hebrew People*, 116; and Karin Schutjer, *Goethe and Judaism: The Troubled Inheritance of Modern Literature* (Evanston, IL: Northwestern University Press, 2015), 5–6.

tendency to identify the Hebrew Bible with an unambiguously "Jewish" position. It is true that *Joram*'s reception displayed, at least in part, some residue from the previous century in its inclination to interpret the work's biblical language as a reflection of the poem's indelible Jewish essence. But the aesthetic program that accompanied *Joram* ultimately neither confirmed nor denied such views. Instead of arguing for or against the existence of a particularly Jewish element in the work and thereby acknowledging the attribution of biblical discourse to Jewish sectarianism, it took what was previously understood by Jews and non-Jews alike as particularly Jewish and used it as the foundation for its notion of a universal German *Kulturnation*. In doing so, Borchardt's program was no less subversive than Buber and Rosenzweig's aspiration to replace—indeed, *supersede*—the Luther Bible for all German readers.

Like Buber and Rosenzweig's return to biblical language, Borchardt's biblical Creative Restoration linked this subversion with a distinctively modernist historico-philosophical question, namely, that of historical supersession and the persistence of superseded elements in seminal modern debates. To be sure, Kracauer's critique refused to recognize archaistic gestures like those of Borchardt or Buber and Rosenzweig as valid contributions to modern public discourse. Yet in raising the issue, he ended up proving the opposite. The widespread debate surrounding both Borchardt's writings and Buber and Rosenzweig's work ultimately shows that an ongoing reflection on modernity's enduring relation to that which it relegated to a superseded past was in fact an integral part of modernist discourse.

2

Opening the Work

The German Oratorio and Paul Ben-Haim's Joram

The afterlife of Borchardt's *Das Buch Joram* elaborates further on the many ambiguities associated with the poem. In 1932, the composer Paul Ben-Haim (at the time, still known as Paul Frankenburger)[1] provided a musical setting to Borchardt's text as the oratorio *Joram*. Ben-Haim was born in 1897 in Munich to a culturally assimilated, liberal Jewish family. He received his musical training in piano and composition at the Music Academy in Munich and quickly became part of the city's vibrant musical landscape. In his early years in Germany, he was active as both composer and conductor. In 1921 he assumed a position as Bruno Walter's assistant at the *Bayrische Staatstheater* and four years later was appointed Kapellmeister at the

---

1. Some studies that discuss Ben-Haim's German period separately use the composer's German last name. For the sake of clarity and continuity, this chapter will use the Hebrew name the composer adopted after his immigration to Mandatory Palestine.

opera house in Augsburg. He remained in Augsburg until 1931, when his position was terminated amid rising antisemitism that coincided with financial cuts to the theater. In 1933, Ben-Haim immigrated to British Mandatory Palestine, a move that was made at the time out of practical considerations rather than ideological conviction, as his biographer points out.[2]

Today, Ben-Haim is known and studied primarily as an Israeli composer. Most of the scholarship dedicated to his work focuses on the compositions he produced after emigrating from Germany and their involvement in the construction of an Israeli national ethos in the state's formative decades.[3] The fate of his earlier work in Germany as well as Ben-Haim's own status as a German composer are subject to some debate. As Ronit Seter notes, the issue of Ben-Haim's Germanness has often been "soft-pedaled" or read as a passing stage on the way to his later contribution to Israeli art music.[4] My analysis of the oratorio *Joram* in this chapter heeds Seter's observation. It aims to avoid a teleological reading in order to consider the oratorio within the more immediate circumstances of its creation.

Ben-Haim composed *Joram* in his last year in Germany. Given Borchardt's outspoken German national sentiment and the circumstances Ben-Haim encountered in Germany in 1932, it might be surprising to learn of his interest in the poem. Borchardt's staunch devotion to the idea of a national German culture might have conflicted with the view of the young composer who had been dismissed by that same culture. However, the fact that *Das Buch Joram* appealed to Ben-Haim indicates that he did not cease to consider

---

2. See Jehoash Hirshberg, *Paul Ben-Haim: His Life and Work* (Tel-Aviv: Israel Music Institute, 2010), 96.

3. See for example, Assaf Shelleg, *Theological Stains: Art Music and the Zionist Project* (Oxford: Oxford University Press, 2020).

4. See Ronit Seter, "Hirshberg's *Ben-Haim*: Three Decades Later," *Min-Ad: Israel Studies in Musicology Online* 9 (2010): 97–113, 101. Seter points out that there has also been a tendency to tone down German aspects of Ben-Haim's later work in Mandatory Palestine and Israel for similar reasons. For a reading of *Joram* against such a teleology, see, for example, Liran Gurkiewicz, "Paul Ben-Haim: The Oratorio *Joram* and the Jewish Identity of the Composer," *Min-Ad* 11 (2013): 106–29; and Yehuda Cohen, *The Heirs of the Psalmist* (Tel-Aviv: Am-Oved, 1990).

himself a participant in German culture immediately after his dismissal.[5] Furthermore, it confirms that the themes of failure, isolation, incommunicability, and individual suffering the poem addresses offer a much more nuanced and unsettled notion of Germanness, one that Ben-Haim could continue to work with almost thirty years after the poem's original publication.

While the poem's solitary qualities may have drawn Ben-Haim initially, they were nonetheless transformed by the decision to set the text as an oratorio. In studying the afterlife of Borchardt's work in Ben-Haim's *Joram*, I propose that we should first ask how the transformation of the poem into a musical piece shapes the new artistic product—the new *work*. By asking this question, we extend our inquiry into the nature of translation from one medium into another, in this case, from poetry to music. I submit that *Joram*'s setting specifically as an oratorio rather than an opera should be examined closely. The translation of *Das Buch Joram* into the form of the oratorio does not merely repeat Borchardt's poem in a different environment, that is, in a different "language" or medium. Rather, the history and distinct attributes of the German oratorio associate the oratorio *Joram* with a specific conception of the artwork as incomplete and fragmented. In this, the composition undermines the classical view of the "work" that Borchardt assigned his poetry, namely, the work as an autonomous, self-contained manifestation existing independently of its reception. The question of Jewish difference in Ben-Haim's musical rendition emerges as part of these aesthetic considerations.

Close to the completion of his oratorio, Ben-Haim wrote to Borchardt to inform him of his undertaking. In a letter from September 30, 1932, the poet replied:

> I learned with pleasure of the great edifice which you intend to erect ... on the modest sketch of an old work of mine. You may take my consent as a matter of course, and I myself cannot contribute anything more than my

---

5. While there are debates on whether Ben-Haim could be considered a "German" composer after his immigration, few scholars would contest Hirshberg's assertion that the pieces composed in Germany, *Joram* among them, are "the German works of a German composer." See further Seter, "Hirshberg's *Ben-Haim*," 101–6.

most heartfelt wishes and my sincere advice to make the freest possible use of the text, according to the demands of your own heart.... It may interest you to know that many years ago a young gentleman from Silesia already wanted to compose music to this little book, as an opera, no less. To this day he still owes me an answer to my question as to how he would compose a baritone aria for our beloved God [für den lieben Gott].[6]

From the tone of the letter, we can infer that the idea of composing *Das Buch Joram* as an opera seemed incongruous even to Borchardt. It is possible that in the eyes of both poet and composer the poem demanded a musical genre that would resonate with its biblical settings. In this case, the oratorio, commonly categorized as "sacred music" with its long history of setting biblical narratives to music, may appear more appropriate than the operatic genre, which concentrated traditionally on profane themes. *Das Buch Joram*, however, is far from an authentic biblical narrative. Its focus on the suffering of the modern individual in a godforsaken world could have made it a proper candidate for an opera. The transformation of Borchardt's poem into an oratorio, therefore, must have a meaning that goes beyond the surface distinction between opera and oratorio as sacred and profane musical dramas respectively.

This chapter will trace this meaning by reviewing the unique characteristics of the oratorio in Germany and concentrating on the passions of Johann Sebastian Bach as a model for the genre in general and for Ben-Haim's *Joram* specifically. My approach to the study of the oratorio is not solely historical. While I consider the history of the genre in the German-speaking space and examine both its "exemplary" case, Bach's passions, and the individual case of Ben-Haim's oratorio against it, my investigation of the German oratorio also follows an aesthetic-theoretical framework, one that was elaborated in Walter Benjamin's work on the post-Reformation theatrical medium and the idea of the incomplete or fragmentary work that it conveyed.

Benjamin's comments on the open-ended nature of the modern artwork relate to his study of the German *Trauerspiel*, a theatrical genre he distinguished from tragedy as an inherently modern form. Benjamin's work on the *Trauerspiel* does not address the question

---

6. Cited in Hirshberg, *Paul Ben-Haim*, 87. Translation altered.

of music directly. In fact, his comments on music and drama set to music, while highly suggestive and extremely insightful, are also relatively sparse throughout his writings. But by situating the *Trauerspiel* deeply within the historical, social-political, and theological circumstances of the post-Reformation era, Benjamin's work points to a link between the *Trauerspiel* and the German oratorio as two forms that consolidated on the basis of very similar circumstances.

Studying the oratorio alongside Benjamin's writings on the *Trauerspiel* will show how the oratorio promoted a similar conception of the artwork whose boundaries are porous and blurred. With its main problematic being the blurred boundaries between the German Lutheran and Jewish communities, however, the oratorio goes beyond the *Trauerspiel* to link the stakes of the open-ended artwork directly with the issue of Jewish difference. It is this background of the oratorio that served Ben-Haim's own artistic response to the rigid notion of Jewish difference prevailing in Germany in the 1930s. Ultimately, it also allowed him to take the ambiguous gesture of Borchardt's poetry a step further.

The inquiry into the composition of *Joram* relies on two additional principles that issue from Benjamin's work. Benjamin's idea of translation as a continuous supplementation rather than a simple restatement in a different language or medium is also intimately connected with his attempt to salvage the German Romantic concept of art criticism and see in it the root of a productive modernist mode of critical engagement with artworks.[7] The concept of art criticism that Benjamin traces in his essay of the same title from 1920 views the work of the critic as an extension of the artwork. Benjamin shows how the early Romantics understood the act of criticism not as passing judgment—the uncomplicated activity of observing a passive object—but rather as the setting in motion of the work's own immanent potential to reach a higher level of self-reflection. This view put artwork and criticism on the same plane; it deemed criticism a kind of continuation of the artwork. Moreover,

---

7. Walter Benjamin, "The Concept of Art Criticism in German Romanticism," in *Selected Writings 1: 1913–1926*, ed. Marcus Bullock and Michael W. Jennings (Cambridge, MA: Harvard University Press, 2004).

criticism's capacity to bring the work to a higher level of reflection also implied that the artwork was a fragment that would always remain incomplete since there could always be another work of criticism that would further complete it.

Benjamin's essay "The Task of the Translator" was published three years after "The Concept of Art Criticism." In many ways, his understanding of translation draws from that of the Romantic concept of art criticism. Translation, which inevitably involves interpretation, is indeed another mode of criticism. In chapter 1 we saw that, like Borchardt, Benjamin understood translation as an artwork on its own merit. Yet the two differed in their views of the translation's relation to the so-called original work. Whereas for Borchardt, each translation stood as an autonomous and complete work, for Benjamin, every translation formed yet another link in the infinite and never truly complete continuum aspiring toward a lost pure language.[8]

To the Benjaminian understanding of criticism and translation this chapter adds the act of providing a musical rendition. Proposing to consider the composition of Borchardt's poetic work as the oratorio *Joram* in light of Benjamin's work on translation and art criticism allows both to set the two works, poem and oratorio, in a similar nexus that presents them both as part of an open-ended continuum of works and simultaneously to emphasize each work's individual condition as a fragment. This approach complements the view of the open-ended artwork that the *Trauerspiel* and the oratorio promote. The stakes of insisting on the interminable nature of the artwork as part of a study of Jewish difference deserve restating here. As the introduction indicated, the philosophical and aesthetic legacy of Richard Wagner's work, specifically his notion of the total artwork, tied the idea of the complete artwork with a rigid conception of Jewish difference. To promote an interminable understanding of the work, as Benjamin did, amounts to unsettling this rigid view of Jewish difference. Since Wagner reframed the question

---

8. See also Benjamin's distinction between the open-ended "idea of art" and the classical understanding of the autonomous and complete "ideal of art." Benjamin, "The Concept of Art Criticism," 257.

of Jewish difference in aesthetic terms, a response to his claims would likewise have to be located in the realm of aesthetic theory.

Excursus I: Benjamin on Post-Reformation Theater

Understanding the rendition of a poetic work as an oratorio in Benjaminian terms requires a closer look at Benjamin's thoughts on post-Reformation theater and the drama set to music as they are expressed in his book *Ursprung des deutschen Trauerspiels* (*Origin of the German Trauerspiel*, 1925). The term "mourning-play" or *Trauerspiel* denotes a type of theatrical play that emerged during the baroque period in the late sixteenth and early seventeenth centuries. In his study, Benjamin focused on some of the lesser-known exponents of the genre, German dramatists like Martin Opitz (1597–1639) and Andreas Gryphius (1616–1664), rather than on more familiar figures like William Shakespeare and Pedro Calderón de la Barca. The German *Trauerspiel* was characterized by a simplicity of action as well as other baroque features like excessively figurative and bombastic language and exaggerated violence. For Benjamin, it was important to return to these otherwise little-appreciated works, as he understood their emergence to represent a certain distilled moment in modernity that he found instructive for his own modernist circumstances in the twentieth century.[9]

Benjamin's study of the German baroque *Trauerspiel* in relation to both Greek tragedy and post-Reformation modern theater is also relevant to our present wish to trace the distinction between opera and oratorio, specifically the German tradition of the oratorio, which, unlike its Italian counterpart, is profoundly shaped by a Lutheran perspective. One of Benjamin's main objectives in his study of the German *Trauerspiel* is to demonstrate the irreconcilable difference between it and the genre of the tragedy with which, as he

---

9. Benjamin's return to the German baroque to salvage a lesser-known form parallels his return to recover the Romantic concept of art criticism. In both cases Benjamin recognized a moment in history as possessing a missed revolutionary potential that had to be reclaimed.

argues, it has often been erroneously conflated. Based on the earlier works of Franz Rosenzweig and Florens Christian Rang, Benjamin argues that the genre of tragedy corresponded to a specific period—a Greek, pagan age—that disappeared after the rise of Christianity in Europe. The significance of the *Trauerspiel* to the modern conception of the work lies, as Samuel Weber lucidly explains, in its emergence at a specific historical moment marked by the simultaneous hegemony of Christianity and the internal fracture of that same hegemony brought on by the challenge of the Reformation.[10]

For Benjamin, the German *Trauerspiel* united aesthetic and political concerns. At stake was the problem of sovereignty and its relation to theater. As a specifically modern form of theater, the *Trauerspiel* emerged in response to a crisis in Christian eschatology. Luther's notion of *sola fide*, "faith alone," as the path to salvation resulted in the deprecation of *good works* as an action that guarantees transcendence. Redemption as ultimate fulfillment became the sole, dubious business of isolated individuals, who were left to an uncertain destiny they were unable to influence with their deeds. The loss of good works was significant for Benjamin since it rendered human action meaningless. *Works* lost their previous *fulfilling* capacity. Their outcome and meaning remained open. Benjamin understood post-Reformation theater as a response to this uncertain, open condition:

> The great German dramatists of the baroque were Lutherans. Whereas in the decades of the Counter-Reformation Catholicism had penetrated secular life with all the power of its discipline, the relationship of Lutheranism to the everyday had always been antinomic. The rigorous morality of its teaching in respect of civic conduct stood in sharp contrast to its renunciation of "good works." By denying the latter any special miraculous spiritual effect, making the soul dependent on grace through faith, and making the secular-political sphere a testing ground for a life which was only indirectly religious, being intended for the demonstration of civic virtues, it did . . . instill into the people a strict sense of obedience to duty, but in its great men it produced melancholy. Even in Luther himself, the last two decades of whose life are filled with an

---

10. Samuel Weber, *Theatricality as Medium* (New York: Fordham University Press, 2004), 160.

increasing heaviness of soul, there are signs of the reaction against the assault on good works.... In that excessive reaction which ultimately denied good works as such ... there was an element of German paganism and the grim belief in the subjection of man to fate. Human actions were deprived of all value.[11]

This new reality had political implications. The isolation of the individual, who lost access to institutions like the Church as facilitators of the redemption of a unified community through rites and sacraments, resulted in a condition of problematic collectivity. As Benjamin explained, "the baroque knows no eschatology; and for that very reason it possesses no mechanism by which all earthly things are gathered in together and exalted before being consigned to their end."[12] This condition affected the authority of the secular state, which arose in Europe around the same time as the alternative to the absolute sovereignty of the Curia. The secular sovereign was subjected, like everyone else, to the same uncertainty of redemption and was therefore unable, as Weber puts it, "to claim a transcendent justification and the [concomitant] power to endow collective life with a meaning that could comprehend and surpass individual mortality."[13] The effect of the Reformation and the deprecation of works was felt throughout Europe, as Benjamin claims. But unlike France, England, or Spain, Germany had neither a national religion nor a solid, unified nation-state to fall back on and therefore experienced the full thrust of this condition.

Importantly, the deprecation of works for Benjamin was not limited to the religious realm. The "assault on works" as a form of rendering action meaningless—the opening of action to a horizon of endless unknown possibilities and outcomes—had a direct effect on the conception of a closed or complete art*work*, and most importantly on the conception of modern theater as the locus of *action*. Benjamin demonstrates this by observing the transformation in dramatic forms:

---

11. Walter Benjamin, *Origin of the German Tragic Drama*, trans. John Osborne (New York: Verso, 2009), 138. Hereafter *OGT*.
12. Benjamin, *OGT*, 66.
13. Weber, *Theatricality as Medium*, 171.

> The developing formal language of the *Trauerspiel* can very well be seen as the emergence of the contemplative necessities which are implicit in the contemporary theological situation. One of these, and it is consequent upon the total disappearance of eschatology, is the attempt to find, in a reversion to a bare state of creation, consolation for the renunciation of a state of grace. Here, as in other spheres of baroque life, what is vital is the transposition of the originally temporal data into a figurative spatial simultaneity. This leads deep into the structure of the dramatic form. Whereas the middle ages present the futility of world events and the transience of the creature as stations on the road to salvation, the German *Trauerspiel* is taken up entirely with the hopelessness of the earthly condition.... The rejection of the eschatology of the religious dramas is characteristic of the new drama throughout Europe; nevertheless, the rash flight into a nature deprived of grace is specifically German.[14]

Indeed, the German baroque *Trauerspiel* was a dramatic genre dedicated to the exposition of a failed, indecisive, secular ("creaturely") sovereignty in a manner that sharply contrasted with the redemptive apotheosis of medieval religious dramas. While Benjamin describes this genre as specifically German, he also emphasizes that the *Trauerspiel* is characteristic of a general aesthetic position in modernity. Opening the work to uncertainty means rendering the work incomplete—a fragment. For this reason, Benjamin also notes an affinity between the baroque and Romanticism as two positions that oppose the classical notion of complete, autonomous works.[15]

Incompletion is expressed in the *Trauerspiel* also in the form of allegory. Rendering action meaningless opened the work to a simultaneous plurality of arbitrary meanings illustrated by the ambiguous figure of the intriguer. Embodying the inauthentic relation between word or action and meaning, the intriguer who speaks one thing and means another was the foremost representative of the genre and the aesthetic-political position it heralded in Benjamin's eyes.

Of particular interest is Benjamin's description of allegory in spatial terms, the "transposition of the originally temporal data," of the temporal problem of eschatology, "into a figurative spatial

---

14. Benjamin, *OGT*, 80–81.
15. See Benjamin, *OGT*, 176.

simultaneity" quoted above. For it is exactly this specific kind of ambiguity, spatially defined, which allows us to consider the German oratorio alongside the theatrical transformation that the *Trauerspiel* introduced into modernity. This spatiality designates the oratorio, in contradistinction to the mass, as a notably theatrical form, and does so in spite of the traditional tendency to consider the oratorio a somber, unstaged musical genre. The mass is a rite fixed in space and time as an event invested with a conclusive meaning. But as we will see, the German oratorio differs from the mass in that it is unable to provide either the same spatial anchoring or the same conclusion; each member of the audience in the oratorio experiences it individually, internally, and indeterminately. This condition has bearing on the spatial nature of the "confines" of the oratorio. The absence of a stable audience as a fixed collective against which the oratorio is performed erodes the distinct spatial boundaries between work and audience. In other words, the porosity of its unfixed audience contributes to the oratorio's own porosity.

As Weber notes, the exposure of the drama to an unfixed, unstable audience is the condition of modern, allegorical theater. Its subversive capacity "consists in the power to *move* and disrupt the consecrated and institutionalized boundaries that structure political space: those, for instance, that separate the sacred from the profane, the 'altar' from the public."[16] The mutability of the allegorical theater's audience affects the stability of the drama itself, which, as Weber indicates, "never definitively takes place . . . because the space of the stage, which it inhabits, is no more definite or stable."[17]

Under the sign of the Reformation, the German oratorio was similarly not only a *work* in the modern, fragmented sense but also a modern theatrical form par excellence. We will return to this observation in the study of Bach's passions as the paradigmatic example that likewise moves and disrupts boundaries. For now, it suffices to note that the depiction of Christ's life in Bach's *Matthäus-Passion* BWV 244 already demonstrates the same tendency toward open-endedness and interminability that Benjamin identified in his *Trauerspiel* book:

---

16. Weber, *Theatricality as Medium*, 37.
17. Weber, *Theatricality as Medium*, 174.

"Even the story of the life of Christ supported the movement from history to nature which is the basis of allegory.... The eternal is separated from the events of the story of salvation, and what is left is a living image open to all kinds of revisions by the interpretative artist."[18] The omission of Christ's resurrection in Bach's passions exemplifies the exact modern condition Benjamin speaks of. In such works, even Christ's life becomes creaturely, untransfigured. By ending with the crucifixion, the passions are left unresolved.[19]

Excursus II: Benjamin, Nietzsche, and the Problem of Opera

Although Benjamin's reflections on music are scarce, they are in fact essential to a full understanding of his insights concerning the concept of the work. Music and sound play a critical role in his observations on the inauthentic relation to meaning that characterizes modern works and, notably, modern theater. Important in this regard is the distinction that Benjamin draws between writing and voicing as two forms of expression with two fundamentally differing relations to meaning. As early as 1916, Benjamin assigned sound a particular importance in two essays: "On Language as Such and on the Language of Man" and the essay that prefigured his later *Trauerspiel* book, "The Role of Language in Trauerspiel and Tragedy." The two early essays depict sound as the final resolve of language. Every being in creation achieves full recognition in the moment of its being named, whereby naming is notably a sounding out or being voiced.[20]

Benjamin continued to develop these early observations in his *Trauerspiel* book by determining the allegorical mode of baroque

---

18. Benjamin, *OGT*, 182–83.
19. This also corresponds to the reading for Good Friday, which constitutes the texts of the passions. Traditionally, the Gospel reading for Good Friday ends with the crucifixion. The resurrection is read only on the subsequent Easter Sunday.
20. See further Eli Friedlander, "On the Musical Gathering of Echoes of the Voice: Walter Benjamin on Opera and the Trauerspiel," *The Opera Quarterly* 21, no. 4 (2005): 631–46, 634–35.

theater as a mode of writing.[21] The allegorical object's relation to meaning is exactly that of writing or script, an arbitrary sign that stores knowledge. Benjamin contrasts the writing of words to their sounding out, which in primordial times was an expression of a being's immanent significance. In the baroque dramas, he says, "written language and sound confront each other in tense polarity."[22] Through the baroque's fascination with onomatopoeia, Benjamin emphasizes sound's inability to form an authentic relation to meaning in modernity. In the baroque, sound reveals itself as a purely sensuous phenomenon. Meaning, now no longer authentic and immanent but rather arbitrary and allegorical, "has its home in written language." The spoken word is "only afflicted with meaning . . . as if by an inescapable disease."[23]

Benjamin calls purely sensuous sound "music." In the seventeenth century, music had no linguistic-philosophical standing. As he writes, music is "the opposite of meaning-laden speech."[24] This observation has an important bearing on the development of opera around 1600, chiefly since opera emerged as a speculative endeavor with the expressed intention of reaching that lost state of completion, of authentic unity of word and sound. Benjamin's historico-philosophical approach rejects the possibility of such unity in modernity. In the post-Reformation world of the *Trauerspiel*, the unity between word and sound that typified Greek tragedy had no footing. Benjamin's position is not far from that of Jean-Jacques Rousseau's "Essay on the Origin of Language" and even that of Wagner, who considered the common origin of music and language to be a lost primordial unity. Yet unlike Wagner, Benjamin believed any attempt at uniting the two in modernity would deny the historical sense of the time. Instead of a revival of Greek tragedy in the form of opera, then, Benjamin writes of "the dissolution of *Trauerspiel* into opera."[25]

Of importance here is Benjamin's extensive quotation from Nietzsche's *Die Geburt der Tragödie aus dem Geiste der Musik* (*The*

---

21. See Benjamin, *OGT*, 185.
22. Benjamin, *OGT*, 201.
23. Benjamin, *OGT*, 209.
24. Benjamin, *OGT*, 211. Notably, Rudolf Borchardt also attributed the transition to language as an inherently written entity to Luther and the Reformation.
25. Benjamin, *OGT*, 212.

Birth of Tragedy out of the Spirit of Music, 1872). Benjamin relies on Nietzsche to emphasize the problematic union of language and music in modernity. He cites Nietzsche's condemnation of the recitative, the *stilo rappresentativo*, which was the main innovation of the emergent genre opera and the technique that was believed to facilitate the same union of word and sound attributed to Greek dramas.[26] As Nietzsche wrote,

> The recitative was regarded as the rediscovered language of this primitive man; opera as the rediscovered country of this idyllically or heroically good creature, who simultaneously with every action follows a natural artistic impulse, who accomplishes his speech with a little singing, in order that he may immediately break into full song at the slightest emotional excitement.... The man incapable of art creates for himself a kind of art precisely because he is the inartistic man as such. Because he does not sense the Dionysian depth of music, he changes his musical taste into an appreciation of the understandable word-and-tone rhetoric of the passions in the *stilo rappresentativo*, and into the voluptuousness of the art of the song.[27]

As Nietzsche argues and Benjamin cites, while the opera claimed to offer harmonious unity, its recitative technique managed only to render its expression more discursive and theoretical.[28] Nietzsche's chastising remarks on the recitative and on what both he and Benjamin understood as the spurious claims of modern opera serve Benjamin in noting an important transition: as a modern theatrical form, opera, in Benjamin's view, was another, later product of the *Trauerspiel*. Yet what the *Trauerspiel* made visible as the main problematic of its age—the fragmented, ambiguous status of works—opera masked with its spurious claims to unity and cohesion. In this sense, opera was the *Trauerspiel*'s dissolution, marking the decline of a form that made visible its historical condition:

---

26. While he leans on Nietzsche's critique of the *stilo rappresentativo*, Benjamin criticizes the young Nietzsche's conviction that Wagner's music drama was able to restore the unity that "frivolous opera" could not.
27. Friedrich Nietzsche, "The Birth of Tragedy out of the Spirit of Music," in *Basic Writings*, 115–17; Also cited in Benjamin, OGT, 212.
28. See Nietzsche, "The Birth of Tragedy," 116.

Just as every comparison with tragedy—not to mention musical tragedy—is of no value for the understanding of opera, so it is that from the point of view of literature, and especially the *Trauerspiel*, opera must seem unmistakably to be a product of decadence. The obstacle of meaning and intrigue loses its weight, and both operatic plot and operatic language follow their course without encountering any resistance, issuing finally into banality. With the disappearance of the obstacle the soul of the work, mourning, also disappears ... now that allegory, where it is not omitted, has become a hollow façade. The self-indulgent delight in sheer sound played its part in the decline of the *Trauerspiel*.[29]

While opera obscured the fragmented condition of the work in modernity, the German oratorio made it visible on several fronts: fragmentation emerged from the predominant role of the chorus, whose music obstructed the hegemony of the operatic aria-recitative model. The role of the chorus in the oratorio also provided an ambiguous representation of the audience—the congregation or community—within the work. This specific detail had implications reaching beyond the musical-formal aspect of the oratorio. From a dramatic perspective, the integration of an unstable image of the community into the oratorio through the chorus coincided with a splitting of the oratorio's drama into a number of separate levels or planes, whose boundaries were continuously unsettled, as Ruth HaCohen has shown.[30] In Bach's passions, these ambiguous features solidified as prime attributes of the oratorio, linking the genre specifically to an unsettled notion of difference between the German Lutheran and Jewish communities. It is these attributes that emerge again in Ben-Haim's oratorio *Joram*.

The German Oratorio: History and Characteristics

Terminology is a perplexing issue in the study of the oratorio. The diversity of musical dramas bearing this title since the seventeenth

---

29. Benjamin, *OGT*, 212–13.
30. See Ruth HaCohen, *The Music Libel against the Jews* (New Haven, CT: Yale University Press, 2011); HaCohen, "Between Noise and Harmony: The Oratorical Moment in the Musical Entanglement between Jews and Christians," *Critical Inquiry* 32, no. 2 (2006): 250–77.

century is coupled with the existence of numerous works that were not so designated, despite the compelling display of features commonly associated with the genre. Howard Smither, whose *History of the Oratorio* remains to date the most comprehensive study of the genre from the seventeenth century to the end of the twentieth century, captured this problem in his opening lines: "What is an oratorio? Is it simply any work that is called an oratorio by its composer? Or can a composition be reasonably classified as an oratorio even though the composer has given it some other designation—such as spiritual madrigal, motet, dialogue, cantata, *historia, actus musicus, drama sacro* ... ? If the last question be answered in the affirmative, what criteria should be used for selecting the works to be classified as oratorios?"[31] These questions are compounded at times by the challenge to distinguish between the oratorio and the opera. Works such as George Frideric Handel's unstaged musical drama *Hercules* (1744), Joseph Haydn's *Die Jahreszeiten* (The Seasons, 1801), and Hanns Eisler's *Die Maßnahme* (The Measures Taken, 1930), to give but a few examples, show that throughout its history, the oratorio was never strictly limited to sacred themes.[32]

What, then, does the term "oratorio" denote? Its widely accepted definition is as follows: an oratorio is a sacred, unstaged musical work with a text that is either dramatic or narrative-dramatic.[33] However, as we just saw, the existence of numerous exceptions suggests that the criteria above are insufficient for conveying the uniqueness of the genre. Musically, after the emergence of opera and its further development in the eighteenth century, the difference between oratorio and opera became ever more elusive. As a general

---

31. A large part of Smither's study demonstrates the difficulty of answering this question. Howard E. Smither, *A History of the Oratorio*, vol. 1, *The Oratorio in the Baroque Era, Italy, Vienna, Paris* (Chapel Hill: University of North Carolina Press, 1977), 3.

32. Although most works titled as oratorios before the twentieth century are indeed based on sacred themes from either the New or Old Testaments or from the lives of saints, the composer and theorist Johann Mattheson (1681–1764) discussed the "secular oratorio" as a category as early as the eighteenth century. See Johann Mattheson, *Der vollkommene Capellmeister*, trans. Ernest C. Harris (1739; repr., Ann Arbor: University of Michigan Research Press, 1981), 447.

33. See Smither, *The Oratorio in the Baroque Era, Italy, Vienna, Paris*, 4.

rule, the oratorio seems to have adopted the musical developments of the opera, including the use of arias and recitatives. Yet a closer look at the German oratorio in the eighteenth century—a significant, formative period in this genre's history—reveals certain musical attributes that are specific to it and distinguish it as a unique form of musical expression.

Indeed, the music of the oratorio in Italy increasingly resembled that of the opera in those centuries. But unlike its Italian counterpart, the German oratorio remained closer to its antecedent sacred forms like the Lutheran *Historie* or the musical recitation of the passion, whose own features undermined the operatic division between aria and recitative. For example, among the most prominent characteristics of the *Historie* remaining in practice in the German oratorio were responsorial singing—a form of call-and-response alternating between soloist(s) and chorus—and the use of an Evangelist, a narrator who recites the biblical verses. The significance of the responsorial style for the German oratorio lies in its incorporation of the congregation into the work. From its inception, the German oratorio was defined by its extension of the musical-dramatic arena to include the audience. This aspect of the oratorio in Germany was advanced to a great degree by a certain subgenre that emerged in the eighteenth century: the German lyric oratorio, which was greatly influenced by the tradition of Pietism and the poetic language of Friedrich Gottlieb Klopstock.[34] Rather than simply presenting the events of the biblical story as the strictly dramatic oratorio did, the lyric oratorio was concerned with conveying the emotional response to events it assumed were already known to the public. The personages expressing their sentiments about the events in the lyric oratorio were unnamed, thus making it easier for the listeners to identify with them. Consequently, the audience was granted an even more active role in the oratorio.

The German oratorio was not entirely impervious to Italian opera influences. The recitative and aria da capo did make their way into it as early as the seventeenth century. However, these "modern" Italian

---

34. Klopstock did not write oratorio librettos, but parts of his epic poem *Der Messias* were set as lyrical oratorios by composers like Georg Philipp Telemann (*Zween Auszüge aus dem Geschichte: der Messias*, 1759).

practices did not overshadow the responsorial singing tradition and the role of the Evangelist. In Heinrich Schütz's *Die Sieben Worte Jesu Christi am Kreuz* (The Seven Words of Christ, 1645), for example, the Evangelist's part was innovatively set in the Italian recitative style instead of the plainsong recitation tone normally used in the liturgy. But the operatic nature of the piece was countered by the division of this part between several soloists of different timbres. Importantly, this division contributed to the uncertainty surrounding the identity of personages in the work.

A coexistence of different practices prevailed on the textual level as well. In its earlier stages, the German oratorio and its various predecessors set biblical prose alone. In accordance with Lutheran tradition, chorales were later interpolated into the prose. Finally, the oratorio in Germany gradually began to incorporate poetic verses.[35] The result was a work that exhibited a number of different textual levels and corresponding dramatic planes.[36] In Bach's passions, these separate planes would come to be occupied by the narrator (the Evangelist), the internal proceeding of the Gospel, and by a community of meditative observers, which is neither fully a part of the Gospel drama nor entirely separate from it.

Through Bach's passions and the oratorios of Handel, the role of the chorus increased in prominence and came to be recognized as one of the genre's most distinctive characteristics. Handel's early oratorios set a precedent for oratorios in the late eighteenth and nineteenth centuries with their use of the chorus. By being modeled in part after the French classical dramas of Jean Racine, they brought the influence of Greek tragedy (or rather, its modern French conception) into the oratorio, and allowed the chorus both to participate and comment on the drama.[37] After the revival of the *Matthäus-Passion* in

---

35. See further Smither, *History of the Oratorio*, vol. 2, *The Oratorio in the Baroque Era, Protestant Germany and England*, 106. In the case of the passion oratorios in Germany, however, one finds the combination of poetic, biblical-prosaic, and chorale texts to be the norm.

36. HaCohen also observes the "plethora of speech acts" in the oratorio, which consist of narration, exclamation, decrees, glorification, blaspheming, etc. See HaCohen, *The Music Libel*, 89.

37. Smither, *The Oratorio in the Baroque Era, Italy, Vienna, Paris*, 189.

1829, Bach's passions, whose chorus fulfilled a similar function, became synonymous with the German oratorio and inspired further generations of oratorio composers from Felix Mendelssohn to Ben-Haim.[38] In nineteenth-century Germany, the oratorio came to be regarded as a national genre through Bach's passions. This can be heard behind the words of the German historian Johann Gustav Droysen, who announced that Bach's *Matthäus-Passion* "does not belong to art and its history alone, but, as the true aim of art can be, to the community and the people."[39]

Musical developments in the nineteenth century provided a variety of alternative forms that ultimately diminished the dominance of the aria-recitative model in opera. The gradual rejection of this binary pattern came to a head in Wagner's music dramas, which featured a continuous melodic line, a kind of unending arioso that was somewhere between song and recitative. This technique attracted the young Nietzsche, who saw in Wagner's music the answer to the ills of opera, not least its formal division of arias and recitatives.[40] But obstruction of this model in a musical-dramatic context emerged much earlier in the oratorio. It was in fact Nietzsche who identified Bach's passions—and in particular the *Matthäus-Passion* and its chorus—as the precursor to Wagner's work and its defiance of operatic frivolity in the name of German Dionysian music.

In April 1870, while formulating the ideas that would later appear in his *Birth of Tragedy*, Nietzsche wrote to his close friend, the classicist Erwin Rohde: "This week I have heard the *Matthäuspassion* by the divine Bach three times, each with the same feeling of

---

38. The revival of Bach's *Matthäus-Passion* was followed by a renewed interest in Bach's oeuvre, resulting also in the performance of the *Johannes-Passion* by the *Singakademie* four years later. See R. Larry Todd, *Mendelssohn: A Life in Music* (Oxford: Oxford University Press, 2003), 42.

39. Cited in Martin Geck, *Die Wiederentdeckung der Matthäuspassion im 19. Jahrhundert* (Regensburg: Gustav Bosse Verlag, 1967), 58. See also Celia Applegate, *Bach in Berlin: Nation and Culture in Mendelssohn's Revival of the St. Matthew Passion* (Ithaca, NY: Cornell University Press, 2005).

40. Interestingly, Wagner gradually refrained from designating his musical works for the stage as operas but rather chose titles such as *Bühnenfestspiel*, *Musikdrama*, and *Handlung*. Perhaps the composer realized that by rejecting the aria-recitative structure, something of the essence of the term opera was also eliminated.

immeasurable amazement. He who has fully unlearned Christianity can truly hear the work as Gospel."[41] Although Nietzsche's *Birth of Tragedy* was dedicated to Wagner's music, the influence of Martin Luther, celebrated by the young Nietzsche as Wagner's own Dionysian precursor, resonates strongly in the essay. In the chorales of the Reformation, as Nietzsche wrote, "the future tune of the German music resounded for the first time. So deep, courageous, and spiritual, so exuberantly good and tender did this chorale of Luther sound—as the first Dionysian luring call breaking forth from the dense thickets at the approach of spring. And in competing echoes the solemnly exuberant procession of Dionysian revelers responded, to whom we are indebted for German music."[42]

The Oratorio as a Meeting Point: Germans, Jews

One of the many manifestations of the communal nature of German oratorios was the genre's function as a mediator between the German Christian and Jewish traditions. As HaCohen shows, this unique feature became paradigmatic in the eighteenth century through the works of Bach and Handel primarily. Among other influences, HaCohen lists the rising conception of sympathy or *Mitleid* and the attendant "inclusive trajectories" that facilitated Jewish involvement in non-Jewish German society during that century as the main cultivators of the oratorio's ability to blur "demarcations between performers and audiences, original and adjacent members," and so to promote ambiguity between the German Christian and Jewish communities implicated in the work.[43]

HaCohen also acknowledges the unique role of the chorus in the oratorio's ability to unsettle boundaries: "Sometimes embodying the community, sometimes inviting it to join forces, the chorus highlights the blurred boundaries of the real and the fictive, the individual and

---

41. Friedrich Nietzsche, *Briefe 1*, ed. Giorgio Colli und Mazzino Montinari (Berlin: de Gruyter, 1977), 120.
42. Nietzsche, "The Birth of Tragedy," 137.
43. HaCohen, *The Music Libel*, 71.

the communal, the sacred and the mundane."[44] For HaCohen, the oratorio's ability to unsettle the difference between German Christians and Jews was tied to the genre's ambiguous conflation of different dramatic personae as well as of different rhetorical and temporal planes in what she terms "oratorical moments."[45] Following studies that contrast the oratorio's different "time zones" to the unified temporality of the opera, HaCohen emphasizes the conflation of past and present as one of the distinguishing aspects of the oratorical moment.[46]

As HaCohen further notes, the focus on heroic figures from the Old Testament in the oratorios of Handel—some of which, like *Esther*, *Israel in Egypt*, and *Judas Maccabaeus*, depict the stories of Jewish holidays (Purim, Passover, and Hanukkah, respectively)—created a body of works whose audience was not limited to a faithful Christian congregation. In such cases, it is easy to see how the oratorio facilitated moments of ambiguous collective identification. Yet even Bach's passions—works that were not only intended expressly for the edification of the Lutheran congregation through the Gospel but that also carry a harsh antisemitic message—presented a site of conflation between the two communities.

From a historical perspective, the account of Mendelssohn's *Singakademie* revival of the *Matthäus-Passion* on March 11, 1829, is pertinent. Accounts of the event, which instigated the resurfacing of Bach's work into the collective German consciousness and the passion's designation as a work of German national-cultural import, can be read in a number of biographies and historical works.[47] In the musical salons of post-emancipation Berlin, the works of the then esoteric composer Johann Sebastian Bach were objects of continued interest to the women of the Itzig family, Felix Mendelssohn's maternal grandmother and great-aunt. Though under the

---

44. HaCohen, *The Music Libel*, 91.
45. HaCohen, *The Music Libel*, 90. See also HaCohen, "Between Noise and Harmony."
46. See for example, John Butt, "Bach's Vocal Scoring: What Can It Mean?," *Early Music* 26 (1998): 99–107; and John Butt, *Bach's Dialog with Modernity: Perspectives on the Passions* (Cambridge: Cambridge University Press, 2010).
47. See for example, Todd, *Mendelssohn*, and Applegate, *Bach in Berlin*.

tutelage of Carl Friedrich Zelter the young Mendelssohn had already been exposed to Bach's choral works, it was from his grandmother Bella (Babette) Solomon née Itzig that Mendelssohn received a transcription of the full score of Bach's *Matthäus-Passion* in 1824.[48] The trenchant antisemitic tone of the work did not deter the unconverted Bella Solomon and her sister Lea Levy from revering Bach's musical heritage and seeing it as their own.[49] During rehearsals for the premiere, Mendelssohn himself acknowledged the significance of the work's revival for the cultural intertwining of the German Christian and the Jewish communities. In his famous words to his friend and collaborator, the librettist Eduard Devrient, he pointed out the irony "daß es ein Komödiant und ein Judenjunge sein müssen, die den Leuten die größte christliche Musik wiederbringen!"[50] (That a comedian and a Jewish boy would be the ones to return the greatest Christian music to the people!)

Mendelssohn's revival of Bach's *Matthäus-Passion* contributed to the more universalist understanding of the work with which we are familiar today. It made the work accessible to future generations of Jewish listeners and musicians who could now see themselves represented not by members of the passion's *turba* crowds of Jews and priests but rather by the faithful congregation.[51] Thanks in part to the rise of *Kulturprotestantismus* in the second half of the nineteenth century, listening to Bach's *Matthäus-Passion* had turned for many German-speaking Jews into an integral part of the experience of being

---

48. The topic of the Jewish involvement in the revival of one of Germany's most monumental works is a delicate one, as Applegate indicates: "This intertwining of Bach cultivation among the teachers and family of Felix Mendelssohn has generated controversy over the years. At stake is the question of who should get credit for the 1829 performance of the *St. Matthew Passion*, and ultimately of course, of whether Jews can be acknowledged to have a place in the genealogy of German culture." Applegate, *Bach in Berlin*, 17.

49. See further Peter Wollny, "Sara Levy and the Making of Musical Taste in Berlin," *The Musical Quarterly* 77, no. 4 (1993): 651–88.

50. Eduard Devrient, *Meine Erinnerungen an Felix Mendelssohn-Bartholdy und seine Briefe an Mich* (Leipzig: Verlagsbuchhandlung Weber, 1872), 62.

51. This statement has become true also for Bach's harsher *Johannes-Passion*. HaCohen points out commonalities in the *Johannes-Passion* between Jewish and Lutheran traditions. See HaCohen, *The Music Libel*, 100. See also Michael Marissen, *Bach and God* (Oxford: Oxford University Press, 2016).

German. It is therefore not entirely surprising that a composer like Ben-Haim would take it upon himself to compose an oratorio that is redolent of Bach's passions. It is nevertheless noteworthy that such an enterprise was undertaken in the political climate of 1932 Germany and under Ben-Haim's personal circumstances as mentioned above.

The elements that Ben-Haim's oratorio shares with Bach's passions are exactly those that turned the passions into exemplary cases of the German oratorio.[52] Even more than the historical conditions that qualified the oratorio as a meeting point for the Christian and Jewish communities since the eighteenth century, it was the oratorio's unique formal attributes and theoretical stance that promoted its ambiguous communal nature. These features and their intentional ambiguity are the focus of my analyses in the remainder of this chapter, first of Bach's passions and then of Ben-Haim's *Joram*. They allow the oratorio to reflect the conception of the fragmented, open-ended work while providing an aesthetic expression of the porous and unsettled notion of Jewish difference that accompanies it. In the passions, ambiguity is manifest both in the strictly formal aspects of the passions' music and text, as HaCohen shows, and in the theoretical relation between music and language that I analyze based on Nietzsche's and Benjamin's writings.

Tracing the perpetuation of these same attributes from Bach to Ben-Haim's *Joram*, then, will not only mark these attributes as essential to the genre, independent of changing epochs and styles; it will also suggest, in the case of Ben-Haim, that the decision to compose Borchardt's poetic work as an oratorio voices a significant statement: the communal notion it promotes is not reactively Jewish, sectarian, but one where Jewish difference is unsettled. The aim, therefore, is not to single out *Joram* as an exceptional work in terms of the genre's historical development. It is rather the traditional elements—what Ben-Haim chose to preserve rather than reject—that are of interest, as they allow us to identify certain unique features of the oratorio while arguing for *Joram*'s significance for the discourse of Jewish difference.

---

52. See also the discussion of the German oratorio and Stefan Zweig's *Jeremias* in Kita, *Jewish Difference and the Arts in Vienna*, 143–56.

The Passion's Unsettled Boundaries

Adherents of the image ban, which prohibits the staging of oratorios, might object to the performance of the *Matthäus-Passion* by the Berlin Philharmonic under Peter Sellars's direction.[53] Sellars chose a unique staging for Bach's masterpiece. Rather than having the traditional arrangement of choruses and soloists facing the audience in the same position throughout the performance, Sellars has all performers engage with each other expressively and constantly. The result, however, is not a simple operatic rendering of the passion. The staging calls for interaction between personages on different dramatic planes. Personages who are considered part of the Gospel interact with those who are considered outside observers, among them the two choruses and the soloists, who represent members of the faithful community. Even members of the orchestra leave their stationary seats to engage with both audience and singers.

One of the most interesting moments in this production is the scene of Judas's betrayal, no. 26.[54] The number is a recitative for three personages: Evangelist, Jesus, and Judas. As the Evangelist announces Judas's arrival with a group of men to capture Jesus, Judas starts pacing toward the Evangelist. The latter continues to inform the audience that Judas gave the men a sign by which to recognize Jesus: "He whom I kiss is the one, seize him." As Judas reaches the Evangelist, he lays his arms on his shoulders and sings his line: "Gegrüßet seist du, Rabbi!" (my greetings to thee, Rabbi!). The Evangelist, kissed by Judas, continues to narrate "und küssete ihn" (and he kissed him). The instruction to kiss the Evangelist rather than Jesus deliberately unsettles the identity of the Evangelist. The latter, not relinquishing his role as narrator entirely, remains

---

53. J. S. Bach, *Matthäus-Passion BWV 244*, performed by the Berlin Philharmonic, conducted by Sir Simon Rattle, recorded April 2010, Berlin Phil Media GmbH, DVD.

54. The numbers follow Johann Sebastian Bach, *Neue Ausgabe Sämtliche Werke II*, ed. Johann-Sebastian-Bach Institut Göttingen and Bach Archiv Leipzig (Kassel: Bärenreiter, 2004).

suspended between the two roles as the bass who sings Jesus's part stands on a balcony, as if observing the drama from outside.

Sellars's artistic choices might be regarded as unconventional. Yet it is exactly these moments of ambiguity where the boundaries between different dramatic planes and dramatis personae are unsettled, as demonstrated vividly in this number, that highlight an essential attribute of the oratorio.[55] As HaCohen indicates:

> In the oratorio, past and distant places are grafted onto the immediate present, creating a nonrealistic, transhistorical chronotopoi. The sacred text delivered by the narrator, however sealed and canonized, becomes . . . a commentary, an interpretation, and a message. Inviting impersonation through distinct vocal intonation, . . . it also calls for textual mediations and meditations on the narrated and enacted subject matter, enhancing the active role of the actual contemporary believer—the designated audience of the performed work. Time . . . becomes further mixed, while representation turns out to be rather loose. Actual voices are potentially divided between personae belonging to different temporal and spatial categories. . . . The same performing voice could, in principle, represent both a *historia sacra* figure as well as a host of contemporary subjective feelings about it, cast in a mixture of expressive ecclesiastic and secular modes.[56]

Sellars's decision to conflate the identities of Jesus and the Evangelist in the scene described above coincides with the general oratorical tendency to unsettle the identities of all voices in the passion. Certain performance choices can of course accentuate moments of unsettlement in the passion, but those are in fact written into the oratorical form. This becomes most obvious in the chorus.

The chorus's dual role as participant in the Gospel drama and external commentator makes it one of the most interesting components in Bach's passions and the most relevant to the inquiry concerning difference between communities. In its meditating capacity, the chorus indicates a separate dramatic plane removed from the internal drama of the Gospel. Bach's librettist Picander (Christian

---

55. See also the analysis of the performance at the Tel Aviv Opera Hall from 2002 in HaCohen, *The Music Libel*, 81.

56. HaCohen, *The Music Libel*, 88–89.

Friedrich Henrici) originally followed the tradition of the Hamburg passion oratorio in his use of the dialogue form between two separate figures, the allegorical *Tochter Zion* (Daughter of Zion) and *Die Gläubigen* (The Faithful Community). Although Bach did not preserve the names Picander assigned to the individual and collective dialogue partners in his setting of the libretto, instead assigning them both to the chorus, he did retain the dialogue form in his decision to split the chorus in the *Matthäus-Passion*.[57] By preserving the dialogue between two separate figures within the chorus but without indicating their names or titles, Bach associated his passion with the German lyric oratorio, where dialogue between unnamed figures contributed further to the ambiguating gesture of the form.

But even within the confines of the Gospel's drama, the chorus is never assigned a fixed role. Rather, the various mobs (*turba*) it represents continuously alternate between Jews, priests, soldiers, and disciples, mostly without clear distinction. The antiphonal interaction between the two choruses in the *Matthäus-Passion* offers a degree of complexity by suggesting that the chorus should not be considered one homogeneous body but rather an ever-shifting collection of various voices and perspectives.

Despite the overtly operatic nature of Bach's music in the passions, the division into multiple dramatic planes contrasts with the single dramatic dimension of the opera. But the passions differ from the opera also in the fluid identity of all its dramatis personae. Personages in Bach's passions serve as points of intersection for multiple dramatic functions. The example of the chorus is perhaps the most obvious, but it is by no means singular. Since, as oratorios, Bach's passions were not staged, soloists were not restricted to depicting one individual character. Studies of performance practice in Bach's time have shown that the composer employed a limited number of soloists in his passions, who had to sing and portray multiple parts.[58] As John Butt argued, what was initially a practical

---

57. See Richard D. P. Jones, *The Creative Development of Johann Sebastian Bach*, vol. 2, *1717–1750* (Oxford: Oxford University Press, 2013), 184.
58. See Daniel R. Melamed, *Hearing Bach's Passions* (Oxford: Oxford University Press, 2005), 34–36.

consideration for Bach nevertheless emerged as a particular aesthetic feature of the passions that produced an array of meanings different from that produced by the opera.

Butt observes further that this fluidity was not limited to the performers; it also affected the audience, which, like the singers, underwent "constant fluctuations of subjectivity: at one moment a passive observer ... he or she is next part of a group within a tradition of worship and then an individual sinner who learns of salvation."[59] Involving the audience in the passions' pattern of unsettlement promoted the modern, theatrical nature of the genre and its affinity with the concept of the open-ended work. Just as the identity of the dramatis personae in the work was unsettled, so was that of its audience. In the absence of a stable audience, the boundaries of the work became porous. The meditative arias and chorales sung by personages representing members of the congregation turned these performers into gateways through which the audience could enter and exit the drama fluidly in a manner reminiscent of Nietzsche's idea of the chorus of satyrs.[60]

This pattern of unsettlement was musically enforced. The short chorus section "Sei gegrüßet, lieber Jüdenkönig" (no. 21b) in the *Johannes-Passion* BWV 245 demonstrates how the music itself confounded the distinction between the different functions of the chorus. The number is conceived as a *turba* chorus representing a group of soldiers (*Kriegsknechte*) who mock the captured Jesus by crying out "Hail to thee, king of the Jews!" The musical treatment of this cry, however, does not confirm the text's derisive tone. The fugal texture Bach frequently uses in the *turba* choruses appears in this number as well. But the bright tonality of B-flat major, affirmed already in the first measures by the leaps in fifths and fourths (B♭–F in the soprano and tenor parts and F–B♭ in the alto and bass

---

59. Butt, "Bach's Vocal Scoring," 106.

60. For Nietzsche, the chorus as a site of audience transformation facilitated a simultaneous setting and unsettling of dramatic boundaries. See Nietzsche, "The Birth of Tragedy," 62–64. Although Nietzsche reflected on the role of the tragic chorus, his conception of theatricality and the unsettling role of the chorus was inherently modern. See also Weber, *Theatricality as Medium*, 41.

Figure 2.1. Bach, *Johannespassion*, BWV 245, no. 21b, "Sei gegrüßet, lieber Jüdenkönig" (mm.1–3).

parts), distinguishes this number from its tumultuous, sometimes roaring fellow *turba* choruses (see figure 2.1).[61]

Even with the brisk movement of the sixteenth notes, the number's general tone is decidedly more stately than restless. The festive nature of the musical expression in this case makes us wonder whether the statement "Sei gegrüßet, lieber Jüdenkönig" is indeed sung in mockery or whether it is the sincere exaltation of Christ. In this moment, Bach's music hinders our ability to determine which specific role the chorus represents. Do we hear the voice of a stirred crowd of soldiers or that of the faithful community? Are we in the dramatic plane of the Gospel or have we moved to that of the meditating community? Bach notably chose to set both "Sei gegrüßet, lieber Jüdenkönig" (no. 21b) as well as the subsequent no. 25b "Schreibe nicht: der Jüden König, sondern daß er gesaget habe: Ich bin der Jüden König" (write not: king of the Jews, rather that he claimed:

---

61. Compare, for example, this chorus with "Wäre dieser nicht ein Übeltäter" and "Wir dürfen niemand töten" (no. 16b and no. 16d in the *Johannes-Passion*) where the restlessness of the perpetual movement in eighth notes is aggravated by the tension of rising chromatic scales that render the chorus tonally unstable, emulating the uproar one expects of a *turba* chorus.

I am king of the Jews) to the same music in the same key. In the second number (no. 25b), it is clearer that the chorus is indeed a *turba* of priests denying Jesus as the King of the Jews. But Bach maintained an irony by setting two potentially contradicting statements to the same music. Doing so, he demonstrated the overall instability of all utterances in the passions.

The oratorical unsettling of boundaries between different communities and individual identities is musically enforced by the ambiguous scoring of numbers like "Sei gegrüßet," but it does not stop there. On a deeper level, the passions' targeted unsettling of the operatic aria-recitative structure contributes to the same aim as it furthers the oratorio's transparent reflection of the fragmentary and open-ended condition of the modern artwork through its own form.

To recall Benjamin's thoughts, the opera's problematic sprang from its innate modes of musical expression, the recitative and aria, whose attendant claim to unite music and meaning masked the fragmented and ambiguous condition of artworks and particularly of theater in modernity. With this in mind, the case of the German oratorio and Bach's passions in particular bears import. While—or perhaps exactly because—the oratorio employs an operatic structure of arias and recitatives, it also visibly obstructs these same patterns. Bach's passions unsettle the division of aria and recitative in the same way they unsettle the boundaries between the passions' different dramatic levels and personages. These moments are instigated by the inherent needs of the genre and therefore become essential to it. In the German baroque *Trauerspiel*, Benjamin identified inherent formal attributes like the use of allegory that designated this theatrical form a sincere reflection of the fragmentary condition of modernity. We see similar dramatic and musical attributes inherent in the oratorio. These attributes render the oratorio another theatrical art form that coveys the porous condition of post-Reformation modernity and thereby questions the coherence of any collectivity that is associated with the work.[62]

---

62. There are indeed other similarities between the *Trauerspiel* and the oratorio. Benjamin in fact mentions the medieval Mystery and Passion plays as predecessors of the *Trauerspiel*. See Benjamin, OGT, 76. And in addition to their

In the *Matthäus-Passion*, the multiple dramatic levels yielded a particular musical form that came to be a characteristic feature of the work. The different textual levels in the passion demanded separate musical treatment. While Bach reserved the *secco* or "dry" recitative for the narration of the Gospel by the Evangelist and the aria for the emotional outpourings of members of the congregation, he required a different form for the meditative-descriptive texts that preceded the arias in Picander's libretto. The motivic *accompagnati* that were matched with these poetic texts in the *Matthäus-Passion* were a musical form unique to this work, differing from the Gospel recitatives in intensity and scope.[63]

Although their less developed predecessors in the *Johannes-Passion* were titled "arioso,"[64] the motivic *accompagnati* of the *Matthäus-Passion* are not simply a more melodic and measured version of the recitative. Their distinctive nature chips away at the binary of the aria and recitative by presenting an elaborate musical setting, which is often as expressive as the words it accompanies if not more so. Bach occasionally employs the technique of word-painting in some of his motivic *accompagnati* (as for example in the alto recitative "Du lieber Heiland du," where the soloist's voice sinks on the words "zum Grabe" [to the grave] to the lowered second scale degree C♯ that creates a darker-sounding diminished seventh chord). But the *accompagnati*'s uniqueness, as I argue, lies in the fact that through the ostinato recurrence of a single motive characteristic of each of them, they allow the music to be equally expressive without resorting to mimetic techniques, which hierarchically subordinate music to text.[65]

By allowing the music to take an equal yet inherently independent expressive share, these *accompagnati* foreground the separation

---

common ancestry, the *Trauerspiel* and Bach's passions also share the relinquishing of eschatology, as previously discussed.

63. See further Werner Neumann, *Handbuch der Kantaten Johann Sebastian Bachs* (Wiesbaden: Breitkopf and Härtel, 1966), 6–7; and Martin Geck, *Johann Sebastian Bach: Life and Work*, trans. John Hargraves (Orlando: Harcourt, 2006), 409.

64. There are only two such cases in the *Johannes-Passion*: no. 19, "Betrachte, meine Seel," for bass, and no. 34, "Mein Herz," for tenor.

65. See also Geck, *Johann Sebastian Bach*, 410.

rather than the unity between text and music. The motivic *accompagnati* in the *Matthäus-Passion* further challenge the traditional recitative by not being dedicated to the promotion of the plot like their operatic counterparts. Their text is at times as reflective as that of the arias that follow. In this, a more equal relation between *accompagnato* and aria is achieved.[66] Nonetheless, the *accompagnati* are not solely meant to convey an emotional response to the Gospel. They rather fall somewhere between description and emotional reaction, as one can see for example in the *accompagnato* "Am Abend da es kühle war" (no. 64).

With the *accompagnati* as one of its most prominent features, Bach's *Matthäus-Passion*, although very operatic in nature, offers an alternative musical dramatic form. The motivic *accompagnato* "O Schmerz" (no. 19) and the subsequent aria "Ich will bei meinem Jesu wachen" (no. 20) demonstrate how the passion challenges the traditional operatic format, this time through one of its most prominent components, the chorus. The integration of the chorus in both numbers unsettles not only the recitative's structure but also that of the da capo aria. Bach begins by inserting fragments of the chorale "Herzliebster Jesu" (no. 3, here paired with Picander's text) into the bass's singing line. By enlisting the chorus, the *accompagnato*, commonly confined to the voice of a single soloist, now permits a dialogue to take place. Bach expands the limits of the *accompagnato* also in terms of its orchestration, which here includes two flute and two oboe parts on top of the orchestra's string section.

The amassing of sound and the conflation of two separate dramatic planes (the meditating recitative of the soloist and the devotional chorale of the chorus) bring the *accompagnato* closer to a collapse of the form, which indeed occurs in the subsequent aria. Attempts to adhere to the da capo structure in the tenor aria no. 20 "Ich will bei meinem Jesu wachen" are thwarted by the integration of the chorus. The back-and-forth movement between soloist and chorus eventually causes Bach to give up the customary da capo

---

66. This is contrasted to the idea of the recitative, which, from a musical perspective, simply functions as a passage leading to the aria.

template and write out the recurrence of the aria's A section, causing the aria to resemble a more through-composed form.[67]

The fractures in the operatic recitative-aria model manifest in the pair "O Schmerz" and "Ich will bei meinem Jesu wachen," marking the beginning of a process of disintegration that culminates in no. 27—the dramatic climax of the first part of the *Matthäus-Passion*—the aria-duet "So ist mein Jesus nun gefangen," which responds to the capture of Jesus. This alto-soprano duet is one of the few arias in this passion not introduced by a motivic *accompagnato*. Unlike the mitigated chorale interjections of the tenor aria no. 20, Bach interrupts the elaborate, melismatic singing line of the soloists with the harsh and abrupt syllabic calls of a *turba* chorus. Yet the afflicted choral cries "Laßt ihn, haltet, bindet nicht!" (Leave him, hold, bind him not!) are not the exclamations of any bloodthirsty crowd depicted in the Gospel but rather those of the congregation. Adding to this unsettled role of the chorus (is it the *turba* or perhaps the faithful community?) is the fact that Bach employs both choruses here (they later engage in a fugal dialogue with one another) rather than the one used earlier in no. 20. After the conclusion of the first part of the aria on the dominant, Bach unleashes the tension that has been hitherto accumulated by the constant interruptions. The aria bursts into a raging fugal section in the choruses, marked vivace ("Sind Blitze, sind Donner," no. 27b), and the da capo form of this aria is never restored.

By undercutting the operatic recitative and aria structure, the passion as the paradigmatic example of the German oratorio distinguishes itself from the opera's aspirations for unity and harmony between music and drama. This renunciation of operatic claims for unity joins a series of parallel identity-unsettling gestures that work to undermine clear distinctions between the communities—specifically, between the German Lutheran and Jewish communities—that are

---

67. In the traditional aria da capo, a single sign at the end of the B section marks the return to the A section, whose second appearance is not written out in the score. The integration of the chorus in the aria in the *Matthäus-Passion* is prefigured by two similar occurrences in the *Johannes-Passion*: "Eilt, ihr angefochtnen Seelen," no. 24, and "Mein theurer Heiland, lass dich fragen," no. 32.

implicated in the passion. Similar gestures can be identified in Ben-Haim's oratorio *Joram*.

Unsettling Difference in the Oratorio *Joram*

Though Ben-Haim never expressly stated a debt to Bach, his oratorio features numerous elements that reveal the direct influence of Bach's passions on his oratorio. Ben-Haim's *Joram* is divided into three parts: The first part corresponds to the first four chapters in Borchardt's *Das Buch Joram*. It begins with an exposition of Joram's lineage and concludes with Joram's return home after his six-year exile. The second part corresponds roughly to the fifth and sixth chapters in Borchardt's poem and focuses on Joram's confrontation with his wife Jezebel. The third part, coinciding with chapters seven to nine of Borchardt's text, relate Joram's unanswered accusations against God and closes with the birth of Joram's son, a Messiah. Ben-Haim complicates the tripartite structure of his oratorio by adding a chorale at the center of the second part, the nadir of Joram's suffering, when he learns during his reunion with his wife that she has been reduced to prostitution. The chorale is set to a separate text by Borchardt. Its placement at the center of the middle act suggests an alternative division of the oratorio that resembles the diptych-like *Matthäus-Passion*, where Ben-Haim's chorale would parallel the great chorale "O Mensch, bewein dein Sünde groß" (no. 29) that concludes the first part of the passion.[68]

As in Bach's passions, the different sections in each part of Ben-Haim's oratorio are grouped according to numbers. Ben-Haim chose to minimize the intervention into Borchardt's text and use it without adaptation. As a result, the piece does not exhibit the overwhelmingly numerous textual and dramatic levels of the passions. However, Ben-Haim's music makes up for this difference by pushing the fluidity of the roles in his oratorio even further. The absence of a reflective textual level also results in the omission of any proper arias from the oratorio. *Joram* is comprised mostly of a concatenation

---

68. See also Hirshberg, *Paul Ben-Haim*, 85.

of arioso sections that dictate the nature of the chorus segments just as much as they do the solo ones. Finally, as part of the few changes he did make to Borchardt's text, Ben-Haim omitted the death of Joram and his wife Jezebel depicted in the poem's ninth chapter. Yet any optimistic or conciliatory approach to the text that may have been implied by this omission is thwarted by the music. Ben-Haim never renounces tonality in the oratorio, but the work displays a pronounced trajectory from a relatively consonant environment at the beginning of the work to an increasingly dissonant form of writing toward its end.[69]

Unlike Bach's passions and their elaborate choral opening, Ben-Haim's *Joram* opens with an orchestral overture ("Vorspiel"). This gives the work a more operatic quality, but the following number immediately assures the listener that *Joram* is no opera. Since the oratorio follows Borchardt's mostly unaltered text, narration becomes its primary mode of expression. *Joram* is indeed centered around the role of an individual narrator, an equivalent of the passions' Evangelist. However, the oratorio does not restrict the narration to this single personage. Its narratory exposition in fact begins with the chorus (no. 2, "Erzählung" or "Narration").[70] Thus, from its opening, *Joram* defines the flexibility and interchangeability of different roles as its most prominent feature.

Chorus and tenor share the narrating role in the second number of the oratorio. The main portion of the number, corresponding to the first twelve verses of chapter one in Borchardt's poem, is an ABA form in which the A sections are recited by the chorus and the B section sung by the tenor-narrator. The B section is marked arietta and is in fact the only one of its kind in the entire work.[71] The arietta's obbligato trumpet part reference Bach's arias in the passions, all of which are written for soloists with obbligato instruments. However, here, it is not the resemblance to Bach's arias but rather what distinguishes Ben-Haim's arietta from Bach's model that is noteworthy.

---

69. See Malcolm Miller, "Munich: Ben-Haim's *Joram*," *Tempo* 63 (2009): 52–53.

70. Numbering is taken from the vocal score edition: Paul Ben-Haim, *Joram: Oratorio for Soli, Choir, and Orchestra* (Tel-Aviv: Israeli Music Publications, 1978).

71. All other solo sections in the oratorio are marked either recitative or arioso.

The arietta introduces the narrator for the first time and thereby unsettles his role. Unlike Bach's Evangelist, who enjoys relative stability in the passion by being bound exclusively to the dry recitative, the first appearance of Ben-Haim's narrator involves singing. By assigning a singing part to the narrator, Ben-Haim counters expectations of listeners, who are already familiar with Bach's passions and could consequently mistake the tenor for a different personage.

Although the oratorio *Joram* is relatively traditional in the musical models it employs, the incorporation of the arietta in the second number serves as an elucidating example of the challenges the work poses to its forebears. The division between recitative and aria, which even in Bach's passions still remained mostly clear, is extensively undercut in Ben-Haim's *Joram*. Solo singing sections like the tenor arietta emerge spontaneously amid the chorale. In a similar manner, the recitative *accompagnato* for the tenor in the last thirty-four measures of the same number moves freely from a strictly declamatory style to a more fluent recalling of the previous arietta theme.[72] The various shifts between singing and reciting in this concluding part are not marked by different titles; they are merely indicated in the score as performance instructions such as "plötzlich langsamer" (suddenly slower), "rezitativisch" (recitative-like), and "Überleiten zum Zeitmass der Arietta" (transition to the aria's tempo).

These fluid transitions between different forms of vocal techniques are combined with the flexible distribution of roles in *Joram*. Together they blur traditional musical-formal boundaries as well as unsettle the relation between music and text in the work. Narration in *Joram* is not restricted to recitative but can also be lyrical. Moreover, unlike in Bach, it is not the domain of a single soloist. By allowing the chorus to participate in the act of narration, the oratorio *Joram* refutes the assumption that the primary purpose of these narration sections is to communicate a coherent plot to the audience. Ben-Haim utilizes the multivocal potential of the chorus by layering different textual segments contrapuntally, making it harder for the audience to follow a single coherent text. Though this

---

72. The recitative *accompagnato* has a stricter rhythm and a slightly more melodic nature than the dry or *secco* recitative, which is closer to speaking.

does not deviate from standard technique in choral writing, the ultimate effect renders the communication of the text and its plot ancillary to conveying the chorus's polyphonic texture. Consequently, the opening of the oratorio unsettles the function of narration itself by presenting us with a narration section whose main purpose is not primarily to narrate.

While the chief purpose of the chorus in *Joram* is to share the narration with the tenor-narrator, its function is by no means restricted to it. Occasionally, the chorus will also voice personages in the internal drama. In no. 9, "Die erste Engelerscheinung" (the First Angel Appearance), for example, the chorus sings both narration as well as the role of the angel who intervenes in the slave's attempt to redeem Joram.[73] Consequently, the chorus in this number must oscillate constantly between two separate dramatic planes, the narration and the internal drama. Ben-Haim's scoring is similar to Bach's passions in calling for a limited number of soloists who occupy multiple personages and dramatic planes in the oratorio. As a result, the stable collective identity of the chorus is unsettled in a manner akin to that of the passions.

Such unsettling moments occur repeatedly in *Joram* and are indeed written into the score. The preceding number has the narrator double as Joram's Chaldean captor. In an *accompagnato* recitative, the narrator describes the rage of the Chaldean over Joram's unfulfilled promise of ransom and subsequently ventriloquizes the same personage: "und hieß Joram bringen vor sein Angesicht, dass er ihn versuchete, und redete hart mit ihm, denn er war voll Zornes und sprach: Du hast mein gespottet." (And he called for Joram to be brought before him so that he may test him, and spoke harshly with him, for he was full of wrath and said: you have mocked me.) Ben-Haim does not separate the two parts in the score but rather writes the entrance of the Chaldean into the same tenor's part to ensure that both roles are sung by the same soloist (see figure 2.2).

Unsettling identities and dramatic planes do not only occur linearly in *Joram*, that is, by assigning different roles from different

---

73. The number corresponds to verses 11 to 22 in chapter four of Borchardt's poem.

Figure 2.2. Ben-Haim, *Joram*, no. 8 "Und der Chaldäer" (piano reduction).

planes to the same vocal part that begins to sing one part and moves on to sing another in the same line. In no. 12, "Vorspiel—Heimkehr" (Prelude—Homecoming), which opens the oratorio's second part, separate dramatic planes also merge into one another polyphonically or vertically. After a short orchestral prelude that opens the number, a recitative for solo narrator and chorus accompaniment depicts Joram's return and his first encounter with his wife Jezebel. The first entrance of the soprano on the words "Lieber, kehre ein unter mein Dach" (Lover, come in under my roof) materializes as though out of thin air. The performance instruction "sehr leise, wie aus weiter Ferne" (very softly as if from far away) and the fact that the voice is not announced or identified first by the narrator indicates that Ben-Haim deliberately sought to obscure the identity of this personage. The tenor, accompanied by the chorus, continues to narrate Joram's return without commenting on the interjection by the soprano. As Joram approaches his home, the soprano repeats its part. The narrator still does not reveal the identity of this personage to be Jezebel. He finally introduces her here only as "ein Weib" (a woman), as if reflecting Joram's struggle to recognize his own wife.

Confusion reigns in this number musically too, as the narrator's and the soprano's parts are sung together. Despite expectations, we are not granted any subsequent musical or dramatic interaction between Joram and Jezebel in this number (in fact, the conversation between them occurs only after the punctuating orchestral interlude and great chorale that follow this number). Instead, Ben-Haim engages the tenor and soprano—narrator and Jezebel—in a duet that merges the inner dramatic level of the latter with the external one of the former, thereby unsettling the identities of all three soloists in this number, the narrator, Jezebel, and Joram.[74]

The absence of arias and the strong emphasis on narration and dialogue in recitative and arioso sections in the oratorio *Joram* do not

---

74. In Borchardt's original text, the words "Lieber, kehre ein unter mein Dach und wasche Deine Füsse" belong to a woman Joram encounters at the well by his house and not to Jezebel. By dissociating the words from their original speaker, Ben-Haim gains further ambiguity in his depiction of the role of the soprano in this number.

mean that the reflective and emotional levels are altogether excluded from the work. These are rather delegated to the orchestra, as in the previous example of no. 12. Were *Joram* set to a more traditional operatic form, one would expect a tormented aria about the fear and apprehension of returning to a no-longer-familiar home from Joram at this point. Ben-Haim provides no such thing. The emotional charge of the narrator's description of Joram's homecoming—a recitative accompagnato, beginning with the words "Joram aber blickte gegen sein Haus" (Joram looked toward his house)—is reserved for the orchestra. In no way auxiliary to the narrator's part, the orchestral expression of the emotional aspect of the number conveys yet another separate dramatic plane.

Such highly charged orchestral "interjections" appear also in the great chorale Ben-Haim inserted at the center of the work. The chorale (no. 13, "Chorspruch") marks the climax of the oratorio. Its arrival immediately after Joram's fraught reunion with his wife prompted the composer to set aside the text of *Das Buch Joram* momentarily and pause to meditate on the gravity of the scene. The meditative chorale—here, functioning similarly to the chorales in Bach's passions—is one of a kind in *Joram* and therefore requires special attention. Although it alludes to the chorale tradition of the passion, the *Chorspruch* displays none of the harmonious sonorities that characterize Bach's chorales. The continuous interruption of the chorus by erratic orchestral interjections—featuring racing sixteenth-note scales in the strings and strident diminished seventh chords in the brass section—emphasizes the equal part the orchestra plays as an independent reflective plane in *Joram*.

While the tonality of C minor is maintained throughout the *Chorspruch*, extensive use of the harsh-sounding augmented fourth interval—particularly on strong beats that accentuate it even more—makes it arguably the most dissonant number in the oratorio. The chorale concludes on a strident cadence that resolves the dominant G–D in the chorus into the dissonant augmented fourth interval D♭–G rather than the harmonious and stable tonic C. This jarring obstruction of auditory expectations leaves the listener with the palpable sonic sensation of the chorale's final word: "Passion."

For the chorale's text, Ben-Haim selected the poem *Einem Jüngeren in den Joram* (To the Youth in Joram), which concludes Borchardt's 1912 *Jugendgedichte* collection.[75] The incorporation of *Einem Jüngeren* in the oratorio allowed Ben-Haim to add a separate reflective-meditative textual plane that shifts the focus from Joram's individual loss and conveys a universal concept of suffering, expressed here through the idea of the passion:

Nicht nur Gott von Gottes Thron
Der gepeitschte mit der Kron—
Alle seid ihr seine Kinder,
Keiner näher, keiner minder,
Keiner dingt vom ganzen Lohn.
Handle: und du opferst schon
Dich für Brüder, dich für Kinder;
Sprich: du bist mit jedem Ton
Überwunden, Überwinder.
Gottes Sohn
Ward es nicht gelinder—
Lebe: und es ist Passion.

[Not only the God from God's throne,
The whipped one with the crown,
All of you are his children.
None be closer, none be lesser
None beaten down from the full wage.
Act: by this itself you sacrifice
Yourself for brethren, yourself for children.
Speak: by this itself you are, with each sound
Subjugated, subjugator.
To God's son
Fell no lighter lot.
Live: and this itself is *Passion*.][76]

---

75. Borchardt also presented the poem in 1911 at a public reading of *Das Buch Joram* in Munich. Yet, other than its title, the poem bears no thematic relation to *Das Buch Joram*.

76. Ben-Haim makes a slight alteration in line 4 of Borchardt's original poem by replacing the word "näher" with "mehr." The version read by Borchardt in 1911

In accordance with the chorale tradition in Bach's passions, Ben-Haim's *Chorspruch* offers a consolatory response to Joram's pain expressed by a community that observes the drama from the outside.[77] Yet it is not only this gesture and the explicit textual reference to the passion that ought to interest us here. The chorus offers a poetic reflection on the same unsettling of difference—most importantly, between communities that have historically been implicated by the passion—that characterizes the form of the oratorio. With the lines "Alle seid ihr seine Kinder, keiner näher, keiner minder," it raises the claim that human suffering, as a modern form of passion, transcends difference. All experience the passion and there is no point in distinguishing between communities to whom the passion belongs. Far from being a Christian universal claim, the poem's profane tone undermines the distinction between God and man, just as it undermines the distinction between a passion that is carried out by dying for another's sins and one that is performed simply by living: "Gottes Sohn ward es nicht gelinder—Lebe: und es ist Passion." With this refutation of the passion's religious exclusivity, the chorus fulfills its oratorical promise as an unsettling agent, conflating various communities and dramatic and textual levels, as well as the very sense of the passion as a stable religious marker.

It is, of course, to be expected that the music of Ben-Haim's oratorio sounds different from that of Bach's passions. Much transpired in the course of the two centuries separating the *Matthäus-Passion* and *Joram* from musical and stylistic perspectives. But the distinct features of the oratorio, those that had solidified in the eighteenth century through works like the *Matthäus-Passion*, persisted even two hundred years later. This continuity is significant for the close link between the questions of modernity and Jewish difference.

In the eighteenth century, the uniqueness of the oratorical genre in the German tradition, coupled with the emerging process of

---

is slightly altered and can be found in Borchardt, *GW: Reden*, 181. The version used in the oratorio and cited here appears in Borchardt, *GW: Gedichte*, 118. English translation by Bathja Bayer, cited in Hirshberg, *Paul Ben-Haim*, 85.

77. See also Hirshberg, *Paul Ben-Haim*, 86.

Jewish emancipation, was tied to an aesthetic conflation of religious communities, first and foremost among them the German Lutheran and Jewish communities. The oratorio thus embedded itself in the heart of modern debates concerning Jewish difference in Germany. In the twentieth century, the same link was not only preserved but also manifested with greater deliberation. Wagner's intervention in the interim planted the intertwined stakes of musical dramatic forms and the problem of Jewish difference in an even broader context, that of the artwork and its perceived boundaries in modernity. Consequently, the conflation of communities offered by the oratorio received a more explicit parallel in the question of the open-ended and fragmentary versus the closed and unified work, upon which Benjamin consciously reflected in his writings from the 1920s. If, through Wagner, the idea of the complete and unified work coincided with a stable notion of a German community that can be unambiguously distinguished from the Jewish community, then the contrasting idea of a work whose boundaries are porous, unsettled, and fluid, would indeed present a challenge to such a view of a stable and unambiguous Jewish difference. And this challenge was in fact what the oratorio brought to the table.

For Benjamin, outlining the specific aesthetic expression of modern existence involved a deliberate return to discrete moments in history like the German baroque, in which modern, fragmentary existence crystallized in certain art forms only to be subsumed again by an inauthentic drive toward totality, self-identity, and completion. The political bearing of the artwork's condition in modernity was evident in Benjamin's linking of the baroque *Trauerspiel* to a crisis of sovereignty and eschatology in modern Europe, especially in Germany. This crisis manifested itself in the inability to form a stable notion of collectivity whose boundaries are settled and clearly defined. The oratorio *Joram* prompted a similar act of deliberate return in this chapter, not to the German baroque *Trauerspiel* but rather to the German oratorio at a particular moment in history, where it likewise reflected a modern condition of problematic collectivity with a transparency that the opera of the time could not parallel.

This chapter opened by asking how we can understand Ben-Haim's composition of Borchardt's work as an act of translation.

In what way does the musical rendition complement the poetry or even "continue" it, to think again like Benjamin? I have proposed to search for an answer by attributing meaning to Ben-Haim's decision to compose *Joram* as an oratorio rather than an opera. The theoretical significance of the oratorio as a genre that openly exhibits the modern condition of unstable collectives and pairs it with a concept of an artwork with unsettled boundaries has been the focus of this chapter. While similar issues of problematic collectivity and Jewish difference pervaded *Das Buch Joram* and its surrounding debates, they were nevertheless still bound to a self-secluded perspective. The lyrical nature of Borchardt's poetry and the poet's own view of the autonomous self-sufficiency of artworks that was expressed in his translation theory could only hint at the further implications of *Das Buch Joram*'s underlying themes. The oratorio *Joram* brought these considerations fully to the surface and stripped away any trace of the autonomy that Borchardt still attached to his work. From the perspective of translation then, we could say that the oratorical rendition of *Das Buch Joram*, far from providing a musical "completion" of Borchardt's poetry, *opened* the work. It emphasized the poem's actual status as a fragment by providing it with a musical rendition that openly conveyed the porous condition of modern artworks and modern collectives.

3

MOSES AND ARON
REPRESENTING THE PEOPLE

For the past six decades, Arnold Schoenberg's unfinished opera *Moses und Aron* (Moses and Aaron) has been fascinating critics and scholars of widely ranging fields.[1] The modernist retelling of central events from the Book of Exodus opens with Moses being called in the desert to free the people of Israel from slavery, a liberation that is more conceptual than physical in its operatic rendering. It continues with Moses and Aron's joint attempt to convey to the people the idea of a God who neither image nor word could represent—this is Schoenberg's radical interpretation of the biblical image ban—and concludes with the worship of the golden calf and its destruction. *Moses*'s composition began with the first drafts of a

---

1. An earlier, abridged version of the chapter was published as Adi Nester, "The End of Abstraction and the Beginning of the People: On Law and Representation in Arnold Schoenberg's *Moses und Aron*," *German Quarterly* 93, no. 1 (2020): 19–36.

libretto in 1928 and accompanied Schoenberg throughout his life. The first two acts were completed by 1932. Schoenberg continued to work on act 3 after leaving Germany the following year. However, to this day, the third act's text remains uncomposed. In 1963, Adorno's essay "Sacred Fragment" was the first work of criticism to link the unfinished state of the opera to Schoenberg's interpretation of the *Bilderverbot* (image ban) and its attack on artistic mimesis. After Adorno, a significant share of *Moses* scholarship was dedicated to the opera's insoluble dilemma, relating Moses's impossible task of proclaiming an ineffable God to a crisis of representation in modernist art and the attention that modernism's self-critique drew to the inadequate relation between concept, image, and reality.

Alongside Schoenberg's remarks on the opera's theological and philosophical thrust, we find his acknowledgment of its "undeniably political" bearing,[2] which leans both on the work's thematic focus—the liberation of the people of Israel from Egypt and its formation as a nation under God's law—and on the historical circumstances surrounding the opera's composition in the 1930s.[3] And indeed, while scholarship has primarily endeavored to relate *Moses*'s modernist critique of representation to theological and philosophical questions, its inquiries could never be pursued independently of the opera's political import. In Jan Assmann's work, for example, this theopolitical entwinement manifests in the recognition that Moses's introduction of monotheism and the image ban was above all a means to distinguish between "us" and "them."[4]

Yet in no other work of criticism is this involvement more pronounced than in Adorno's 1963 study of *Moses* as an opera "after

---

2. See Joseph Auner, *A Schoenberg Reader: Documents of a Life* (New Haven, CT: Yale University Press, 2003), 330.

3. See Michael A. Rosenthal, "Art and the Politics of the Desert: German Exiles in California and the Biblical *Bilderverbot*," *New German Critique* 118, no. 40 (2013): 43–64. The opera has been analyzed from a political perspective in various studies. See, for example, Ute Holl, *The Moses Complex: Freud, Schoenberg, Straub/Huillet*, trans. Michael Turnbull (Zurich: Diaphanes, 2017).

4. Jan Assmann, *Moses the Egyptian: The Memory of Egypt in Western Monotheism* (Cambridge, MA: Harvard University Press, 1997); Jan Assmann, "Die Mosaische Unterscheidung in Arnold Schönbergs Moses und Aron," *Musik und Ästhetik* 33 (2005): 5–29.

Wagner." "Sacred Fragment" asks whether sacred art is even possible today. For Adorno, the "sacred" condition of great artworks—and *Moses*, as he acknowledges, clearly *appears* to be such a work—relied on a sense of transsubjective authority attributed to the work as a convener and organizer of public life. The model for such sacred, collective art was of course Greek drama, where the bond between art, politics, and religion was inaugurated in the arena of the theater. It was to this sacred status that Wagner's music drama laid claims. But although Adorno poses the possibility of attaining this status as a question, he already knows that such claims in Wagner's case are false. While reliance on myth endowed Wagner's music dramas with the anonymous voice of the people, it simultaneously bound his work to a specific kind of bourgeois subjectivity: that of Wagner the poietic subject, for whom the realm of passions prevailing in his music dramas represented the essence of isolated, individual expression. Wagner's work, Adorno insists, is the product of a bourgeois era whose idea of the "sacred" is the all-commanding individual genius. True collective art and its accompanying vision of a harmoniously organic people were no longer available in Wagner's time. The monumentalizing gesture of his work had only the potential to evoke a disastrous aestheticization of fascism. Could Schoenberg, a successor of Wagner in many respects, be granted a different verdict?

The impossible yet unavoidable task of representing what cannot be represented, which underlies Schoenberg's opera, leads Adorno to a further deliberation on the work's historical impossibility as a monumental "great work" in an era that is unable to sustain great, collective artworks. Yet while Adorno admits that Schoenberg's work cannot escape its own historical circumstances, he nevertheless notes a fundamental difference between Wagner's mythology and Schoenberg's theology. "An immense gulf opens up between the trans-subjective of the Torah, on the one hand, and the free aesthetic act which created the work on the other," he writes, but notes further that it is exactly this gulf that reveals *Moses*'s negative theology.[5] The possibility of sacred or collective art today is

---

5. Theodor W. Adorno, *Quasi Una Fantasia: Essays on Modern Music*, trans. Rodney Livingstone (New York: Verso, 2002), 227.

disclosed through an "inverted mirror-image" of what is confessed to be unattainable.

The fact that *Moses* is a fragment is crucial for Adorno. Fragmentation mitigated the totality that Adorno otherwise saw in the opera's twelve-tone composition method, which, despite its progressive atonal nature, did not stray too far from Wagner's notion of the total artwork.[6] For Adorno, fragmentation made the opera's sacred aspirations appear more legitimate. But more than that, what appealed to Adorno was the dominance of the chorus in *Moses*. Unlike Wagner's music dramas, Schoenberg's opera lifted the voice of the people—the chorus—above the combined voices of Moses and Aron.[7] The pervasiveness of the chorus in the opera places the formation of a people—the paradoxical act of liberation and setting boundaries—at the center while challenging the very possibility of providing a homogeneous and organic notion of the people. *Moses* conveys the representation of the people as another insoluble problem. And it is this impossibility, exposed in the opera's attempt to represent the people onstage, that endows the work, albeit only negatively, with the status of a collective work, or rather, a sacred fragment.

Adorno's essay serves this chapter as a starting point for a reflection on the relation between artworks, collectives, and representation. In Wagner's wake, the pressure that the modernist opera fragment brings to bear on concepts like the "great artwork" is inseparable from the challenges it poses for notions of homogeneous and restricted collective identities. The historical realities of *Moses* grant these considerations a specific critical charge: at stake are homogeneous and restricted conceptions of so-called German and Jewish collectives. These are implicated by the relation between the artwork and the notion of the people that *Moses* invokes.

---

6. See Theodor W. Adorno, *Philosophy of New Music*, trans. Robert Hullot-Kentor (Minneapolis: University of Minnesota Press, 2006).

7. In an interview that accompanied his performance of *Moses* at the Salzburger Festspiele in 1996, Pierre Boulez noted that there are indeed three different persons in the opera: Moses, Aron, and the People, which serves as arbitrator between the first two. See Arnold Schönberg Center, "Pierre Boulez on Arnold Schoenberg's Moses und Aron," accessed October 27, 2023, https://www.youtube.com/watch?v=2IpFPDnVX1s.

This chapter explores these themes by focusing on laws and their capacity to create both unity and distinction among peoples in the opera. Such concerns find their aesthetic manifestation in the laws that govern Schoenberg's twelve-tone composition method. On the political front, the opera's reference to Moses's law calls for its consideration in relation to a series of reflections on law and difference from Freud and Thomas Mann to Jacob Taubes. Schoenberg's opera lends its fragmentariness to its people too. The opera's evocation of Moses's law and its history of ambiguating and unsettling rather than reifying difference between peoples resists the conceptualization of stable collective identities. *Moses*'s people cannot be represented homogeneously. Their boundaries are volatile and porous, and they cannot be defined against a stable other.

The people's mutability in *Moses* call for further deliberation on the question of political representation. Once we establish that Schoenberg's people cannot be grouped together under a stable, rigid identity, however broad, the question of the people's representability emerges. Guided by Schoenberg's political drafts with an emphasis on his critical view of democracy as the vaunted representation of the general will, this chapter also explores the problem of representing the people both politically and onstage. It considers the opera in relation to critical views of democracy and political representation in the Weimar Republic, where Schoenberg lived between 1926 and 1933. Thus, it introduces *Moses* to a much broader political-theoretical debate on the nature of representation.

Schoenberg, Schmitt, and the Challenge of Democracy

That Schoenberg was indeed concerned with the people, and more specifically, with the question of the Jewish people, is evident from the numerous drafts of essays, addresses, and letters pertaining to Jewish political affairs he left behind. These materials, which Schoenberg produced mostly in France and the United States after leaving Germany, bespeak the anxiety of an exile stripped of an Austro-German cultural legacy he previously believed to spearhead. The composer discussed having experienced antisemitism even early in his youth.[8] But a series of events beginning in the early 1920s ultimately confirmed to him that even conversion, which he himself undertook in 1898, could not aid Jews in Europe.[9] In 1921, Schoenberg was denied lodging on account of his being Jewish while vacationing in the Austrian town of Mattsee. Just a few years later, in 1926, he faced fierce antisemitic opposition to his appointment at the Prussian Academy of Arts.[10] These experiences resulted in his intensified interest in the fate of European Jewry. The rise of antisemitism in Vienna, which coincided with a growing Zionist consciousness among many Austrian Jews, had further influenced Schoenberg's political inclination in the years prior to his move to Berlin in 1926.

Although he had some contact with figures in the Zionist movement, Schoenberg's political excerpts are primarily instances of isolated reflection. For the most part, these writings were not published during his lifetime. Schoenberg was never an active participant in the movement but rather an outside observer who had his own ideas about how to address the plight of European Jews. Nevertheless, he continued to labor on his political writings until as late as 1947, a year before it was made clear that a Jewish state was becoming a reality and he was not to play a leading role in it. His commitment and dedication were such that, in an unpublished draft from 1934, Schoenberg claimed to be willing to forsake his music in favor of political work.[11] In yet another fragment from 1937, he continued to emphasize: "A statesman has one ideal: His People; one ethics: His People; one thought: His People; one feeling: His People."[12]

Next to notes elaborating on his position vis-à-vis Zionism, Schoenberg's scattered political excerpts comprise materials such as an emergency four-point program for Jewry on the way to erect an

---

8. See Arnold Schoenberg, "Jeder junge Jude," *Journal of the Arnold Schoenberg Institute* 17, nos. 1–2 (1994): 452–55.
9. On Schoenberg's conversion and reaffirmation of the Jewish faith, see Malcolm MacDonald, *Schoenberg*, 2nd ed. (Oxford: Oxford University Press, 2008), 93.
10. See Alexander Ringer, *Arnold Schoenberg: The Composer as Jew* (Oxford: Clarendon, 1993), 56.
11. See Klára Móricz, *Jewish Identities: Nationalism, Racism, and Utopianism in Twentieth-Century Music* (Berkeley: University of California Press, 2008), 212.
12. Arnold Schoenberg, "Two Fragments on Jewish Affairs," typed manuscript, Archive of the Arnold Schönberg Center, Wien.

independent Jewish state and an outline for an envisioned Jewish *Einheitspartei* (unity party). The writings called for unanimity among the different political and ideological Jewish factions who, unable to reach a consensus among themselves, hindered the work they set out to accomplish. Depicting the challenging task of bringing together a group of people that carried as many different opinions as the number of individuals within it, Schoenberg wrote:

> The Jewish body is divided in a very complex way. Primarily, the whole body is divided into three principal sections hostile to each other, according to religion: orthodox, reformist, atheist; then each of these groups is broken according to socio-political principles into conservatives, liberals, socialists. Further, the origin of the Jews as Western, Eastern, Oriental, again subdivides every group. And finally, each one of these geographic groups includes "nationalities" eager to preserve their respective splinter into an almost unlimited number of "isms."[13]

Many of Schoenberg's essays revisited themes that appeared earlier in his play *Der biblische Weg* ("The Biblical Way," 1927), which prefigured *Moses und Aron* with its focus on the attempt to unite a disparate and contentious population under Moses's law.[14] The contemporary political setting of the play, which deals with the establishment of a Jewish state in a fictitious African country, is presented with a biblical subtext. Max Aruns, the protagonist who seeks to create this modern state, is an amalgam of both Moses, the visionary, and Aron, the practical man. Like *Moses und Aron, Der biblische Weg* explores the limits of spiritualization and its suitability for the project of constructing a people.

Schoenberg's quest for unity brought him to dismiss any political logic that did not originate in a single, individual will. His belief that this unity could only be realized through the figure of a single,

---

13. Arnold Schoenberg, "A Four-Point Program for Jewry (1939)," in *Arnold Schoenberg: Stile herrschen, Gedanke siegen: Ausgewählte Schriften*, ed. Anna Maria Morazzoni (Mainz: Schott, 2007), 305.

14. Arnold Schoenberg, *Der biblische Weg, Schauspiel in 3 Akten*, typed manuscript, Archive of the Arnold Schönberg Center, Wien. For an English translation, see Moshe Lazar, "The Biblical Way," *Journal of the Arnold Schoenberg Institute* 17 (1994): 162–330.

authoritative leader—certainly a problematic conclusion for someone in Schoenberg's position—has been construed by scholars either as a celebration of the openly militaristic views of the revisionist Zionist leader Vladimir Ze'ev Jabotinsky (1880–1940) or as evidence of an "uneasy parallel" with the politically aggressive model of Hitler's Germany.[15] It is possible to see how Schoenberg's recurring remarks on the shortcomings of the democratic system and his fascination with authoritative models might lead one to conclude that the composer could not help but replicate the fascism he was escaping from in Germany. Yet a closer look at his writings would suggest that it is in fact Schoenberg's experience of democracy in the Weimar Republic—the democracy that, in the name of a majority regarded as the will of the people, enabled Hitler's ascension—that informed the composer's critique.

In a draft titled "Notizen zur jüdischen Politik" (Notes on Jewish Politics), written in 1933, Schoenberg expressed skepticism toward democracy and its ability to represent the general will in a language that appeared to be taken directly from his opera:

> Ein Gedanke entspringt einem Hirn; mit seinen Vorzügen; mit seinen Mängeln. Wenn andere sich dreinmengen, so werden die Fehler nicht verbessert. Ein aus dem Hirn gesprungener Gedanke, ist nur so zu brauchen, wie er sich seinem Schöpfer darstellt. . . . Die Demokratie aber handelt auf Grund von Gedanken, die niemand gehabt hat; die keines einzelnen Hirn entsprungen sind; . . . sondern: die—angeblich—dem geeinigten Willen der Gesamtheit entsprechen—in Wirklichkeit aber nur jener Zufalls-Majorität, die sich für sie entschieden hat—wobei die vielen Minoritäten unwirksam geblieben sind, die dagegen gestimmt; und mehr noch, diejenigen, die gar nicht den Versuch gemacht haben sich zu äußern. Dieser Wille der Gesamtheit aber ist nichts Faktisches, sondern kommt nur durch Kompromisse zustand. . . . Die Demokratie erzeugt künstlich einen Gesamtwillen, der nichts anderes ist als das Verwesungsprodukt vieler verderbter Einzelwillen.[16]

---

15. See respectively Ringer, *Arnold Schonberg*, 130; and Móricz, *Jewish Identities*, 214.

16. Schoenberg, "Notizen zur Jüdischen Politik," typed manuscript, Archive of the Arnold Schönberg Center, Wien. The passage, dating from the summer of 1933 spent in the French town of Arcachon, was written in preparation for the eighteenth

[An idea springs from one mind with its merits and its shortcomings. If others were to meddle [with it] they will not improve its flaws. An idea that has sprung from the mind is to be used only as it presents itself to its creator. . . . Democracy however operates on the basis of ideas, which no one has had; [ideas] which did not spring from a single mind, . . . but rather: which—allegedly—correspond to the unified will of the whole—but in reality, only belong to that chance-majority that decided upon it, whereas the many minorities that voted for the opposite remain ineffective, not to mention those who did not make the attempt to express themselves at all. This general will however is nothing factual, but rather comes to be through compromise. . . . Democracy artificially begets a general will which is none other than the spoiled product of many corrupted individual wills.]

The reservations about democracy that Schoenberg voices here have long preoccupied political theorists, for whom concepts such as the general will, law, and representation must be reevaluated and relegitimized time and again. Schoenberg was distressed by what he saw as the impossibility of providing a faithful and accurate representation of the will of the people due to the divergence of opinions that is an inevitable part of any given *Gesamtheit* (totality). This brought him to deem the compromise generated by democracy to be artificial and corrupt.

Whether he intended to or not, Schoenberg's intimation that the solution to such a problem could be located in the person of an authoritative leader tapped into a broader debate, spearheaded by his contemporary Carl Schmitt, on the conditions that validated democracy as a form of representative government in the Weimar Republic. While he did not acknowledge Schmitt's direct influence on his political thought, it is not implausible that during the years Schoenberg was involved in Jewish politics, he was exposed to the

---

Zionist Congress that was to take place in Prague the same year. These thoughts were never read in the forum for which they were intended. Schoenberg eventually chose not to attend the conference when he realized that he had been invited as a Jewish composer and that he would not be given the right to speak, vote, and make proposals like other elected members of the movement. See also Michael Mäckelmann, *Arnold Schönberg und das Judentum: Der Komponist und sein religiöses, nationales und politisches Selbstverständnis nach 1921* (Hamburg: K. D. Wagner, 1984).

fundamental arguments—whether in conjunction with Schmitt's name or not—of one of the central debates around the nature of democracy.[17]

A letter to Thomas Mann from January 1939 attests that Schoenberg did not dismiss democracy unconditionally, although he was aware of the exact weaknesses that informed its critique during the Weimar Republic. "Please do not misunderstand me," he wrote to Mann, "I know to value the worth of democracy, although I am not in a position to overlook its weakest points: included in the orthodox exaggeration of its principles is the possibility of overthrowing it. The free expression of opinion allows anyone to make propaganda for a change in the form of government, and as a result democracy everywhere has proven itself unable to deal with opposition."[18] Though he did not use the same terminology, Schoenberg expressed concerns identical to those that undergirded Schmitt's articulation of what the latter took to be the weakness of the Weimar brand of liberal democracy: the basic assumption that any political party, even one that is bent on subverting the state, is permitted to compete for parliamentary representation.[19]

Schoenberg's depictions of a sovereign ruler come close to the decisionist, indivisible concept of sovereignty developed in Schmitt's *Politische Theologie (Political Theology*, 1922). The coherent, incorruptible idea—be it musical or political—could only emanate from a single authoritative mind for Schoenberg, just as legislation, the implementation of the law, and its suspension in the case of the

---

17. From Jacob Taubes we know that Schmitt's work was known in Jewish political circles. Taubes recalls that in 1948, Pinhas Rosen (formerly Felix Rosenblüth), Israel's first minister of justice, relied on Schmitt's *Verfassungslehre* in order to draft Israel's constitution (which, to this day, still does not exist). Importantly, this anecdote serves Taubes's ongoing opposition to an understanding of inherent difference between a "German" or "Christian" and a "Jewish" position. See Jacob Taubes, *To Carl Schmitt* (New York: Columbia University Press, 2013), 50.

18. Cited in Auner, *A Schoenberg Reader*, 232.

19. In 1932, while Schoenberg was composing the second act of *Moses* in Berlin and a year prior to the writing of "Notizen zur jüdischen Politik," Schmitt argued that only parties that are not inherently anti-republican should be allowed to compete for representation. See Carl Schmitt, *Legalität und Legitimität* (Berlin: Duncker und Humblot, 1932), 30–40.

exception (as well as the decision on the exception itself) was attributed by Schmitt to the indivisible person of the sovereign.[20]

Schmitt encountered the same challenge that heterogeneity posed to the concept of the general will and responded with an identitarian conception of democracy. Jean-Jacques Rousseau's notion of the *volonté générale* served as the foundation for Schmitt's views on identity among a people as a representable political body. In his interpretation of Rousseau's *Social Contract*, Schmitt argued that democracy and the representation of the general will are only possible when one conceives of the people as a homogeneous body, thus conceptualizing a contradiction between democracy and parliamentarism's presupposed heterogeneity.[21]

With the prerequisite of homogeneity as a complete identity within a people, Schmitt managed to override the problem of representation altogether since unanimity further implied a complete identity between the authoritative ruler and the ruled.[22] For Schoenberg, however, this was not a viable solution. As an analysis of representation in *Moses* reveals, while the composer might have considered this option briefly, he ultimately could not deny the people's heterogeneity. The people in Schoenberg's operatic depiction are anything but homogeneous. This is where aesthetics parts ways with political theory. For where the latter aspires toward a resolution of contradictions, Schoenberg's modernist opera can convey the exigencies of representation and its inherent corruptions without the need for synthesis. Rather than settling representation's inherent contradictions, the opera turns them into its subject matter.

The problem of representation that emerges in Schoenberg's opera is double: first, the difficulty of representing (*darstellen*) Moses's God is related here as the problem of representing the law. Where Schmitt relies on Hobbes in his assertion that a sovereign authority precedes the law, *Moses*, on the contrary, emphasizes the impossibility of a

---

20. Carl Schmitt, *Political Theology*, trans. George Schwab (Chicago: Chicago University Press, 2005), 33.
21. Carl Schmitt, *The Crisis of Parliamentary Democracy*, trans. Ellen Kennedy (Cambridge: MIT Press, 1988), 13.
22. See Carl Schmitt, *Constitutional Theory*, trans. Jeffrey Seitzer (Durham, NC: Duke University Press, 2008), 266.

place "before the law." In the opera, the law itself becomes inaccessible and its interpretation and implementation—its representation as *Darstellung*, a rendering of the law—is subject to an inevitable corruption. Moreover, through the figure of Aron, the problem of representing the people as *Vertretung*—as the reductive substitution of the many by the few or the single—is revealed. For as much as Aron's role is to serve as a mouthpiece for Moses, he is also tasked with transmitting and representing the people's demands back to his brother. Here the challenge to democracy's claim of representing a general will, the same challenge that prompted Schmitt's prerequisite of complete homogeneity for a viable representation of the people by the ruler, is met with a refusal to reduce the heterogeneity of the people of Israel. *Moses und Aron* thus retains its role as a modernist critique of representation precisely in its refusal to resolve the problem of representation and in its admission that representation is simultaneously inadequate and yet indispensable.

Law and Unity

As befits a work that is concerned with the formation and unification of a people, *Moses und Aron* places great emphasis on the link between law and unity. Moses's and Aron's task of uniting the people around the idea of a single God is equal in the opera to the act of unification under law. The formative, unifying act is to be sealed in the opera by the gifting of the Tables of the Law to the people. Gods and laws in *Moses* are interchangeable. Their equivalence is made manifest in the people's demand: "Gebt uns unsere Götter wieder, daß sie Ordnung schaffen! Oder wir zerreißen euch, die ihr uns Gesetz und Recht genommen habt!" (Give us back our gods, let them bring us order! Lest we tear you limb from limb, you who took law and command away from us!)[23]

---

23. Arnold Schoenberg, *Moses und Aron Oper in drei Akten: Textbuch* (Mainz: Schott, 1957), 20. English translation by Allen Forte in Arnold Schoenberg, *Moses und Aron Oper in drei Akten: Klavierauszug von Winfried Zillig* (Mainz: Schott, 1957).

Spiritual liberation and purification of thought in the desert, all that Moses offers as a promise to those who have until recently been slaves in Egypt, are clearly not enough. What is required is a law that will validate the liberated rabble's new condition as a people. And so, in the second act of the opera, Moses ascends the mountain, not to help the people better understand the idea of the singular, eternal, omnipresent, invisible, and inconceivable God but rather to return with laws that would confirm the people's new unified status. "Vierzig Tage warten wir nun auf Moses," sings an impatient priest, "und noch immer weiß keiner Recht und Gesetz!" (Forty days now we have awaited Moses, and still no one knows either law or command!)[24]

Schoenberg's opera adopts a political thinking that has existed in Western thought since the Greeks and persisted in the works of political philosophers like Hobbes. Discussions on the origin and purpose of the law are placed, as early as Plato's *Republic* and *The Laws*, in relation to a need to ensure peace and cooperation between the different elements of a given whole. Hobbes's *Leviathan* depicts the law as the element that binds all the subjects of the commonwealth together as one body, a mortal God.[25] The first scene of the second act in *Moses* describes a state of conflict in anticipation of the law that is reminiscent of Hobbes's *bellum omnium contra omnes*, the war of all against all that Hobbes saw in the state of nature:

EIN ÄLTESTER: Immer besetzt Juda die
besten Weideplätze!
EIN ANDERER: Ärger als Ägypten,
zu Fron ohne Ruhetag zwingt Ephraim
Benjamins Söhne!
EIN DRITTER: Benjamins Söhne haben
Ephraims Weiber geraubt!
DIE 70 ÄLTESTEN: Gewalt regiert! Unzucht
kennt ihre Strafe nicht, Tugend nicht ihren

---

24. Schoenberg, *Moses Textbuch*, 19.
25. See Thomas Hobbes, *Leviathan*, ed. Richard Tuck (Cambridge: Cambridge University Press, 1991), 185.

Lohn! Vierzig Tage warten wir vergebens
vor dieser Höhe![26]

[AN ELDER: All the best pastures are occupied
by Judah!
ANOTHER: Far worse than in Egypt, to toil
without day of rest, as Ephraim makes
Benjamin's sons do!
A THIRD ELDER: Ephraim's women have
been stolen by Benjamin's sons!
THE SEVENTY ELDERS: Thus, might now
reigns! Lewdness knows not its punishment,
virtue knows not reward! Forty days we
have waited vainly before this summit!]

Conflict and disunity are recurrent challenges Schoenberg confronted along various paths of his work. It is therefore fitting that *Moses und Aron*, an opera whose underlying problem is unity, would also be Schoenberg's first (and only) twelve-tone opera to be based on a single row. Questions of unity and coherence guided Schoenberg's theoretical writings on music as early as his *Harmonielehre (Theory of Harmony*, 1911), where he dismissed the opposition between consonance and dissonance, claiming that the distinction between the two categories is not one of kind but rather of degree, of familiarity and proximity in relation to the series of overtones contained in each tone ("they are no more opposites than two and ten are opposites").[27]

By rejecting the idea of nonharmonic tones, a situation emerged wherein former hierarchies were annulled without leaving any alternative system of organization to supplant them. As Schoenberg explained:

> With the renunciation of the formal advantages inherent in tonal cohesion, presentation of the idea has become rather harder; it lacks the external rounding-off and self-containedness that this simple and natural

---

26. Schoenberg, *Moses Textbuch*, 19.
27. Arnold Schoenberg, *Theory of Harmony*, trans. Roy E. Carter (Berkeley: University of California Press, 1983), 21.

principle of composition brought about better than did any of the others used alongside it.... For in a key, opposites are at work, binding together. Practically the whole thing consists exclusively of opposites, and this gives the strong effect of cohesion. To find means of replacing this is the task of *the theory of twelve-tone composition.*[28]

Schoenberg's "Method of Composition with Twelve Tones Which Are Related Only with One Another" provided a comprehensive principle of organization without jeopardizing the newly achieved emancipation.[29] The method's requirement to use all tones of the chromatic scale in each basic row without repetition ensured that no accidental hierarchies could be created among them. It also guaranteed that all the "laws and rules that govern the form" were to be derived from the material itself (from the row) rather than from any external principle.[30] The order of the row dictated all of its other possible permutations: the inversion, retrograde, and their respective transpositions.[31] With the twelve-tone method, Schoenberg was able to unite the otherwise diffused musical material under the law of "the first creative thought," a single musical idea, the basic or prime row, which operated as a multidimensional unit commanding vertical and horizontal planes:

THE TWO-OR-MORE-DIMENSIONAL SPACE IN WHICH MUSICAL IDEAS ARE PRESENTED IS A UNIT.... All that happens at any point of this musical space has more than a local effect. It functions not only in its own place, but also in all other directions and planes, and is not without influence even at remote points.... A musical idea, accordingly, though consisting of melody, rhythm, and harmony, is neither the one nor the other alone, but all three together.... The mutual relation of tones regulates the succession of intervals as well as their association

---

28. Arnold Schoenberg, *Style and Idea: Selected Writings*, ed. Leonard Stein, trans. Leo Black (Berkeley: University of California Press, 1984), 209.
29. Schoenberg, *Style and Idea*, 218.
30. Schoenberg, *Style and Idea*, 218.
31. In twelve-tone technique, the original row (prime) could appear in reverse order (retrograde), or with all intervals inverted, for example the first interval of an ascending third would appear as a descending third (inversion), or in retrograde inversion (a combination of the two above).

into harmonies; the rhythm regulates the succession of tones as well as the succession of harmonies and organizes phrasing.[32]

This desire to find a system of laws that will govern an otherwise disparate material did not go unnoticed by Adorno. In his *Philosophy of New Music*, he critiqued Schoenberg's twelve-tone method as the extreme and inevitable product of an Enlightenment process in which the subject, in an inexhaustible effort to gain full command over nature—in this case, the musical material—is ultimately subdued by its own prescribed laws. Adorno commended Schoenberg for liberating Western music from a tonal system of hierarchies that was no longer historically valid in his eyes, but he noted that the composer could not maintain this state of freedom. Schoenberg's search for an alternative compositional method that would regulate the musical material in the wake of tonality's dethroning was in fact far from qualifying as a Benjaminian "general strike." For Adorno, although he never used this exact terminology, this was indeed another example of "law-making violence," the breaking of an old law in order to replace it with a new one.[33]

Adorno's observations provide a penetrating view of totality in Schoenberg's work. The strictness Adorno associated with the twelve-tone method relied on the composer's ubiquitous references to "laws" that govern music. The fact that the composition of *Moses* was guided by a single twelve-tone row supports the claim that the opera is focused on the exigencies of an uncompromising law.[34]

---

32. Schoenberg, *Style and Idea*, 220. Schoenberg continued to explore the idea of unity in his unfinished oratorio *Die Jakobsleiter*. On the relation between *Moses* and *Die Jakobsleiter* and the dialectic between freedom and organization in both works, see Mark Berry, "Arnold Schoenberg's Biblical Way: From 'Die Jakobsleiter' to 'Moses und Aron,'" *Music and Letters* 89, no. 1 (2008): 84–108.

33. See Adorno, *Philosophy of New Music*; and Walter Benjamin, "Critique of Violence," in *Selected Writings I: 1913–1926*, ed. Marcus Bullock and Michael W. Jennings (Cambridge, MA: Harvard University Press, 2002).

34. On the parallels between Schoenberg's compositional rules and the law, see, for example, Alexander Ringer, "Schoenberg and the Concept of Law," in *Bericht über den 1. Kongress der Internationalen Schönberg-Gesellschaft Wien 4.–9. Juni 1974*, ed. Rudolf Stephan (Wien: Verlag Elisabeth Lafite, 1978), 165–72; and Matthias Schmidt, "Vor dem Gesetz: Zur religiösen Dimension eines musika-

Yet Schoenberg's understanding of the law, as one gathers from his writings and from a further study of his opera, is far more intricate. In a short piece titled "Wiesengrund" from 1950, the composer responded to Adorno, clarifying that his method "is not the only way to a solution of the new problems [that arose when tonality was relinquished] but just one of the possibilities."[35] The retort dismissed Adorno's view of the tyranny of the method. For Schoenberg, laws were means of organization and regulation. Their rigidity was an invitation to break and overthrow them. The seemingly "natural" laws that govern and regulate music, as Schoenberg explained in *Harmonielehre*, originated in the human mind: "What we claim to perceive as laws may perhaps only be laws governing our perception, without therefore being the laws a work of art must obey."[36] Even with their human origin, the laws that govern music did not lose their status in Schoenberg's eyes; they remained laws by the fact that they could be broken and replaced.

The exchange between Schoenberg and Adorno prompts us to consider the complexity and ambiguity that accompanies the law in Schoenberg's work. The realization that the law always contains within itself the possibility of its own overthrowing makes us wonder what other contradictions it may hold. *Moses* rises to this challenge by tightening the link between laws in the political and aesthetic contexts. With its archaic, biblical settings, the opera seeks to study the role of the law in the formation of peoples by returning to the law's point of origin and attempting to reconstruct the hypothetical place "before the law."

Law and Difference

Moses und Aron joins several contemporaneous works that similarly seek to examine the concept of law by venturing into the place

---

lischen Begriffs bei Schönberg," in *Arnold Schoenberg und sein Gott, Bericht zum Symposium 26.–29. Juni 2002* (Wien: Arnold Schönberg Center, 2003), 299–310.
35. Cited in Auner, *A Schoenberg Reader*, 338.
36. Auner, *A Schoenberg Reader*, 91.

"before the law." This type of inquiry involved a renewed interest in Moses's law with a specific focus: the ambiguous relation between law and difference. By their power to establish peoples, laws create distinctions as well as unities. They are responsible for uniting the individuals that adhere to them while simultaneously determining who is admitted into the community and who is refused entrance to the law. This is what informs Jacques Derrida's remark on the man from the country seeking entrance into the law in Kafka's parable "Before the Law": "The man from the country does not know the law which is always the city's law, the law of cities and edifices protected by gates and boundaries, of spaces shut by doors."[37]

The discourse of law and difference had a specific historical relevance for debates on Jewish difference. Law loomed large in discussions about Jewish integration into modern European society and shaped the anti-Jewish position of German idealists concerning the distinct nature of Judaism. For the Christian Bible scholar and Orientalist Johann David Michaelis, Mosaic law presented an obstacle to Jewish emancipation. In his polemic against Christian Wilhelm von Dohm's call for the civic betterment of Jews in Germany, Michaelis insisted that Mosaic law made citizenship and full integration of Jews in Germany impossible since its purpose was "to maintain the Jews as a people almost completely separate."[38]

Kant's and the young Hegel's similar notions of Jewish heteronomy supported their view of Judaism as irreconcilably distinct from the moral values of European Enlightenment and from the spirit of Christianity respectively. Kant's conception of Jewish obedience to an imposed law deprived Judaism of freedom as an inner moral imperative.[39] Hegel's early works continued Kant's line in denounc-

---

37. Jacques Derrida, "Before the Law," in *Acts of Literature*, ed. Derek Attridge (New York: Routledge, 1992), 195. On the *Gesetzlichkeit* (legality) of exile and the camp before the law, see Holl, *The Moses Complex*, 15. On Kafka's *Vor dem Gesetz* and Schoenberg's twelve-tone method, see also Schmidt, "Vor dem Gesetz."

38. Christian Wilhelm Dohm, *Ueber die buergerliche Verbesserung der Juden* (Berlin: Nicolai, 1783); Johann David Michaelis, "Herr Ritter Michaelis Beurtheilung," in *Ueber die buergerliche Verbesserung der Juden*, vol. 2, 33–51.

39. Kant considered Judaism a polity rather than a religion for the same reasons. See Immanuel Kant, "Die Religion innerhalb der Grenzen der blossen Vernunft," in *Werke in 12 Bänden*, ed. W. Weisched (Frankfurt: Suhrkamp, 1964), 8:789–93.

ing Judaism as the religion of posited law. For Hegel, this condition engendered a distinction between Judaism and the Hellenic spirit, which Christianity, Protestantism, and especially the German people had come to absorb.[40]

Yet even as early as the eighteenth century, the period that saw the initiation of debates on Jewish emancipation, the discourse on law and Jewish difference was ripe with ambiguities. Michaelis's voluminous treatise on Mosaic law, *Mosaisches Recht* (1770–1771), was itself a modern political intervention calling for the abrogation of Mosaic laws that were in effect in certain German states. Michaelis's treatise may have argued for the incompatibility of Mosaic law with the modern German state, but in doing so he exposed its deep involvement in the formation of the modern German nation.[41] The relation between Judaism, Christianity, and reason was confounded by Moses Mendelssohn's response to claims of Jewish heteronomy. Mendelssohn's notion of Mosaic law as "revealed law" substituted Judaism for Christianity as the religion more compatible with the values of German Enlightenment since, unlike Christianity, which was never able to reconcile revelation with the Enlightenment premise of universal reason, Judaism as revealed law did not require revelation as a category of knowledge.[42]

Against this background, we can understand why critical reflections on Moses's law were renewed around the time when decisions were being made in Europe concerning difference, that is, concerning who was granted admittance to the law and who was excluded by it. In the first half of the twentieth century, the object of such critical reflections was to further complicate and confound the nature of difference that was linked with Moses and his law. In this respect, Schoenberg's opera joins the works of Freud, Mann, and, later, Taubes, who were all interested in the ambivalent kinship between

---

40. Hegel, "The Spirit of Christianity and Its Fate"; Hegel, "Die Positivität der christlichen Religion," in *Gesammelte Werke, Frühere Schriften I*, ed. Friedhelm Nicolin et al. (Hamburg: Felix Meiner, 2014). On the view of Judaism in German idealist philosophy, see also Michael Mack, *German Idealism and the Jew* (Chicago: Chicago University Press, 2003).
41. See Hess, *Germans, Jews*, 60; Ilany, *In Search of the Hebrew People*, 43–62.
42. See further Yovel, *Dark Riddle*, 10–14.

separation and commonality that the figure of Moses the lawgiver embodied.

The coinage "Mosaic Distinction" (*Mosaische Unterscheidung*) introduced by Assmann, one of Taubes's intellectual disciples, informs the study of difference here.[43] Assmann's Mosaic Distinction denotes a separation between different religious communities (Jews and Gentiles, Christians and pagans, etc.) issuing from Moses's initial act of distinction through the introduction of monotheism. On its volatile nature Assmann commented: "Once the distinction is drawn, there is no end of reentries or subdistinctions." Since drawing these distinctions yields not only the creation of meaning and orientation but also conflict and violence, it demands constant reexamination.[44] Although Assmann's term places weight on a separation between true and false in religion, we should note that the Mosaic Distinction's association with the biblical lawgiver inevitably establishes an intimate affinity between difference and the law. Moses's status as lawgiver and the founder of a people turns the Mosaic Distinction into a distinction that is also grounded in the concept of lawgiving. It is this affinity between law and difference that also determines the critical thrust of engagements with the figure of Moses by Freud, Mann, Taubes, and Schoenberg.

Freud's *Der Mann Moses und die Monotheistische Religion* (*Moses and Monotheism*, 1939) investigates the origins of the distinct nature of the Jewish faith. The law of distinction accompanies the idea of Moses's "unique, omnipresent, unapproachable God" from the outset.[45] As in Schoenberg's *Moses und Aron*, monotheism in Freud's study involves a set of laws that are intended to distinguish the adherents of Moses's new faith from Egypt and its many religions. The law of circumcision unites members of the Jewish faith—members previously comprising two different groups, the one that left Egypt and the one that was met in Canaan—while simultaneously serving as a separating mark. Freud's essay seeks to reveal

---

43. See Assmann, *Moses the Egyptian*; and Jan Assmann, *The Price of Monotheism*, trans. Robert Savage (Stanford, CA: Stanford University Press, 2010).

44. Assmann, *Moses the Egyptian*, 1.

45. Sigmund Freud, *Moses and Monotheism: Three Essays*, trans. James Starchey (London: Hogarth, 1974), 18.

the root of the distinction between the German-speaking Jewish and Christian positions of his own time. Assmann observes that the study of Moses had specific relevance to the historical moment in which it was written. Freud's aim was indeed to use this hypothetical essay as a means of comprehending Jewish difference in 1939. As Assmann stresses, "Despite his historical attitude, Freud consistently and consciously insists on speaking with regard to Moses and his time of 'Jews' instead of 'Hebrews' or 'Israelites,' which would be the historically correct designation."[46] In Freud's work, the Mosaic image ban, a direct product of a remote and repressed event that has been experienced by one group, is discovered to dictate a fundamental difference that sets this group apart from the other. Laws that prohibit representation distinguish between two groups residing in two different planes of spirituality, which results in separate subsequent laws that govern the psychology of each group.[47]

Concerned more with questions of politics and morality than religion and group psychology, Mann's novella *Das Gesetz* (*The Tables of the Law*) shifts the focus from monotheism to moral law as the facilitator of communal life. Mann's novella was commissioned and written in 1944, yet in its retelling of the story of Moses it continues the same line of inquiry pursued by Freud and Schoenberg.[48] *Das Gesetz* presents a vivid picture of Moses the lawgiver, who, at great pains, shapes raw human material into a unified nation. In Mann's version of the biblical story, Moses's law represents the transition from a kinship of blood (*das Geblüt*) into an organized community adhering to moral laws (*das Volk*). Although the laws in Mann's novella function as a kind of threshold, gatekeepers granting entrance into a moral society, they are also depicted as universal.[49] However, it is important to note that Mann's treatment of

---

46. Assmann, *Moses the Egyptian*, 148.
47. See also Yosef Hayim Yerushalmi, *Freud's Moses: Judaism Terminable and Interminable* (New Haven, CT: Yale University Press, 1991).
48. See also Rosenthal, "Art and the Politics of the Desert," 53–60.
49. See also Tobias Boes, *Thomas Mann's War: Literature, Politics, and the World Republic of Letters* (Ithaca, NY: Cornell University Press, 2019), 158. Boes also notes Mann's ambiguous depiction of Moses in the novella as a figure that is both the liberator of an oppressed people and the dictator himself.

Moses's law disregards the traditional Christian distinction between eternal moral law (the Decalogue) and temporary political and ritualistic laws (Mosaic law), which Christianity attributed solely to Judaism. Most of the laws that Moses labors to install among his new people in Mann's narrative are laws of purity and cleanliness taken from Leviticus. In the novella, the law in its entirety works to distinguish not between man and man but rather between man and beast; it is in fact "die Quintessenz des Menschenanstandes" (the quintessence of human decency).[50]

The works of Freud and Mann present a complex image in which every distinction that the law erects is promptly undermined. Behind the many distinguishing laws in Freud's *Moses and Monotheism* stands the figure of Moses the Egyptian and the implication that the origin of the people set apart by such laws is to be found precisely in the community rejected by those people. Mann neutralized the distinction that Moses's law entails by suggesting that the moral standards set by this law are universal. Forty years later, the same principle guided the image of Paul the Apostle from the Jews to the Gentiles that Taubes painted in his Heidelberg lectures.[51] Taubes, who continued to develop the figure of Paul that Freud depicted in part 3 of *Moses and Monotheism*, approaches the apostle from a Jewish perspective.[52] In the hands of Paul, the Roman Jew from Tarsus who, alongside Moses, is attributed with the founding of a new People of God, the critique of law turns into a political act. Taubes opposes the prevailing view of the apostle as the founder of a community whose retreat into inner faith supposedly did not challenge the ruling Roman authority. As he notes, Paul rejected the Mosaic conception of a law that unites a people and separates it from others in order to cre-

---

50. Thomas Mann, *Das Gesetz* (Stockholm: Berman-Fischer Verlag, 1944), 133.

51. Jacob Taubes, *The Political Theology of Paul*, ed. Aleida Assmann et al., trans. Dana Hollander (Stanford, CA: Stanford University Press, 2008).

52. The emphasis Taubes places on the Jewish origin of Paul, the founder of Christianity, as a universal, world-political order, resembles that found in Freud's discussion of the different states of Jewish and Christian collective memories. See Freud, *Moses and Monotheism*, 109. Taubes cites Freud and points out further that Paul's universalism was predated by a universal sense of guilt. See Taubes, *The Political Theology of Paul*, 93.

ate a universal community. Yet this very act contested the Roman Empire's claim to the title of a sole universal order. Paul, in other words, asserted a difference between his new community and the Roman Empire while claiming to abolish all difference.

Taubes's insight into the Moses-Paul comparison implies that even Paul's transfigured "*pas* Israel" or "all Israel," a universal community joined in love and solidarity that rejects the law-bound distinction between Jew and Gentile, is irrevocably implicated in the political act of asserting difference. Taubes views Paul's critique of law as an internal Jewish polemic. He rejects the Augustinian distinction between Judaism and Christianity as communities of law and grace respectively and highlights their interchangeability, noting that "Judaism can't lay exclusive claim to ritualistic religiosity any more than Christianity can lay exclusive claim to a spiritual religiosity that liberates from the law."[53] With his recognition that the boundless community is not truly boundless, nor is the distinct truly distinct, Taubes provides an additional layer of ambiguity to debates on Moses's law and Jewish difference.

Schoenberg's *Moses* provides yet another layer. Different communities and cultures merge within the opera: Moses and Aron's joint attempt to form a people on the basis of a prohibition on images places the Jewish community alongside the Christian—primarily the Protestant—one, rather than in contradistinction to it. The Pauline-Augustinian distinction *sub lege, sub gratia* (under law, under grace) is overridden by the codependence of the two brothers. Both Moses's *Gesetz und Gedanke* (law and idea) and Aron's *Grazie und Gnade* (grace and clemency) are required for the task as the opera sets Aron's expressed love of the people ("Ich liebe dieses Volk!," act 2, scene 5) next to Moses's continued demand to regiment thought.[54]

Schoenberg's monotheism, a conflation of the first and second commandments ("thou shalt have no other gods before me" and "thou shalt not make unto thee any graven image"), joins Jewish

---

53. Taubes, *The Political Theology of Paul*, 116.
54. Consider Aron's line in act 1, scene 4: "Er hat euch vor allen Völkern auserwählt und will euch allein seine Gnade schenken." Jan Assmann also calls attention to the performance instruction *Grazioso* on Aron's first entrance in act 1, scene 2: Moses and Aron's encounter in the desert. See Assmann, "Die Mosaische Unterscheidung," 11.

and Protestant iconoclasm together. In fact, the abstraction of *Moses* exceeds both approaches to representation and its restrictions. Informing the composer's radically abstract notions of God and the image ban is an apophatic theology originating in Greek thought. Abstraction, as it appears in both Schoenberg's and Freud's works, is an element that was introduced into Jewish theology during the twelfth century through the work of the Jewish Neoplatonist Maimonides.[55] The famous filmed rendition of *Moses und Aron* by Jean-Marie Straub and Danièle Huillet (1975) develops this Jewish Greek (and Jewish Roman) conflation by filming the first two acts in the Alba Fucens amphitheater in Abruzzo, east of Rome. Observing this fact, the philosopher Philippe Lacoue-Labarthe further complicates the Jewish Greek conflation by evaluating *Moses und Aron*, a biblical opera, as a tragedy according to Hegel's definition of the genre.[56] Assmann also points toward Jewish Greek conflation in his application of Hans Blumenberg's concept of "Arbeit am Mythos" (work on myth) to Schoenberg's treatment of the Moses story.[57] As "work on myth," *Moses* differs from the exegetical or Midrashic engagement with the biblical story since, according to Assmann, it crosses ethnic, national, political, and religious boundaries.[58]

A similar attitude pervades the formal aspects of the opera's composition. The unity that Schoenberg achieved in his twelve-tone opera by deriving the entire musical material from a single row immediately lends ambiguity to difference—understood here as formal division—within the work. The uniformity of the row in the opera attenuates the means of formal articulation. In most tonal operas, punctuation of larger segments within the work is accomplished through transitions to different key areas. In the absence of a tonal

---

55. See also Yosef Hayim Yerushalmi, "The Moses of Freud and the Moses of Schoenberg: On Words, Idolatry, and Psychoanalysis," *The Psychoanalytic Study of the Child* 47, no. 1 (1992): 1–20.

56. Philippe Lacoue-Labarthe, "The Caesura of Religion," in *Opera through Other Eyes*, ed. David J. Levin (Stanford, CA: Stanford University Press, 1993).

57. See Hans Blumenberg, *Arbeit am Mythos* (Frankfurt am Main: Suhrkamp, 1979).

58. See Assmann, "Die Mosaische Unterscheidung," 7. On blurring the boundaries between Graecophilia and the Old Testament, see also Holl, *The Moses Complex*, 57.

infrastructure, segments in *Moses* are differentiated instead as separate "row areas."⁵⁹ Such areas are dictated by a certain row permutation or a fragment thereof, but they always remain subject to the same primary row. The twelve-tone law is accordingly a law that generates unstable differences. It provides a way to carve out separate combinations from the prime row and consequently to mandate points of division in the opera. Yet it never obscures the common source and subsequent tenuous distinction between each section.

Difference, this time between voices and instruments, is obstructed in the very first measures of *Moses*. The sounds in measures 1–5 are meant to be perceived in darkness. The eye cannot serve as an auxiliary means to distinguish between singer and instrumentalist as the instruction to lift the curtain is given in the score only in the sixth measure.⁶⁰ This effect is expressly desired by Schoenberg, who specifies in the performance instructions prefacing the score:

> 6 solo voices: Soprano, Mezzosoprano, Alto, Tenor, Baritone, Bass.
> They sit in the orchestra thus: the soprano with the second flute, mezzosoprano with the second clarinet, alto with cor anglais, tenor with second bassoon, baritone with bass clarinet, bass with second cello. Throughout, when these six voices sing, the given instruments play the same part in unison with them.... Where the singers and the instruments are supposed to be differentiated from each other in performance (particularly in terms of dynamics) it will be clearly marked. Otherwise the sound should blend together as closely as possible.⁶¹

As Ute Holl observes, language, as that which introduces distinct meanings and vowel sounds that are separated by sharp consonances,

---

59. See formal analysis of the opera in Pamela C. White, *Schoenberg and the God-Idea: The Opera Moses und Aron* (Ann Arbor: University of Michigan Research Press, 1985), 138–46. The punctuation between the first seven measures and the new segment beginning with Moses's entrance in measure 8, for example, is achieved by presenting the prime row and its retrograde inversion in mm. 1–7. The new section beginning in measure 8 presents the retrograde inversion of the first transposition of the aggregate (broken to tetrachords). This transition is also accompanied by a change in rhythm and texture.

60. See also Holl, *The Moses Complex*, 40.

61. Arnold Schoenberg, *Moses und Aron: Oper in drei Akten*, ed. Christian Martin Schmidt (London: Edition Eulenburg, 1984), x.

is also banned from the first measures. The six soloists representing *die Stimme aus dem Dornbusch* (The Voice from the Burning Bush) vocalize a continuous "O" whose beginnings and endings in the different parts elude the listener. In her analysis of the vocalise, Holl notes Schoenberg's strategy of "removing tone quality from the human body." The avoidance of consonants and adherence to "non-incriminating" vowels that will not betray the origin of a speaker through their accent and place them in a specific geographical region serves, according to Holl, as another means of unsettling difference.[62]

Compared to the blending of voices and instruments in the opening vocalise, the clear distinction between the musical characterization of Moses's and Aron's respective parts seems indisputable. Aron's eloquent melodic line is sharply contrasted to Moses's *Sprechstimme*, a singing technique closer in nature to metered speech. In this technique, pitches are marked on the score but are in practice only approximated by the performer. Here too, however, what was initially created as a form of distinction (between Moses's speech and Aron's singing) produces the opposite. Moses's ungainly *Sprechstimme* muddles the difference between frequencies and intervals and challenges the authority of the twelve-tone row.[63]

The approximation Schoenberg called for in Moses's part requires that the singer not adhere to the separate pitches as they are written in the score but rather, in his imitation of speech, blur the difference between them. Previous remarks by Schoenberg about the execution of *Sprechstimme* in earlier works like the *Gurre-Lieder* and *Pierrot lunaire* wavered between a demand to maintain the written pitch and to approximate without hitting it exactly. In *Moses und Aron*, however, Schoenberg was explicit about his wish. A footnote he added to Moses's part in the score clarifies: "Here as everywhere else, please never sing the speech notes! They do not

---

62. See Holl, *The Moses Complex*, 45–51.

63. The notation of Moses's part substitutes x-marks for traditional round note heads, though these are still placed accurately on the stave. In act 2, scene 4, note heads are omitted altogether, leaving only the stems to indicate rhythm.

correspond to the rows!"⁶⁴ *Sprechstimme* in the opera thus results in a suspension of the row and its interval-based organizational law.

With the distinction between Moses's and Aron's musical characterization, the opera resurrected the debate on the supremacy of music or language that had accompanied the genre since the seventeenth century.⁶⁵ Wagner's notion of drama purportedly put the matter to rest by attributing music's and poetry's common origin to the stroke of a single genius. Yet whatever union Wagner may have restored was again undone by *Moses*'s polarization of language and music as two opposing figures whose tragic conflict was destined to remain unresolved. The law that prohibits representation does not allow Aron's round and seductive melismas to corrupt Moses's rigid and angular declamation. As Adorno stressed, music, not immune to historical process, became "interwoven with the pictorial arts" as that which "makes sensuous something other than itself."⁶⁶ This entanglement with the prohibited act of representation barred music from entering Moses's world of abstract concepts and left the latter with a form of expression that is limited to the declamation of text. The link to the previous conflict in opera between music and language as thought and emotion respectively is also manifest in the characters' opposed exclamations. To Aron's sentimental "Kannst du lieben, was du dir nicht vorstellen darfst?" (Can you love, what you may not conceive?) Moses provides the intellectual rejoinder: "Reinige dein Denken, lös es von Wertlosem, weihe es Wahrem."⁶⁷ (Purify your thought, free it from worthless things, let it be righteous.)

---

64. See further Peter Stadlen, "Schoenberg's Speech-Song," *Music and Letters* 62, no. 1 (1981): 1–11.

65. A famous example is the *Querelle des Bouffons*, a debate that took place in early 1750s Paris between proponents of French and Italian opera. The *Querelle* sparked a controversy that prompted Rousseau, close to thirty years later, to publish his *Essay on the Origin of Language* (1781) suggesting that language originated in song as an emotional utterance radically different from language's contemporary conceptual sense. Ninety years later, Nietzsche continued to consider the original relation between language and music in *The Birth of Tragedy* (1872), which he wrote under the influence of Wagner's music dramas.

66. Adorno, "Sacred Fragment," in *Quasi Una Fantasia*, 230.

67. Schoenberg, *Moses Textbuch*, 7–8.

Figure 3.1. Schoenberg, *Moses und Aron*, act 1, scene 2 (mm. 183–86).

Yet Moses's *Sprechstimme* and Aron's elaborate singing, though sharply different from each other, are still united in another way. Remaining as close as possible to the speechlike pronunciation of words to avoid any semblance of melody, Moses's part cuts through bar lines and rhythmic divisions. Accents and inflections are dictated by textual meter, overriding the measured rhythmic division of the score. Thus, Moses's words, "Unvorstellbar, weil unsichtbar, weil unüberblickbar, weil unendlich, weil ewig, weil allgegenwärtig, weil allmächtig" (inconceivable because unseen, can never be measured, everlasting, eternal, because ever present, and almighty), in the second scene of act 1 appear as an endless succession of attributes whose components do not always overlap with the set time signature, creating syncopations and confounding strong and weak beats (see figure 3.1).[68]

The obstruction of rigid rhythmic structures by language directs Aron's singing as well. His melismas operate in a manner similar to that of Moses's speech, stretching vowels over bar lines to create a far from symmetrical melodic line, whose punctuation is not constrained by any distinct periodical structures (see figure 3.2).

In *Moses und Aron*, differences created by musical laws are disruptive. Just as the separation between song and speech unsettles the difference between various pitches and various intervals, so too does it work to undermine melodic topographies and distinct rhythmic patterns. Introducing this ambiguity of musical laws is the opera's unique contribution to the discourse on law and difference.

---

68. Schoenberg, *Moses Textbuch*, 7.

Figure 3.2. Schoenberg, *Moses und Aron*, act 1, scene 2 (mm. 130–138).

Deconstructing Moses: The Inaccessibility of Law

Schoenberg's observations on democracy intersect with the discourse on law and difference in the problem of political representation. If law-bound difference is an unsettled difference, the collective identities that the law asserts are likewise unsettled. This inevitably prompts the problem of representing collective identities unequivocally and unproblematically. In *Moses und Aron*, political representation appears as a twofold problem. The possibility of adequate representation, of *Vertretung*, was questioned in Schoenberg's expressed mistrust of democracy. For how can the people or the general will be represented if they are in fact fictitious abstracts? The opera's depiction of Moses as a failed representative of his people gives one expression to this problem. But representation is also complicated in the opera as *Darstellung*, this time of the law itself, whose abstract conception is dissociated from its implementation or realization in particular cases.

What emerges here as the twofold problem of representation, the *Darstellung* of the law and the *Vertretung* of the people, was addressed by Rousseau in his discussion of the lawgiver. To ensure their efficacy, Rousseau observed, the lawgiver must be removed from the people as "a superior intelligence that beheld all the passions of men without feeling any of them; . . . It is a particular and superior function that has nothing in common with the dominion over men."[69] Rousseau's lawgiver resembles Schoenberg's Moses, in whose person the inaccessibility of both lawgiver and his law are manifest. The remote and inaccessible station of the lawgiver in Rousseau's *Social Contract* was a direct result of the problem he found in the body politic's capacity to proclaim laws as a unified whole: "Will it be a common accord, by a sudden inspiration? Who will give it the necessary foresight to formulate acts and promulgate them in advance?"[70] The lawgiver appears as a kind of instant solution to the problematic agency of the abstract "whole," which troubled Schoenberg as well.

Next to the difficulty of identifying a consolidated, undivided "will of the people," another fundamental question arose for Rousseau regarding the act of lawgiving. To have the "necessary foresight" that allows one to promulgate a law *in advance*, one would have to be in that exact impossible place "before the law." Impossible, since for the law to apply to all cases, it must be absolute and nameless. It cannot be gradually and empirically decreed following each specific incident but rather remain general. A general, abstract law, however, is one whose emergence, to use Derrida's terms, is an event that cannot be accessed, a "non-event." Derrida's study of the law resembles his language criticism. Like the hypothetical emergence of language Derrida finds in Lévi-Strauss, the law too could only have been born "in one fell swoop," since upon its emergence it had to be generally applicable, that is, applicable to all cases and also to no specific case.[71] Derrida's deliberations here are not too far from Rousseau's words: "When I say that the object of the law is always general, I have in mind that the law considers subjects as a body and actions in the abstract, never a man as an individual or a particular action."[72]

---

69. Jean-Jacques Rousseau, "The Social Contract," in *The Basic Political Writing*, trans. Donald A. Cress (Indianapolis: Hackett, 1987), 163.

70. Rousseau, "The Social Contract," 162.

71. Jacques Derrida, "Structure, Sign, and Play in the Discourse of the Human Sciences," in *Writing and Difference*, trans. Alan Bass (Chicago: University of Chicago Press, 1978).

72. Rousseau, "The Social Contract," 161.

Much of the fascination that deconstructionists like Derrida had with the law was owed to what they perceived as the inaccessibility of the law as a body of text. Through a deconstructive lens, the law as text evinces an indefinite postponement of its origin. This is how the law gains authority. The law of the law, according to Derrida, is to be intolerant of its genesis. It is no coincidence, then, that Freud, as Derrida notes, defined the condition "before the law"—the actions that brought about the installment of laws in Freud's *Totem and Taboo*—as one of repression, an inaccessible memory of a past event. This, of course, did not prevent the psychoanalyst from attempting to access that exact moment of origin in both his studies of Moses. *Moses and Monotheism*, despite its author's claims that the work has historical and archaeological validity, remains a speculative thought experiment. "Wenn Moses ein Ägypter war . . ." (if Moses was an Egyptian), the title of the second part of *Moses and Monotheism*, is a hypothetical that betrays the work's earlier conception as a historical novel and makes clear that the matter cannot be determined conclusively. Similarly, Freud's objective in his earlier 1914 essay "The Moses of Michelangelo" is to reconstruct a no-longer-accessible chain of events that preceded the one moment the artist left suspended in marble.

Next to Freud's work, Schoenberg's opera is another attempt to return to the moment before the law so as to inquire after its nature. Such an impossible task dictates that the opera will be riddled with many other impossibilities that will ultimately prevent its completion, including the compulsion to represent what cannot be represented.

In their rejection of Moses, the people in Schoenberg's opera express a legitimate concern regarding abstract law. Paul de Man's reading of *The Social Contract* voices the same reservation: "No law is a law unless it also applies to particular individuals. It cannot be left hanging in the air, in the abstraction of its generality. Only by thus referring it back to particular praxis can the *justice* of the law be tested."[73] In Mann's *Das Gesetz*, Moses's God is indeed invisible

---

73. Paul de Man, "Political Allegory in Rousseau," *Critical Inquiry* 2, no. 4 (1976): 649–75, 669. See also Samuel Weber, "In the Name of the Law," *Cardozo Law Review* 11 (1990): 1515–38, 1527.

but the laws given to the people are designated "zeigbar" (showable), a visibility that is demonstrated by the direct link between an action and its consequence: "Das Volk kommt zu mir, dass ich richte zwischen einem Jeglichen und seinem Nächsten, und zeige ihnen Gottes Recht und seine Gesetze."[74] (The people come to me that I will judge between one and his neighbor, and show them God's law and command.) This visibility is perceived as justice: reward for the righteous and punishment for the unjust.[75] But it is exactly this that the people are denied by Schoenberg's Moses: "unvorstellbares Gesetz des unvorstellbaren Gottes" (unperceivable law of the unperceivable God), Moses's law does not satisfy the people's demand for a perceptible economy of equivalences and exchange rates, where wrongdoings and good deeds are measured and repaid according to their exact worth.[76]

In the first act, the law of exchange was promised to the people by Aron, who sought to increase the appeal of Moses's abstract God: "Der Allmächtige verwandelt Sand in Frucht, Frucht in Gold, Gold in Wonne, Wonne in Geist."[77] (The almighty changes sand to fruit, fruit to gold, gold to rupture, rupture to soul.) It is this unkept promise that the people later demand of Aron when Moses tarries on the mountain. The alternative that Aron offers in the form of the golden calf seems to compensate for what Moses's abstract law was lacking all along. As the people dance around the golden calf, they chant in praise of the same visibility of exchange that constitutes quantifiable justice:

CHOR: (*Bässe*): Menschentugend gleicht Gold!
(*Sopran und Alt*): Gold gleicht Lust!
(*Bässe*): Lust ist Wildheit!
(*ein Sopran*): Gold glänzt wie Blut!

---

74. Mann, *Das Gesetz*, 93.
75. It is true that Mann also acknowledges the possibility of a miscarriage of justice, where a wrong verdict is reached. But Moses's system of justice guaranteed that every action brought before his court generated a certain response. See, for example, chapter 13.
76. See also Holl, *The Moses Complex*, 160.
77. Schoenberg, *Moses Textbuch*, 16. Translation altered.

(*ein Alt*): Gold ist Herrschaft!
(*ein Tenor*): Hingabe!
(*Bässe*): Gerechtigkeit!⁷⁸

[CHORUS: (*Basses*): Human virtue equals gold!
(*Sopranos and Altos*): Gold equals Lust!
(*Basses*): Lust is wildness!
(*One Soprano*): Gold gleams like blood!
(*One Alto*): Gold is sovereignty!
(*One Tenor*): Devotion!
(*Basses*): Equity!]

Reward and punishment are examples of particular, localized applications of the law. This kind of *Gerechtigkeit*, which is associated with the visibility and tangibility of the golden calf, appears to be the opposite of Moses's abstract law/God. Of this Aron is repeatedly reminded:

ARON: Unvorstellbarer Gott:
Du strafst die Sünden der Väter an den
Kindern und Kindeskindern!
MOSES: Strafst Du?
Sind wir fähig zu verursachen, was Dich
zu Folge nötigt?
ARON: Gerechter Gott:
Du belohnst die, die deinen Geboten gehorchen!
MOSES: Gerechter Gott! Du hast gerichtet,
wie alles geschehen soll:
Gebührt dem Lohn, der gern anders möchte?
Oder dem, der nichts anders vermag?⁷⁹

[ARON: Inconceivable God:
Thou punisheth [*sic*] sins of the father on his
children and children's children.
MOSES: Punish?
Are we able to originate what thou demand'st as outcome?
ARON: O righteous God:

---

78. Schoenberg, *Moses Textbuch*, 25. Translation altered.
79. Schoenberg, *Moses Textbuch*, 7.

Thou rewardest those who are faithful to thy commandments!
MOSES: Righteous God: Thou hast directed
how ev'rything must befall.
Then to whom is the reward presented,
him who wants or cannot want things else?]

In the tension between the generality of the law and the necessity to represent its application in individual cases, Derrida found an indefinite postponement of the law: "For a decision to be just and responsible, it must . . . be both regulated and without regulation, it must preserve the law and also destroy or suspend it enough to have to reinvent it in each case."[80] Here too, in order to be just, law is unavoidably dependent on its representation, as Moses is dependent on Aron. But through that dependency, law itself is suspended. This is what the people fail to understand as they sit and wait for Moses's law, which will always remain postponed: "Vierzig Tage liegen wir nun schon hier! Wie lange noch?"[81] (Forty days now that we wait here! How much longer?) This constant suspension of the law by its successive individual representations gives new meaning to Rousseau's remark that the law involves a certain setting in motion.[82] Since the law can only be encountered in particular cases that, in turn, render its generality inaccessible, it is explored in *Moses* as what Samuel Weber termed "institutionalization of conflict" between the general and the particular, between abstraction and its necessary representation.[83]

The identity between the law and the text is embodied by the Decalogue. The long Jewish and Christian exegetical traditions attest to the fact that, as text, the law requires interpretation. More precisely, the representation of the law in particular cases is the product of an act of interpretation. This was also clear to Hobbes,

---

80. Jacques Derrida, "Force of Law: The Mystical Foundation of Authority," in *Acts of Religion*, ed. Gil Anidjar (New York: Routledge, 2002), 251. See also Joseph Vogl, *On Tarrying*, trans. Helmut Müller-Sievers (Calcutta: Seagull Books, 2011), 9.
81. Schoenberg, *Moses Textbuch*, 19.
82. Rousseau, "The Social Contract," 160. Consider also Derrida's *à-venir* of justice. Justice is always postponed, always to come. Derrida, "Force of Law," 256.
83. Weber, "In the Name of the Law," 1526.

who recognized the law's reliance on the word and its subsequent subjection to the perils of signification. "All laws," Hobbes writes, "have need for interpretation" since they are "easily misinterpreted from the diverse signification of a word or two." In its pure, abstract form, the law as text holds numerous potential meanings. But, as Hobbes concludes, there ultimately must be "only one sense of the law."[84] Whereas general law is not anchored in one meaning or another, justice cannot tolerate ambivalence. For the sake of justice, an authorized interpreter is required.[85] Yet interpretation itself is considered corruption, since it involves a certain act of force.[86] This "interpretative violence" is what Aron is accused of in the opera.

Aron: Interpretation, Representation

Lacoue-Labarthe's critical reading of Adorno's "Sacred Fragment" is a warning call against the disastrous potential of the notion of the "great artwork" after Wagner.[87] Like Adorno, Lacoue-Labarthe believes that in post-Enlightenment modernity, works that are presented as "great" or "collective" betray a dangerously regressive political notion of an organic, homogeneous people intolerant of difference. In Wagner's work, the drive toward homogeneity manifested in the music itself or, more precisely, in what Lacoue-Labarthe calls "musical saturation," an absorption and synthesis of all diverse parameters of the music drama—of all difference—into the sameness of an endless melody.

Lacoue-Labarthe critiques Adorno for understanding Schoenberg's opera in similar terms—for treating *Moses*, that is, as another instance of musical totality or musical saturation à la Wagner. His disagreement with Adorno hones in on the break between the second and third acts. While Adorno's melocentric approach—an approach that focuses on music as the primary component of the

---

84. Hobbes, *Leviathan*, 190–91.
85. See also Weber, "In the Name of the Law," 1519–20.
86. See Derrida, "Force of Law," 241.
87. Lacoue-Labarthe, "The Caesura of Religion," 47. See also Alain Badiou, *Five Lessons on Wagner* (London: Verso, 2010), 18.

drama set to music—leads him to locate the opera's conclusion at the end of the second act, where the music concludes, Lacoue-Labarthe insists that the third, uncomposed act cannot be extracted from the work. He emphasizes furthermore that it is in fact the transition into bare speech in the third act that constitutes a "scar" that redeems the work from becoming a totality. He calls this transition the "caesura" of religion, an interruption of the problematic claim to convey the absolute in art.

Despite this dispute over the opera's conclusion, Lacoue-Labarthe's and Adorno's projects remain fairly similar. In his reliance on Benjamin's notion of the caesura, which the latter defined precisely as a distinguishing mark of great works, Lacoue-Labarthe, like Adorno, is unable to relinquish a critical position that is bound to a validation of the work's greatness in spite of itself.[88] Lacoue-Labarthe's rigorously Benjaminian program is indeed a form of authentication of a great work. For Benjamin, the act of criticism and interpretation that the critic performs reveals the work itself as "criticizable." "Criticizability" is Benjamin's criterion for the great artwork. This approach moves away from the totality and autonomy of the classical view of the artwork, but nevertheless still refuses to relinquish the category of greatness altogether.[89]

Benjamin attenuated the totality of the artwork by making it dependent on corresponding acts of criticism or, in other words, on acts of interpretation. But such an approach still maintains a hierarchy between work and interpretation that preserves some of the coherence and integrity of the "work." We can find an alternative, far more radical relation between work and interpretation if we consider music as a performing art. After all, Benjamin formulated his idea of art criticism in relation to literature, and the question remains

---

88. See Walter Benjamin, "Goethe's Elective Affinities," in *Selected Writings I*. Here I follow Kirk Wetters's observations on critical theory's struggles to relinquish the traditional idea of the great artwork. Kirk Wetters, "*Bilderverbot*: The Straub/Huillet Film of Schoenberg's *Moses und Aron*," colloquium presentation at the annual meeting of the American Friends of Marbach, Marbach am Neckar, Germany, June 10, 2016.

89. See Walter Benjamin, "The Concept of Criticism in German Romanticism," in *Selected Writings I*, 159–60, 179.

whether this model transfers unproblematically to musical works.[90] Lacoue-Labarthe disregards this difference by not considering that, when it comes to music, synthesis and completion are never truly available. For unlike a work of literature, Schoenberg's opera (and in this regard, Wagner's music dramas too) relies on interpretation as performance, in a manner thoroughly different than the interpretative act of the critic.

Ironically, it was Adorno who started a project whose conclusions, had they been fully drawn, might have been able to provide such a view of musical works. In a short fragment on music and language from 1956, Adorno had already asserted the different function that interpretation fulfills in relation to language and music: "Interpretation is essential to both music and language, but in different ways. To interpret language means: to understand language. To interpret music means: to make music. Musical interpretation is performance."[91] This essential difference is further developed in the posthumously published *Towards a Theory of Musical Reproduction*.[92] The project sought to determine the relation between the conceptual and physical-sensual aspects of a musical work. While these writings still do not fully relinquish the purported autonomy of the unperformed score, they nevertheless locate musical works in the intricate dialectic between notation and its sensual realization: the performance. Music, as Adorno writes,

> is not purely legible or purely imitable as language. It therefore divides itself into the sound-ideal and the writing, and requires interpretation as the ever-renewed effort to achieve a reconciliation of these divergent elements.... This necessity of interpretation shows a fundamental difference between music and literature. The latter permits interpretation, yet

---

90. I respond here to Wetters's question concerning the application of Benjamin's notion of criticism specifically to operas, whose intricacy of genre comprises a "text, a diegesis, and a staging." I contend that Wetters's challenge persists also when one considers "absolute" (textless, unstaged) music, since completion is achieved only through the ephemeral act of performance.

91. Theodor W. Adorno, "Music and Language: A Fragment," in *Quasi Una Fantasia*, 3.

92. Theodor W. Adorno, *Towards a Theory of Musical Reproduction*, ed. Henri Lonitz, trans. Wieland Hoban (Cambridge: Polity Press, 2006).

without absolutely requiring it.... Music, however, as the paradoxical sign language of something non-intentional, requires something that lies beyond itself and fulfills the signs.... The necessity of interpretation manifests itself as the neediness of musical texts. It is a law that any such text contains a zone of indeterminacy ... that cannot be answered directly through the ideal of sound, and which requires interpretation as something that augments the text in order to achieve its objectification in the first place.[93]

The interdependence of score and sound undermines the status of the work as a stable, fully synthesized, coherent totality. The ephemerality of performance ensures that even if Adorno still believed he could theorize a *wahre Aufführung*, a "true performance," as one of his earlier titles for this project indicates, the work's dependence on such an unstable act would render it equally unstable.

In this regard, the opera *Moses und Aron* is an exemplary case since it radicalizes the question of completion through its performance. The dispute between Lacoue-Labarthe and Adorno concerning the fate of the uncomposed third act exposes this dependency on performance by reopening the question of logo- and melocentrism in opera. Understanding the third act's reintroduction of language as a redemption of music and its attributed threat of saturation, Lacoue-Labarthe merely replaces Adorno's melocentrism with a renewed focus on language. Music drama reverts to poetry; *Moses* remains a great work. Yet the understanding of *Moses* as a work that needs to be performed makes possible an alternative. When the decision as to whether to include the third act is made in the impermanent act of performance, the choice between music and poetry is suspended. *Moses* can be either or both simultaneously. The work itself becomes unsettled.

Schoenberg left no conclusive statement concerning the performance of the third act. His comments on the matter seem contradictory. In light of his struggles to complete the opera, the composer recommended in 1950 that the work be performed without the third act. A year later, however, he indicated that the third act could be performed as spoken dialogue. In a posthumous note to act 3 in the libretto,

---

93. Adorno, *Towards a Theory*, 180.

Gertrud Schoenberg cites various letters by her husband in an attempt to elucidate the composer's elusive intention regarding the third act. She concludes with the observation: "As is so frequently the case with Schoenberg, an unequivocal answer is to be ruled out here."[94]

Ultimately, *Moses*'s completion remains a matter to be decided in performance. Where the jurisdiction of the composer ends, the work continues to be fashioned in the hands of different interpreters, who reveal that choosing musical totality by omitting the third act or choosing poetic redemption by including it are both ephemeral decisions. The openness that *Moses* acquires shifts the opera's focus from the individual genius and their struggles to a people, not of passive listeners, but of active interpreters and therefore cocreators. Their indispensability to the work confirms that the notion of the single opera *Moses und Aron* is itself an abstraction validated only through its diverse representations on the stage.

Despite the authoritative image that is often ascribed to him, Schoenberg was aware of this dependency. His extensive performance instructions support this claim. A composer who was certain of the autonomy of his score would not have troubled himself with such an elaborate address to his performers unless he deemed their contribution to the work indispensable. Consider some of his remarks:

> Arioso sections also occur however within the recitatives. They are recognizable (usually) from a more "fixed" accompaniment, the continuity of which will not permit any disruption of the tempo. Nevertheless, an attempt should always be made to give the singer a certain amount of freedom in performance so that the impression is different from the larger set forms.
>
> . . .
>
> In some scenes the place of action must change. I have nothing against the producer using separate areas for different parts of a scene so long as it is done with tact, taste and moderation. Anything which brings out the thought is appropriate.
>
> . . .

---

94. See Christian M. Schmidt's preface in the Eulenburg edition of the score.

Act II scene 5
> In this scene the musical characterization is intentionally worked out in a way that the two performers (Moses and Aron) have far more freedom than usual.... Much is left open, particularly in the transitions, and even the moods are not absolutely fixed. For these two performers have a task here that cannot be accomplished without bringing to it something of their own.[95]

Just as the composer relies on the performer to complete the work by executing his ideas, so too is Moses dependent on Aron.[96] But this symbiosis is not one between two individual leaders. Aron the interpreter-performer is as much the representative of the people as he is the interpreter of Moses's law. This equivocal directionality of representation is a residue from *Moses*'s oratorical prehistory and speaks to the fluidity of roles that is characteristic of the genre.[97]

Derrida suggests that a potential corruption embeds itself in each interpretative instance when one speaks of the representation of laws. Moses's objection to Aron's interpretative-representative drive reflects this exact reservation: "Ich soll den Gedanken verfälschen?" (Am I to falsify the idea?) Yet de Man's reflections on the representation of the law challenge this notion by acknowledging that a general law as pure idea nevertheless excludes any possibility for justice. The same potential for corruption resurfaces when one turns to consider the representation of the people. The problem Aron faces as the people's representative is defined as the substitution of irreducible heterogeneity with a homogeneous concept or entity. It is, in other words, the substitution of heterogeneity's ephemerality with the stability of identity. Schoenberg's opera captures this problem with its own musical representation of the people.

---

95. Schoenberg, "Instruction for Performance" and "Stage Directions" in the Eulenburg edition, 1–5. See also discussion on musical aspects of *Moses* that undermine Schoenberg's authority in Daniel Albright, "Butchering Moses," *The Opera Quarterly* 23, no. 4 (2007): 441–54.

96. See also David Lewin, "Moses und Aron: Some General Remarks, and Analytic Notes for Act 1, Scene 1," *Perspectives of New Music* 6, no. 1 (1967): 1–17.

97. See my discussion of the oratorio in chapter 2. One of the earlier drafts of *Moses* is a twenty-seven-page typescript written by the composer around 1928 and titled "Moses und Aron: Oratorium." For a complete chronology of the work's genesis, see White, *Schoenberg and the God-Idea*, 7–48.

Representing the People

The opening lines of the chapter on representation in Hobbes's *Leviathan*, "Of Persons, Authors, and things Personated," immediately establish skepticism toward the concept. Defining the representative as an "actor" whose actions and words belong to another, Hobbes acknowledged the inherent potential for corruption this transaction entails. The representative is not considered a "natural person" but rather "feigned or artificial." Hobbes designates the act of representation with the verb "to personate." Its root *Persona*, he observes, "signifies the *disguise*, or *outward appearance* of a man, counterfeited on the stage."[98]

Not unlike the intricate dependency between composer and performer, the necessary relationship that Hobbes outlines between author and actor, as that between the owner of words and actions and the executor who is trusted with them, presupposes a fictitious element. Rousseau is also interested in the definition of the representative as actor, though with a different aim. While for Hobbes it indicates a false aspect of representation, it facilitates for Rousseau a reflection on the people's sovereignty. Representation, Rousseau notes, involves a commission by the people for the execution of actions of which it is the owner.[99] The people as commissioner thus occupies a dual position: it is both subject and sovereign.

In *Moses*, this duality is implied by the identical musical depiction of the Voice from the Burning Bush and the people of Israel. Both parts are sung by the chorus, which, unlike Moses and Aron, is not limited to either speech or song.[100] The predominance of the chorus in *Moses* calls to mind the fact that, in its earlier stages, the work was conceived as an oratorio. Vestiges of the oratorio are found not only in the ubiquity of chorus sections but also in the chorus's function as a single entity channeling the perspectives of multiple personages.[101]

---

98. Hobbes, *Leviathan*, 111–12.
99. Rousseau, "The Social Contract," 173–74.
100. See for example act 1, scene 4 (mm. 630–31).
101. See my discussion of the oratorio in chapter 2.

This fluidity suggests that, in the opera's first scene, the voice that commands Moses to promulgate the law that will free the people belongs to none other than the people itself.

Moses's negative theology guarantees that God, though referenced repeatedly, is never truly present in the work. The dialogue between Moses and the Voice in the opening scene does not indicate to whom the voice belongs. This in itself is nothing out of the ordinary for oratorios, where it is uncommon, despite the fact that the genre is primarily celebrated as "sacred music," for the voice of God to be sung onstage.[102] But the Voice's extraordinary musical depiction seems exceptionally unordinary. Its distribution among the six soloists, who are later joined by the entire chorus, contradicts the idea of the single God that is otherwise conveyed by Moses. Its heavy polyphonic texture promotes not unity but rather a plurality befitting a polytheistic notion of the divine or, better yet, a pluralist depiction of a people and its many opposing perspectives.

Contrary to previous understandings of the role of the people in the opera as mere *turba*, a passive, fickle, and gullible rabble that is easily swayed by others, this fusion of the people's voice with the Voice from the Burning Bush conveys an image of the people as a sovereign body endowed with the power to appoint representatives.[103] When Moses appears to betray his appointment by rejecting both act and representation, the people turn to Aron, who, with the Golden Calf, presents the people an image not of a foreign god but of itself:

ARON: Dieses Bild bezeugt,
dass in allem, was ist ein Gott lebt.
Unwandelbar, wie ein Prinzip,
ist der Stoff, das Gold,
das ihr geschenkt habt;
anschaulich—wandelbar,

---

102. See Assmann, "Die Mosaische Unterscheidung," 10.

103. For a reading of the people's role as *turba* in *Moses*, see Bluma Goldstein, "Schoenberg's Moses und Aron: A Vanishing Biblical Nation," in *Political and Religious Ideas in the Works of Arnold Schoenberg*, ed. Charlotte M. Cross and Russell A. Berman (New York: Garland, 2000), 159–92, 183.

wie alles andere: Zweite,
ist die Gestalt, die ich ihm gegeben.
Verehrt euch selbst in diesem Sinnbild![104]

[ARON: This gold image attests
that in all things that are, a god lives.
Unchangeable, as principle,
is the matter, the gold
that you have given.
Seemingly changeable,
As all else must be. Secondary
is the shape that I have provided.
Revere yourselves in this symbol!]

Unlike the withdrawn Moses, Aron, the representative of the people, is a man of deeds, as he himself attests: "Das Wort bin ich und die Tat!" (I am the word and the deed!) It is he who, in Schoenberg's version, performs the miracles that first win the people's trust. Moses's remove from mundane activities is clearly expressed in his response to a priest who asks how the people are to sustain themselves in the desert—"In der Wüste wird euch die Reinheit des Denkens nähern, erhalten und entwickeln" (In the wasteland pureness of thought will nurture, sustain, and advance you)—which Aron summarily supplements by reassuring: "Er [Gott] wird es euch auch in der Wüste an Speise nicht fehlen lassen"[105] (He [Moses's God] will not fail to provide you with food also in the wasteland).

Aron's dual function as interpreter of the law and representative of the people designates him, following Rousseau's definition, as the one responsible for communication. The communicative nature of Aron's musical characterization, his alluring melodic line, supports this assertion. Assuming that Moses, like his brother, was appointed lawgiver by the people, as the identity between the musical representation of the Voice and the people implies, Aron's role emerges as one of mediator not between Moses and the people but between the people's two functions as subjects and as sovereign.

---

104. Schoenberg, *Moses Textbuch*, 22. Translation altered.
105. Schoenberg, *Moses Textbuch*, 16.

The musical-dramatic representation of the people in the opera accounts for such intricacies of representation and places emphasis on contention and debate as signs of sovereignty rather than submission. The introduction of the people in the third scene of the first act demonstrates this. On their first appearance onstage, the people are involved in a protracted debate aimed at deciding whether to accept Moses, Aron, and their God or to reject them. With the varying divisions of the chorus and swift alternations between chorus and soloists who represent individual dissidents, Schoenberg exposes the formative stages in the crystallization of a general will, a process that, though postulated, remains obscure in Rousseau's *Social Contract*.

CHOR (*in vielen Gruppen*): . . .
Ein rettender Gott!
Er wird uns befrein!
Vielleicht ist er stärker als Pharao!
Glaubt den Betrügern nicht!
Wir wollen ihm dienen!
Wir wollen ihm opfern!
Wir wollen ihn lieben!
CHOR (*in zwei Gruppen*): Glaubt nicht den
Betrügern! (*recit.*)
Er wird uns befrein!
Die Götter lieben uns nicht!
Wir wollen ihn lieben!
Wer ist es, der stärker sein—
Wir wollen ihm opfern!
—will als Pharaos Götter?
Laßt uns in Frieden!
Wir wollen ihn lieben!
Zurück zur Arbeit!
Wir wollen ihm dienen!
Sonst wird sie noch schwerer![106]

[CHORUS (*in many groups*): . . .
A god that will save!

---

106. Schoenberg, *Moses Textbuch*, 10. Translation altered.

He shall make us free!
Perhaps he is stronger than Pharaoh!
Heed not the deceivers!
We give him obedience!
We want to make off'rings!
We want to give worship!
CHORUS (*in two groups*): Heed not the
deceivers! (*recit.*)
He shall make us free!
The gods do not love us!
We want to give worship!
Who is this, that would mightier be—
We want to make off'rings!
—than Pharaoh's gods?
Leave us in peace!
We want to give worship!
Back to work!
We give him obedience!
Lest it become harder!]

The process that Schoenberg traces does not suggest that the apparent consensus reached in the subsequent scene is the result of a miraculously attained unanimity. What starts as the people's resistance to three soloists—advocates of Moses and Aron—turns quickly into an internal dispute that is never truly resolved into unison at any point. Dissent fissures the chorus, creating numerous divisions and subdivisions; factions emerge and dissolve, members continually leave one group and join another, the chorus expands and contracts again. Melodic lines and declamatory *Sprechstimme* alternate indiscriminately between the different chorus sections. Schoenberg, the celebrated emancipator of dissonance, has concocted a commotion that represents the people as a sovereign body of noise.

It is no coincidence that Schoenberg's extensive stage directions call for numerous reconfigurations of the chorus onstage (see figures 3.3 and 3.4). The desire to depict the people as a mutable body in motion complements the opera's refusal to reduce the inherent contradiction of representation—its simultaneous necessity and inadequacy—by providing a homogeneous image of a static, unified chorus. The emphasis on the agency of the people exposes the political stakes of aesthetic dilemmas like the attempt to move beyond the restrictive notion of the great artwork. The opera's critical stance exposes the closely linked inadequacies of political representation both as *Darstellung* and *Vertretung*. Yet it refuses to settle the conflicts it invokes: those between the generality and specificity of the law, between the people and their representation, or between the compulsion toward and prohibition of the image. It reminds us that fragmentation, incompleteness, and contradiction are the very substance of aesthetic expression. Whereas political theory endeavors to resolve conflicts like those posed by the problem of representation, works like *Moses und Aron* are able to retain such tensions without the urge to diffuse them.

The antinomies of Schoenberg's opera, as both Adorno and Lacoue-Labarthe observed, demonstrate that the work cannot be contemplated independently of Wagner's intervention into our conception of artworks and their political bearing. To compose an opera after Wagner means to respond in some way to claims about the totality and authority of the artwork as well as the identity and homogeneity of the people it invokes. This becomes more concrete when we consider the historical circumstances surrounding the opera's composition. To evoke Wagner in a biblical operatic fragment in the 1930s means to respond unequivocally to the claim concerning the irreconcilable difference between the "German" and the "Jewish," or more accurately, to claims about the identity of the German people that Wagner constructed against a Jewish foil.

Wagner's "sacred art" assumed a complete identity—in the Schmittian sense—among a homogeneous *Volk*. To this problem of identity *Moses* offers a double rebuttal: by complicating the possibility of representing the people, it also challenges the expectation of homogeneity among the so-called German people. The antifascist potential of the opera lies in its insistence on conveying the inability to represent fully the diversity of people who consider themselves German. Moreover, it raises the question of Jewish difference and Moses's law and joins other contemporaneous reflections on this issue in revealing the ambiguity at its heart.

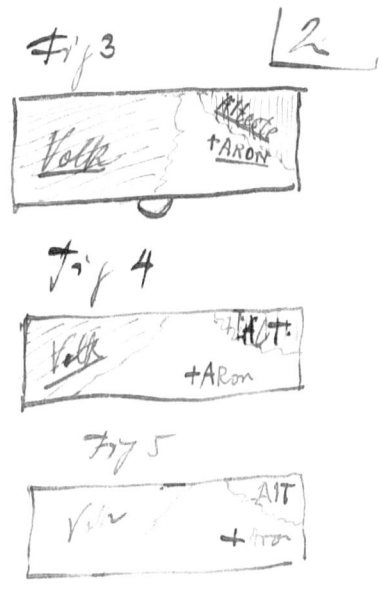

Figure 3.3. Schoenberg's hand-drawn sketch from a typescript for *Moses und Aron* ("Typoskript 2 des Textes zum Oratorium"). Image credit: Arnold Schönberg Center, Wien (T09.05). Used by permission of Belmont Music Publishers, Los Angeles.

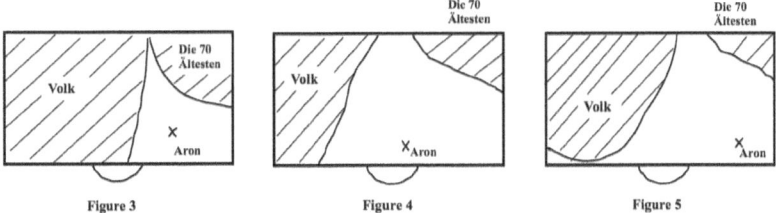

Figure 3.4. Divisions and shifting borders, the people as a body in motion in Schoenberg's stage directions.

Schoenberg is often quoted in his ardent renunciation of the German nation and culture following his escape from Germany in 1933. Yet the composer, who subsequently pledged himself to none other than the Jewish people, never truly ceased to be a "German composer." Nor did he have to. The unsettled difference between Jews and other Germans embedded in the opera's reflection on Moses's law precludes the assumption of two originary and distinct identity positions, for what made the German "German" could in many ways be described as Jewish. The ambivalent Mosaic Distinction characterizes the identity of the people in the opera as fluctuating or interchangeable. This ultimately becomes another reason for their irrepresentability. To convey this problem, perhaps no art is more suited than music. Despite the dangers that Lacoue-Labarthe saw in the "musical saturation" of Wagner's music dramas, the homogenizing potential of the most sensuous of all arts, music always also held the potential of self-critique. Adorno recognized this in noting that music is the language that utters the absolute while simultaneously imparting the imperfection of its own communication, or as he himself put it, "it is the human attempt, doomed as ever, to name the Name."[107]

---

107. Adorno, "Music and Language," 2.

4

ON BEING SUPERFLUOUS

Integration and Excess in Joseph Roth's Hiob

Compared with Schoenberg's *Moses und Aron* and its monumental aspirations, Joseph Roth's 1930 novel *Hiob: Roman eines einfachen Mannes* (*Job: The Story of a Simple Man*) and its operatic rendition by Eric Zeisl discussed in the next chapter are striking in their seemingly modest scope. Roth's *Hiob* turns away from grandiose theopolitical claims to convey the plight of a single individual. This gesture of contraction marks a turning point in Roth's work. Beginning with the novel *Hiob*, Roth seems to relinquish the overt political engagement of his earlier novels and journalistic work in favor of what appears to be a regressive nostalgia for monarchist times. Yet, in actuality, Roth's novel is not strictly traditional, nor does it really eschew social and political critique. Rather, it responds to the rise of nationalism and the nation-state system in the aftermath of the First World War and the fraught position of Eastern European Jews within this system.

Schoenberg's more than ten years of flirtation with Zionism and the political writings it begot situated his opera between the critiques of political and aesthetic representation. Grappling with the notion of homogeneity, a necessary condition for representation for contemporaries like Carl Schmitt, Schoenberg linked the burning political and aesthetic questions of his time to a discussion on Jewish difference. His response to the rising drive toward homogeneity in Germany was a notion of radical heterogeneity that the irrepresentable image of the people in *Moses* allowed him to express. This heterogeneity had an ambiguating power; it resisted the imagining of fixed and restricted collective identities and thereby ruled out the possibility of a settled, unambiguous difference between them.

Roth's novel and Eric Zeisl's opera both respond to the same problematic drive toward homogeneity and organicism that dominated social, political, and aesthetic discussions, this time in the territories formerly belonging to the Austro-Hungarian Empire. However, Roth's and Zeisl's respective contributions introduce a new critical perspective. Rather than addressing the question of difference between peoples, they both, mutatis mutandis, challenge the integrative paradigm that underlies every collective's claim to homogeneity.

With "integrative paradigm" I mean the assumption that heterogeneity indeed exists, but only as a transient condition awaiting dissolution into homogeneity. This paradigm does not mean that there can be no difference, no exceptions. Those may very well be present, but they must be contained; they must exist in some form of relation to an integrated whole. The integrative paradigm can only allow for a contained notion of difference. Contained difference is always perceived against a broader horizon of identity and homogeneity from which it gains its meaning. When we speak of a major-minor or a dominant-marginalized relation, we are bound to a contained notion of difference. The relevance of this theoretical problem of difference to our inquiry into Jewish difference issues from the recognition that Jewish difference is unsettled and therefore uncontained. To remain bound to a contained understanding of difference is to restrict the discussion of Jewish difference. This approach gains us access to Jewish difference only insofar as we hypothesize a stable category of identity, for example, "German" or "Austrian," against which we can consider Jewish difference. To unsettle Jewish difference, on the other hand, means to find alternative ways to speak about difference that recognize the mutability of categories like "German," "Austrian," or "Jewish."

As an alternative to contained difference, my analysis of Roth's *Hiob* and Zeisl's operatic rendition of the novel in the following two chapters explores and develops the category of superfluousness, which I link here to the notion of an uncontained exception, a form of difference that is not subordinate to an integrative paradigm. Roth's novel confronts integration as the paradigm of the nation-state—the form of collective identity that proliferated in the former territories of the Dual Monarchy after World War I—with the image of the Eastern European Jewish immigrant. Far from an example of any innate Jewish incapacity for integration, immigrant and refugee *Ostjuden* represented for Roth a revolutionary potential that was altogether emancipated from any relation toward integration. They were superfluous to the nation-state model, uncontained exceptions to a system that purported to contain all.

Roth had a personal connection to those Eastern European immigrant Jews who inspired not only his novel *Hiob* but also his numerous journalistic essays from the decade preceding it. He was born to Nahum and Miriam Roth as Moses Joseph Roth in 1894 in Brody, Galicia, a town that was then part of the Austro-Hungarian Empire, "just back of the Russian border, on the edge of Europe if not the civilized world," as Michael Hofmann puts it.[1] Like many of the subjects of his writings, Roth's life stations outlined a haphazard westward movement from Galicia, through Vienna, to Berlin, Frankfurt, and Paris, the city that signaled hopeful optimism during his first visit there in the mid-1920s, and later, after 1933, despondency, exile, and destitution.

A self-proclaimed "hotel patriot," Roth's frenzied to-and-fro between those cities, together with his innumerable journalistic visits to the Soviet Union, the South of France, the Balkans, Italy, and

---

1. Joseph Roth, *A Life in Letters*, trans. and ed. Michael Hofmann (New York: Norton, 2012), xii.

Poland, rendered him a constant transient. As Hofmann notes, Roth was a "Jew in Austria, an Austrian in Germany, and a German in France."[2] Being out of place was no unusual experience for Roth, but not because he actually identified with any of those labels. The need to label and identify was itself peculiar to him. "We are surrounded by a fence," he wrote to the German readers of the *Frankfurter Zeitung* on whose commission he traveled to give reports from French cities in 1925. "In Germany it's practically impossible not to catch the eye unless I playact. . . . For, even if I don't represent any type, any genus, any family, any nation, any tribe, any race, I am still forced to be representative of something. We are forced to 'show our colors,' and not just any color either, but one off the official color chart. . . . It's a mark of a narrow world that it mistrusts the undefined."[3]

While Germany appeared to Roth as a leader in the obsession for all-encompassing classification, it was not alone. The rise of numerous nation-states after the collapse of the Austro-Hungarian Empire signaled for Roth that the desire to subsume every individual under a specific nation was spreading into the territories of Eastern Europe too, where there had formerly been no need for rigid classifications. Roth was not the only one to recognize that the new conditions inevitably marked former Jewish subjects of the Dual Monarchy as exceptions to this system of classification. Studying the same historical period a few decades later, Hannah Arendt would comment extensively on the notion of the Jew as a social and political exception.

In both Roth's and Arendt's writings, we can see how Jewish difference came to be shaped by such concepts as exception and superfluousness in the interwar period. Superfluousness and excess had previously supported antisemitic images of Jews. Nineteenth-century novels like Gustav Freytag's *Soll und Haben* (*Debit and Credit*, 1855) or Wilhelm Raabe's *Der Hungerpastor* (*The Hunger Pastor*, 1864) associated Jews with excessive capital. In his controversial *Geschlecht und Charakter* (*Sex and Character*) from 1903,

---

2. Roth, *A Life in Letters*, xv.
3. Joseph Roth, *The White Cities: Reports from France 1925–39*, trans. Michael Hofmann (London: Granta, 2005), 72.

Otto Weininger identified Jews with the feminine character and its imputed excessive sexuality. Schoenberg's music has often been accused of exhibiting an excess of rationality even by figures like Adorno.[4] But the pejorative sense is transformed in Roth's and Arendt's work. For Roth, being superfluous becomes a desired condition and the only true form of emancipation from contained systems like the nation-state.

The division of Europe into nation-states and the creation of countless stateless refugees, many of them Jews from Eastern European territories, promoted a perception of Eastern Jews in particular as incapable of integration. Roth and Arendt both address this condition to reveal a broader concern. The unintegrated position of the *Ostjude*—a term that often carried negative connotations and used by both Western European Jews and non-Jews—serves to expose the entrapment of Western society within totalizing, dialectical systems intolerant of remainders or excess. For Roth, therefore, it was not simply the depiction of Jews as "marginalized" or "others" that was of interest but precisely the condition of being superfluous—a condition he regarded as a merit rather than a curse. It allowed him to think of a way out of totalizing systems, be they social, political, or aesthetic.

From Socialism to Monarchic Nostalgia: The Potential of Outdatedness

In its efforts to provide a comprehensive overview of his diverse literary and journalistic output, Roth scholarship traditionally regards 1930, the year of *Hiob*'s publication, as a turning point.[5] The division of Roth's work into two distinct periods representing

---

4. See Adorno, *Philosophy of New Music*.
5. See, for example, Sidney Rosenfeld, *Understanding Joseph Roth* (Columbia: University of South Carolina Press, 2001). A few publications, however, highlight continuities in Roth's work. See, for example, Kati Tonkin, *Joseph Roth's March into History: From the Early Novels to Radetzkymarsch and Die Kapuzinergruft* (Rochester, NY: Camden House, 2008); and Ilse Josepha Lazaroms, *The Grace of Misery: Joseph Roth and the Politics of Exile, 1919–1939* (Boston: Brill, 2013).

two separate literary styles as well as two modes of political engagement began as early as the 1950s with the writings of Hermann Kesten, Roth's friend and the publisher of the first edition of his collected works. "In the fifteen years in which he published books," Kesten wrote in 1959, "Roth turned from a skeptic, at times pessimistic moralist into a legitimist Catholic, from a radical leftist into a right [wing] conservative."[6] According to this division, the works written in the prior decade, from *Das Spinnennetz* (*The Spider's Web*, 1923) and *Hotel Savoy* (1924) to the novel loosely based on the life of Leon Trotsky, *Der stumme Prophet* (*The Silent Prophet*, 1929), exhibit a direct political—more precisely, "socialist"—engagement with current issues.[7] While *Das Spinnennetz* evokes the sociopolitical turbulence that ultimately brought about the collapse of the Weimar Republic, *Hotel Savoy* is centered around the transient existence of a First World War veteran and his fellow hotel residents in a nameless city (Łódź) "at the gates of Europe."

Hotel Savoy and the subsequent novels from the same period, *Die Rebellion* (*Rebellion*, 1924) and *Die Flucht ohne Ende* (*Flight without End*, 1927), offer a critical depiction of a crumbling postwar European bourgeois society through their focus on the unsuccessful integration attempts of those returning from the Great War. Written at the height of Roth's journalistic career, these novels appeared alongside essay series like *Die weißen Städte* (*The White Cities*, 1925) and *Juden auf Wanderschaft* (*The Wandering Jews*, 1927), the products of Roth's numerous travels across Europe reporting for the *Frankfurter Zeitung*. As they resembled Roth's reportages in their presentation as eyewitness accounts of social conditions in postwar Europe, the early novels led some critics to identify Roth with the

---

6. Hermann Kesten, "Joseph Roth," *Wort in der Zeit* 9 (1959): 6.
7. There is support for this classification in the author's own remarks. While working on *Das Spinnennetz*, Roth announced his intention to terminate his employment as a journalist with the conservative newspaper *Berliner Börsen-Courier*. In a letter to his colleague Herbert Ihering from September 1917, he explained that he was "no longer able to share the outlook of a bourgeois readership and remain their Sunday chatterbox" without denying "his socialism on a daily basis." See Roth, *A Life in Letters*, 26.

New Objectivity movement.[8] With *Hiob* and the works that followed in the 1930s, however, Roth abandoned this documentary style in favor of what is described by some scholars as conservative nostalgia and by others as delirious and phantasmagoric.[9]

As reportage gave way to a more subjective form of writing, so, at least outwardly, did Roth's direct literary engagement with the current sociopolitical climate concede to an evocation of a lost monarchic period. From *Radetzkymarsch* (*Radetzky March*, 1932) to its unofficial sequel *Kapuzinergruft* (*The Emperor's Tomb*, 1938), the theme of the declining Habsburg Monarchy dominated Roth's writing. Although these novels concentrated on the Austro-Hungarian Empire's inevitable disintegration, one cannot overlook their prevailing yearning for a return to the supranational principle that the kaiser's Austria represented for Roth.

Such sentiments are openly expressed in the 1934 novella *Die Büste des Kaisers* (*The Bust of the Emperor*). The novella allowed Roth to voice his own misgivings about the rise of nationalism in post–World War I Eastern Europe through his protagonist, Count Franz Xaver Morstin, a scion of a Polish family originating in Italy who considered himself neither Polish nor Italian but rather "the purest type of Austrian there can be, which is to say: . . . a man beyond nationality and therefore an aristocrat in the true sense."[10] Count Morstin, a loyal supporter of the emperor even after the collapse of the empire, refuses to accept the new world order that has been imposed on him and his land. In his home village Lopatyny—formerly part of the Dual Monarchy and now, through "recent unnatural caprices of world history," belonging to the

---

8. See Rosenfeld, *Understanding Joseph Roth*, 28; and Jürgen Heizmann, *Joseph Roth und die Ästhetik der neuen Sachlichkeit* (Heidelberg: Mattes, 1990).

9. See Rosenfeld, *Understanding Joseph Roth*, 35; Tonkin, *Joseph Roth's March into History*, 1; and Lazaroms, *The Grace of Misery*, xxvii. Roth later rejected the claims to authenticity laid by the New Objectivity. See Joseph Roth, *Werke 4*, ed. Fritz Hackert und Klaus Westermann (Köln: Kiepenheuer und Witsch, 1991), 250. See also Sarah Fraiman, "Joseph Roth: Dichter des Offenen," *Bulletin des Leo Baeck Instituts* 76 (1987): 35–50.

10. Joseph Roth, "The Bust of the Emperor," in *The Collected Stories of Joseph Roth*, trans. Michael Hofmann (New York: Norton, 2002), 228.

new Polish Republic—things continue as though the Great War had never transpired. At the entrance to his house, Morstin places a sandstone bust of the kaiser, which he salutes as he comes and goes, dressed in his old dragoons' captain uniform. A relic of the past, Count Morstin has only one passion, his opposition to the "nationality question": "If one had asked him, for instance—but who would have wanted to ask such a nonsensical question?—to which 'nationality' or people he felt he belonged, the count would have looked blankly and uncomprehendingly at the questioner, or perhaps even with a measure of irritation. By what criteria should he have had to nominate his allegiance to this nation or that?"[11]

Roth's growing concern with rising nationalist sentiments in Europe may explain the transition from a relatively socialist stance in the 1920s to the avowed monarchist declarations that one finds, for example, in his letter to the literary scholar Otto Forst-Battaglia from 1932: "The most powerful experience of my life was the war and the end of my fatherland, the only one I have ever had: the Dual Monarchy of Austria-Hungary. To this date I am a patriotic Austrian and love what is left of my homeland as a sort of relic."[12] Considering Roth's position as an assimilated Austrian Jew of Eastern European birth, such statements are not entirely surprising. Perhaps no other group benefited more from the Austrian supranational model than the Jews of the Habsburg Empire. In this Austrian antithesis of the nation-state, the Jewish population not only enjoyed the protection of Emperor Franz Joseph but they also embodied the empire's nation-transcending principle. The correspondence between this principle and Jewish presence as a nationless population throughout the Austro-Hungarian Empire reinforced a sense of loyalty that increasingly came to contrast with the surge of national conflicts in the empire's borderlands in the years prior to the war.[13] And indeed, in *Die Büste des Kaisers*, Count Morstin's only ally is the Jewish innkeeper Solomon Pinio-

---

11. Roth, "The Bust of the Emperor," 232.
12. Roth, *A Life in Letters*, 221.
13. See further Carl E. Schorske, *Fin-de-Siècle Vienna: Politics and Culture* (New York: Knopf, 1980); and Robert S. Wistrich, *The Jews of Vienna in the Age of Franz Joseph* (Oxford: Oxford University Press, 1990).

wsky, who, like Roth himself, shares Morstin's nostalgic lament for this lost transnational ideal.[14]

With all this in mind, critics have often discussed Roth's transition into antimodern monarchism in relation to an identity crisis the author experienced.[15] Having lost his former sense of identity as a Jewish subject of the cosmopolitan Austro-Hungarian Empire, the argument goes, Roth succumbed to the comforts of a utopian past in the form of the Habsburg Myth.[16]

The nostalgic monarchism of Roth's works after 1930 might appear reactionary, as though the author who had abandoned his former socialist convictions decided to turn away from politics altogether and indulge in lost memories of a bygone era. Yet far from a regressive refusal to engage in contemporary political discourse, Roth's so-called monarchism was in fact revolutionary in its own way.[17] Count Morstin may seem like a detached relic, but his position is of utmost political relevance. Through him, Roth plainly and unequivocally articulates a critique of nationalism's self-presentation as a natural, inalienable human right (the right to belong to a nation).

As Morstin reflects, not without a good measure of cynicism, "it has been discovered and brought to people's attention in the course of the nineteenth century that in order to possess individuality as a citizen every person must belong to a definite nationality or race."[18] Roth was not the only one who felt the need to refute the belief that nationality was essential to being considered a proper human being

---

14. See also David Bronsen, "Der Jude auf der Suche nach dem Vaterland: Joseph Roths Verhältnis zur habsburgischen Monarchie," *Wiener Tagebuch* 8 (1979); and the chapter "Imperial Swan-Song: From Stephan Zweig to Joseph Roth," in Wistrich, *The Jews of Vienna in the Age of Franz Joseph*, 621–65.

15. See David Bronsen, "Austrian versus Jew: The Torn Identity of Joseph Roth," *Leo Baeck Institute Year Book* 18 (1973): 220–26; and Andreas Herzog, "'Der Segen des ewigen Juden': Zur 'jüdischen Identität' Joseph Roths," in *Habsburger Aporien? Geisteshaltungen und Lebenskonzepte in der multinationalen Literatur der Habsburger Monarchie*, ed. Eva Reichmann (Bielefeld: Aisthesis, 1998).

16. See Claudio Magris, *Der Habsburgische Mythos in der österreichischen Literatur* (Salzburg: Otto Müller Verlag, 1966).

17. On the difficulty of associating Roth with any clear political position, see Rares G. Piloiu, "The Paradoxes of Left Socialism in Interwar Austria: Joseph Roth and Austro-Marxism," *Modern Austrian Literature* 40, no. 3 (2007): 21–41.

18. Roth, "The Bust of the Emperor," 232. Translation altered.

and that those who did not possess a nationality needed to be emancipated and (re)introduced to this "innate" right to belong to a specific nation. Twenty years later, Arendt would express a similar view in observing the problematic conditions that this assumption created in the former territories of the Dual Monarchy after World War I. Since, as Arendt writes, the Declaration of the Rights of Man was combined with national sovereignty in the French Revolution, it became a common understanding "that true freedom, true emancipation, and true popular sovereignty could be attained only with full national emancipation, that people without their own national government were deprived of human rights."[19] The results of this mode of thinking, as Arendt shows, were in fact devastating to those who were inevitably left without clear national attachments after the division of the former monarchic territories into nation-states.

This short example is already enough to demonstrate how the ostensibly reactionary tone of Roth's later works was as politically trenchant and critical as his writings before 1930. Roth's particular interest in the Austro-Hungarian Empire "as a relic," something apparent in his descriptions of a staunch, decrepit, and outdated Austro-Slavic nobility, is no simple nostalgia. Nor are they evidence of a stylistic regression to antimodern conservatism. Rather, by raising the Habsburgian corpse out of its Capuchin crypt, Roth asserts the revolutionary potential of outdatedness in the spirit of Adorno's reflections on excavation. "This is the way of all outdatedness," Adorno writes, "its expression in things is the shame that overcomes the descendent in the face of an earlier possibility that he has neglected to bring to fruition. What was accomplished can be forgotten and preserved in the present. Only what failed is outdated, the broken promise of a new beginning."[20]

Roth strives for something similar by capturing the Austro-Hungarian Empire not in its heyday but in its decline. In this moment of collapse and failure, he uncovers a critical, revolutionary potential. The collapse of the Dual Monarchy into nation-states

---

19. Hannah Arendt, *The Origins of Totalitarianism* (New York: Harcourt, 1994), 272.

20. Theodor W. Adorno, *Minima Moralia: Reflections from Damaged Life* (New York: Verso, 2005), 93.

affords a glance into the making of the nation-state system and its sweeping claims to be an organic, integrated, remainderless, and exceptionless order. This glance challenges us to envision a line of escape, a way out of such an order. Such critical potential could not be articulated through what Roth himself identified as the inauthenticity of New Objectivity's eyewitness account—the realistic description of what is or was—but only through conjuring the legend of a historical moment of decline.

This desire to provide a critical account of contemporary conditions through outdated forms persisted until Roth's very last work. In the *Legende vom heiligen Trinker* (*The Legend of the Holy Drinker*), his last novella from 1939, Roth prefigured his own death in Parisian exile in the collapse of the drunken "saint" Andreas. Andreas dies during an attempt to repay a debt to his benefactress, the statue of the little St. Thérèse de Lisieux, believed by him to have come to life. His precarious life consists of a series of miracles whose occurrence is arbitrary. His circumstances change abruptly from riches to complete destitution without any clear trajectory. For Roth, Andreas's condition reflected that of a contemporaneous, vagrant humanity, of countless refugees dispersed, this time not as a result of the collapse of monarchies but of a new totalitarian threat from Germany, of a humanity whose sole existence relied likewise on miracles. This condition, too, could be conveyed only when shrouded in the outdated, medieval Catholic tradition of the *Legende*, the archaic literary genre depicting the miraculous lives of saints.

The *Legende vom heiligen Trinker* presents the precarious situation of many living in Paris in 1939 by evoking a medieval genre, a Catholic legend, to portray the life of a modern drunken saint. Its organizing principle is the miracle, which allows for the protagonist time and again to regain the money he repeatedly loses and finally repay his hallowed benefactress. Although the novella was written with an eye to different historical events, it shares a great deal with the novel *Hiob*, written nine years earlier. In the drunk vagrant Andreas, Roth, who was struggling with chronic alcoholism before his death, may have seen himself. The Catholic air of the *Legende* reflects the author's growing interest in Catholicism in the final years of his life in Paris, as the threat of a Second World War became clearer. Those were different circumstances than the ones surrounding the writing of *Hiob* in 1930, where precarity was still primarily associated with the aftermath of the First World War, and the fate of Jewish refugees led Roth to evoke not the Catholic legend but the Old Testament afflictions of Job.[21] In both works, however, the arbitrary nature of the miracle operates as an organizing principle that defies dialectical systems like the nation-state and allows the outdated religious features of their respective literary models—the *Legende* or the biblical narrative—to penetrate contemporary conditions and the social and political problems at their heart.

Hiob: A "Jewish" Novel between Particularity and Universality

The novel *Hiob* transports the biblical Job story to the rural parts of czarist Russia at the beginning of the twentieth century. Its protagonist, Mendel Singer, is an impoverished *Melamed*, a Jewish Bible teacher who faces a series of calamities that begin to plague him in his hometown of Zuchnow and continue after he immigrates to America. One of Mendel's greatest afflictions is the reportedly incurable epilepsy of his youngest son Menuchim. But danger also threatens Mendel's other children. His two older sons, Jonas and Schemarjah, are to be conscripted into the czar's army, while his daughter Mirjam fosters a series of unsavory associations with local Cossack soldiers. Hoping to prevent his daughter from eloping, Mendel and his wife Deborah decide to emigrate and escape to America, where their son Schemarjah, who was smuggled out of Russia, awaits them. The Singers reluctantly leave the sick Menuchim behind, fearing he would not survive the journey. Along with Menuchim, the family also parts with the oldest son Jonas, who, preferring a peasant's life over his father's traditional Jewish occupation, decides to stay behind and

---

21. Despite Roth's increased interest in Catholicism in his last years, including rumors that he may have even converted before his death, Catholicism did not seem to replace Judaism for Roth; it rather alternated with his notion of Judaism. As Michael Hofmann noted: Catholicism was to Roth a "European expression of universal Jewishness." See Hofmann's preface in Roth, *The White Cities*, 18.

join the czar's army. The second part of the novel finds the Singer family in America, where Schemarjah joins the American forces fighting in the First World War and perishes. Learning of his death, Mendel's wife dies instantly from grief, and his daughter is subsequently admitted to a mental asylum. The novel concludes, however, with a fantastical resurfacing of the long-lost son, Menuchim, now a world-renowned musician who was healed miraculously and reunites with his bereaved father.

Hiob, as we have seen, was the first novel to abandon the sociopolitical thematic of the 1920s and thus pave the way for the historical works that followed. Yet even in relation to Roth's later monarchist works, *Hiob* stands out. The Habsburg novels, while turning away from the present in search of an irretrievable moment of collapse in the past, are nevertheless more explicit in their critique of rising nationalism in Europe in the 1930s. This feature relates them directly to Roth's time despite their historical settings. *Hiob*'s reception, on the other hand, has tended to consign the novel to the category of "shtetl literature" alongside the works of Yiddish- and German-language authors like Sholem Aleichem, Isaac Leib Peretz, and Karl Emil Franzos.[22] As a "Jewish" novel, *Hiob* came to be seen as a work concerned predominantly with the vanishing world of Eastern European Jewry, a classification that overshadowed other, more universalist readings that might have connected it with broader contemporaneous issues.[23] When universalist readings of *Hiob* were attempted, they primarily concerned themselves with the novel as an expression of human suffering by focusing on elements in the work that transcended its "Jewishness" under the assumption that the two categories, Jewishness and universality, are mutually exclusive.[24] It is

---

22. See Rosenfeld, *Understanding Joseph Roth*, 44.
23. The novel's reception has been influenced primarily by its classification as an "arch-Jewish" work in David Bronsen's biography. See David Bronsen, *Joseph Roth: Eine Biographie* (Köln: Kiepenheuer & Witsch, 1974), 11. See also Geoffrey P. Butler, "'It's the Bitterness That Counts': Joseph Roth's 'Most Jewish' Novel Rediscovered," *German Life and Letters* 41, no. 3 (1988): 227–34; and Ritchie Robertson, "Roth's *Hiob* and the Traditions of Ghetto Fiction," in *Co-Existent Contradiction: Joseph Roth in Retrospect*, ed. Helen Chambers (Riverside, CA: Ariadne, 1991), 185–200.
24. Lazaroms observes this problematic distinction and notes further that when the film rights to the novel were purchased by Fox Entertainment, the script rewrote

exactly this exclusive restriction of the Jewish element to a position of particularity—a form of difference that can be understood only against and across from a stable, all-encompassing concept of universality—that my reading of *Hiob* counters.

As Guy Stern notes, Roth was not the only author who turned to the Hebrew Bible and specifically to the Book of Job in response to cataclysmic events. Stern positions Roth next to German-speaking Jewish exiles such as Nelly Sachs, Yvan Goll, and Karl Wolfskehl, who, as he argues, all referenced the biblical figure in a kind of turn inward, a rediscovery of Jewish tradition in the face of a perceived exclusion from German-language culture.[25] According to Stern, this "turn" amounted to an acknowledgment of the fragility of the Enlightenment project of Jewish emancipation and its hope for equal Jewish participation in German-speaking society.

While it is not difficult to see how the Book of Job lends itself as a means of expression for figures like Roth, one should nevertheless be wary of the broader implications of claims like the one Stern makes. The problem lies in the fact that reading the turn to the Bible as a direct reaction to an exclusion from German-language culture inevitably renders the biblical text an alternative not only to German-language culture but also to the Enlightenment values of universality and to modernity at large. This reading renders the "turn" the result of a disillusionment with the Enlightenment values of universal humanism. Thus, not only are these values rejected and replaced, the wish to have a stake in modernity by engaging with the present moment is also denied. Denying the present, one is inclined to seclude oneself through a return to biblical themes.

It is, in fact, precisely the choice of Job over a variety of other biblical characters that seems to refute this assumption. In contrast to the figure of Moses, Job represents a potential for bridging gaps between different religions, peoples, and epochs that can itself be traced back to the Enlightenment. While eighteenth-century discourse

---

the character of Mendel Singer and stripped him of any Jewish markers. As a Catholic man from south Tyrol in the 1936 production *Sins of Man*, Mendel Singer's troubles were expected to appeal to "all men." See Lazaroms, *The Grace of Misery*, 71–74.

25. See Guy Stern, "Job as Alter Ego: The Bible, Ancient Jewish Discourse, and Exile Literature," *The German Quarterly* 63, no. 2 (1990): 199–210, 201.

surrounding the figure of Moses concentrated on notions of Jewish legal and theopolitical distinction, the German conversation around the Book of Job was paired with one of the Enlightenment's most idiomatic concepts: *Mitleid*, or sympathy.[26]

The interest in sympathy (or its synonyms: pity and compassion) as the innate capacity to relate to another's emotions was widespread in moral and aesthetic discussions around the mid-eighteenth century. In his *Treatise of Human Nature* (1739), David Hume described sympathy as that which allows us "to feel the pains and pleasure of others, which are not in being, and which we only anticipate by the force of imagination."[27] Adam Smith's notes on sympathy, opening his 1759 *Theory of Moral Sentiments*, likewise praised that "fellow-feeling" that enables us to switch places with the sufferer and "conceive ourselves enduring all the same torments."[28] Sympathy was noted to span not only across synchronic but also across diachronic distance. In Germany, it was Gotthold Ephraim Lessing who discussed *Mitleid* as the ability to relate to the torments of the Trojan Laocoön (*Laokoon: Oder, Über die Grenzen der Malerei und Poesie*, 1766) and later to the circumstances of figures in tragedies and mourning plays (*Hamburgische Dramaturgie*, 1769), thereby emphasizing *Mitleid*'s role in man's aesthetic education.

Yet while *Mitleid* and sympathy indicated a capacity for identification and commonality, they also presupposed an indelible element of distance. Thus, Smith remarks that "though our brother is upon the rack, as long as we ourselves are at our ease, our sense will never inform us of what he suffers."[29] And although in his *Hamburgische Dramaturgie* Lessing identifies the source of *Mitleid* in an inalienable love of fellow men, he also emphasizes distance as its precondition.

---

26. See, for example, Schiller's *Die Sendung Moses* (1789) and Michaelis's *Mosaisches Recht* (1785), the latter discussed in the previous chapter.

27. David Hume, *A Treatise of Human Nature*, ed. L. A. Shelby-Bigge (Oxford: Clarendon, 1968), 385.

28. Adam Smith, *Theory of Moral Sentiments*, ed. Knut Haakonssen (Cambridge: Cambridge University Press, 2002), 12.

29. Smith, *Theory of Moral Sentiments*, 11. See also Dror Wahrman, *The Making of the Modern Self: Identity and Culture in Eighteenth-Century England* (New Haven, CT: Yale University Press, 2004), 188.

This he concludes from the fact that the spectator is also able to derive aesthetic pleasure from the depicted suffering of Laocoön or of tragic figures on the stage.[30]

The rising interest in the Book of Job in eighteenth-century Germany should be considered against this background. Through translations like those of Simon Grynäus and Johann Cube, *Mitleid*'s dialectic of proximity and distance came to the fore.[31] Inspired by a turn away from an antiquarian and philological interest in English Job translations, German translators strove to emphasize the affective nature of the biblical story. Stylized as "poetic," their translations worked to eliminate the gap between the Hebrew and the modern while maintaining a level of foreignness.[32] *Mitleid* consequently became a model for poetic translations, which sought to bring the Hebrew Bible's distant landscape closer to the modern German explorer while still retaining its foreign provenance.

The compelling depiction of human suffering in the Book of Job served as an ideal example of the Hebrew Bible's (i.e., the Jewish Bible's) universalist potential. Understanding the Book of Job through the prism of *Mitleid* meant that such Job translations did not deny the particularity of the text—its foreignness—but rather highlighted the concurrence of the Hebrew Bible's foreignness and its distant provenance with a simultaneous universality, an appeal to all humankind.

The aesthetics of sympathy that flourished during the eighteenth century are also present in Roth's reference to the Book of Job. The outdatedness that characterizes his evocation of biblical texts is anything but a turn away from contemporary events. Its critical potential rejects any mutually exclusive relation between a "return" to the Bible and engagement with current political and social conditions, just

---

30. Gotthold Ephraim Lessing, *Werke in acht Bänden 4*, ed. Herbert Göpfert (München: Hanser, 1979), 203–4. See also Thomas Martinec, "The Boundaries of 'Mitleidsdramaturgie': Some Clarifications Concerning Lessing's Concept of Mitleid," *The Modern Language Review* 101, no. 3 (2006): 743–58.

31. Simon Grynäus, *Das Buch Hiob: In einer poetischen Übersetzung nach Schultens' Erklärung* (Basel, 1767); Johann Cube, *Poetische und prosaische Uebersetzung des Buches Hiob* (Berlin, 1769).

32. See further Sheehan, *The Enlightenment Bible*, 160–68.

as it resists the assumption that, in order to locate the universalist import of *Hiob*, it is necessary to concentrate on elements that transcend its Jewish attributes. With its modern reimagining of Job, Roth's *Hiob* invokes rather than denies the Enlightenment discourse of *Mitleid* as it pertains to the simultaneity of particularity and universality of the Hebrew Bible and its implication for our understanding of Jewish difference as a difference that is not perceived in opposition to a distinctively non-Jewish universality. Taking up this model of sympathy with its simultaneous retention of both identification and distance, Roth's modern Job universalizes Eastern European Jewish particularity, notably by positioning the trials and tribulations of the *Ostjude* Mendel Singer at the center of Western upheavals in the early twentieth century.

Nation-States, Integration, and the Uncontained Exception

Hiob's broader political significance emerges from a reading of the novel that emphasizes a continuity between the literary and journalistic works preceding and following it in Roth's oeuvre. Uniting *Hiob* with earlier and later works by Roth is the novel's own critical position vis-à-vis nationalism and the nation-state model that was growing in popularity in eastern and central Europe after the First World War. The aversion to nationalism that permeates Roth's monarchist works from the 1930s can be traced back to the essay collections written during his travels in Europe in the 1920s. Among these essays, the collection *Juden auf Wanderschaft* best demonstrates the pertinence of the *Ostjude* to a critique of what was becoming a predominant form of collective identity in the twentieth century: the nation-state. As the novel *Hiob* would later do, *Juden auf Wanderschaft* confronts this form with the figure of the immigrant or the stateless refugee that the *Ostjude* embodied for its author. This confrontation allows Roth to expose the contradiction that accompanied the model of the nation-state: with its underlying assumption that every person should possess a certain nationality and belong to a certain corresponding state, the nation-state system presented itself as a hermetically contained order. However, this purportedly contained system was bound to produce exceptions—nationless people, whose "excessive" existence exceeded its order. While this paradox already existed during the rise of nation-states in the previous century, it was only after the First World War that it became undeniably visible.

Juden auf Wanderschaft was the product of Roth's continued interest in the fate of refugees and stateless people suffering the aftermath of World War I. His aim in this essay series was to report on the conditions of immigrant Jews in several locations around the world where his occupation as a journalist had taken him. Beyond demonstrating his sympathy and implicit affinity with the people who shared his own Eastern European background, Roth's focus on the fate of Eastern Jews in three major Western European capitals (Berlin, Vienna, and Paris), in America (which he never visited in person), and in the Soviet Union reveals his discomfort with rigid institutionalized modes of collective identity that he indiscriminately associated with the West and an apathetic and increasingly homogenous bourgeoisie.

Eastern European Jews, forming unassimilated enclaves in the ghettoes of Western capitals, represented for Roth an idealized form of resistance not only to nationalism and nation-states but also to any other form of organized social or political movement. Planted as a foreign object in the West, the *Ostjude*'s ignorance of the West's divisions and norms served in Roth's eyes as a disruptive force. The promises that the West held in the imagination of by those coming from the East betrayed a naivety that ultimately revealed what Roth saw as the West's bitter rigidity. Eastern European Jews, as he observed, know "nothing of the social injustice of the West; nothing of the habitual bias that governs the actions, decisions, and opinions of the average Western European. . . . The Eastern Jew looks to the West with a longing that it really doesn't merit."[33] Roth's Eastern Jews immigrate to the West to improve their own individual fates. The social injustices that are being combated in the West are of no concern to those who constitute the focus of his study.

---

33. Joseph Roth, *The Wandering Jews*, trans. Michael Hofmann (New York: Norton, 2001), 5.

They are, in most cases, workers with no desire to engage in actions for the betterment of a particular class. They are mobilized by the desire to alleviate their individual plights. Taking part in collective, organized work toward social and political change seems suspicious to them: "The majority are working class or lower-middle class, without proletarian consciousness. Many are instinctively reactionary . . . from the not unjustified apprehension that change would not necessarily improve things for the Jews."[34]

Even at the height of his socialist period, Roth saw the true alternative to the ills of the West not in the structured socialism of the Soviet Union but rather in a structurelessness he associated with Eastern European Jewish immigrants. The author, who traveled to the newly established Soviet Union in 1926, expressed disappointment with the nation that was meant to oppose all Western principles. The Soviet Union, as he later noted, did nothing more than replicate Western bourgeois models.[35] A real counterimage was to be found in the figure that resisted any kind of classification into existing forms of collective organization: the *Ostjude* who was chased away from both villages and big cities. As unintegrated pariahs, *Ostjuden* belonged nowhere. They dwelled "in dirty streets and collapsing houses. Their Christian neighbor threatens them. The local squire beat them. The official has them locked up. The army officer fires his gun at them with impunity. The dog barks at them because their garb seems to provoke animals and primitive people alike."[36]

Observing the aversion that *Ostjuden* evoked, Roth was able to identify some political aspects of the antisemitism that was directed at Eastern European Jewish immigrants: because they could not be associated with a particular nation-state and because they seemed

---

34. Roth, *The Wandering Jews*, 12.
35. A draft of an address reporting on Roth's visit opens thus: "Meine Herren, ich werde mich bemühen, Ihnen heute abend zu beweisen, daß das Bürgertum unsterblich ist. Die grausamste aller Revolutionen, die bolschewistische, hat es nicht zu vernichten vermocht." Joseph Roth, "Der neue Tag," cited in Werner Sieg, *Zwischen Anarchismus und Fiktion: Eine Untersuchung zum Werk von Joseph Roth* (Bonn: Bouvier, 1974), 95.
36. Roth, *The Wandering Jews*, 6.

incapable of integration, *Ostjuden* were deemed unworthy of basic rights.[37] This position both troubled and fascinated Roth since, in his view, the mere presence of *Ostjuden* challenged an ossified sociopolitical system. Confronted with unintegrated excess in the form of Eastern European Jews, this system, in Roth's view, desperately attempted to contain the excess, only to discover that in its efforts to fence in (or out) the infiltrating other, it actually quarantined itself: "Anyone deserves the West who arrives with fresh energy to break up the deadly, antiseptic boredom of its civilization, prepared to undergo the quarantine we prescribe for immigrants. We do not realize that all our countries have become barracks and concentration camps, admittedly with all the modern conveniences."[38]

In 1951, close to twenty-five years after the appearance of *Juden auf Wanderschaft*, it was Arendt who described the same interwar conditions in *The Origins of Totalitarianism*. Although Arendt was granted a perspective that Roth, having died in 1939, could not acquire, her rigorous analysis of the nation-state's intolerance of superfluous, uncontained exceptions shared many similarities with Roth's observations. The second part of Arendt's extensive study draws a direct link between the peaking number of refugees and stateless people after the First World War and the rise and collapse into totalitarianism of the European nation-state system.[39]

---

37. The problematic relation between belonging to a nation and human rights is discussed extensively by Arendt. I do not suggest here that this type of antisemitism was directed only at Eastern European Jews, nor that this was the only source of hatred against them, but rather wish to clarify the appeal that *Ostjuden* had for Roth. Moreover, as Shulamit Volkov shows, aversion toward *Ostjuden* was often also expressed by *Westjuden*. See Shulamit Volkov, "The Dynamics of Dissimilation: *Ostjuden* and German Jews," in *The Jewish Responses to German Culture*, ed. Jehuda Reinharz and Walter Schatzberg (Hanover, NH: University Press of New England, 1985), 195–211.

38. Roth, *The Wandering Jews*, 11.

39. Arendt's link between the decline of the nation-state and the rise of totalitarianism has been thoroughly critiqued. See for example Margaret Canovan, *The Political Thought of Hannah Arendt* (New York: Harcourt, 1974); and Peter Staudenmaier, "Hannah Arendt's Analysis of Antisemitism in 'The Origins of Totalitarianism': A Critical Analysis," *Patterns of Prejudice* 46, no. 2 (2012): 154–79. Steven Aschheim summarizes the critique of Arendt's reliance on a "now almost universally rejected socio-psychological model of mass society" as well as her conception of the decline of

Arendt shows how, following the liquidation of the Dual Monarchy and the Czarist Empire, the establishment of the succession states was pursued with the expectation that a division of Europe in correspondence with rising national sentiments would bring stability to the area. The actual result of this transition, however, exposed the incompatibility of demographic conditions in postwar Europe with the desire to apply a grid model to former monarchic territories under the assumption that these could be neatly divided into distinct, homogeneous nation-states. In this, Arendt pointed out what Zygmunt Bauman would later generalize as modernity's greater problem of categorization and ambivalence: "Geometry shows what the world would be like were it geometrical. But the world is not geometrical. It cannot be squeezed into geometrically inspired grids."[40] The need for minority treaties to safeguard the rights of groups who suddenly found themselves without government representation exposed a condition that had accompanied the nation-state system from its inception but was only now made indisputably palpable: the nation-state was inescapably paired with the creation of exceptions, people who did not possess a legal status in the state and therefore required special protection from without.

---

the nation-state model and remarks: "Consonant with her view of mass society, the rise of totalitarianism is linked to a very unclear account of the decline and collapse of the nation-state system. Even if one accepts the dubious premise that such a decay took place, it is not at all apparent why particular societies (rather than others) ended up as totalitarian" (125). While I do not wish to contest these claims, my reading of Arendt focuses on the relation she draws between antisemitism and inherent problems of the nation-state model. I do not read Arendt as claiming that the nation-state is in decline but rather that from its inception, it was based on a paradox. Aschheim's lines, written in 1997, may sound somewhat remote in the current political climate. Today it is becoming increasingly and painfully obvious that the model of the nation-state, while still nowhere near a decline, continues to generate impossible situations for refugees and stateless people. Aschheim's cited remarks, which support a critique of Arendt by observing that some nation-states were able to avoid declining into totalitarianism, sound problematic today, where the danger of slipping into a totalitarian regime in many countries that in 1997 seemed impervious to such an eventuality is unfortunately very real. See Steven E. Aschheim, "Nazism Culture, and the Origins of Totalitarianism: Hannah Arendt and the Discourse of Evil," *New German Critique* 70 (1997): 117–39.

40. Zygmunt Bauman, *Modernity and Ambivalence* (Cambridge, UK: Polity Press, 1991), 15.

While this already indicated a kind of paradoxical basis for the nation-state (for how can a system that purports to be all-encompassing produce exceptions?), it also announced a shift in understanding of who deserves certain rights.[41] The existence of people who required an exception, an auxiliary guarantee in order to secure their rights, implied that as a rule, only those who belonged to the nation-state were entitled to such rights. This new conception formed without regard for the fact that in some cases a significant section of a state's population was comprised of what Arendt called "nationally frustrated peoples."[42]

The existence of minorities or "nationally frustrated" peoples, however, was not enough to fully expose the paradox of the nation-state system. The assumption behind the minority treaties, as Arendt shows, was that exceptional measures were only temporary, and that eventually nationally frustrated people would successfully integrate into the nation-state grid either through naturalization or repatriation. It was the arrival of the stateless people, a population that according to Arendt consisted primarily of Jews and Armenians, that finally broke the illusion of the nation-state, whose policy of exception for minorities, as long as it was deemed temporary, still upheld the validity of its integrative paradigm. The existence of stateless people demonstrated unequivocally that neither naturalization nor repatriation had the ability to integrate and thereby contain the exception. Stateless people could not be repatriated since they had no country of origin to which they could be "returned." At the same time, they could not be naturalized due, in some cases, to their large numbers or, in others, to their refusal to assimilate.

According to Arendt, the conception that rights were only accessible to those who were nationally emancipated played a dominant

---

41. See also Zygmunt Bauman, "The Fate of Humanity in the Post-Trinitarian World," *Journal of Human Rights* 1, no. 3 (2002): 283–303; and Seyla Benhabib and Raluca Eddon, "From Antisemitism to 'the Right to Have Rights': The Jewish Roots of Hannah Arendt's Cosmopolitanism," in *Antisemitism and Philosemitism in the Twentieth and Twenty-First Centuries: Representing Jews, Jewishness, and Modern Culture*, ed. Phyllis Lassner and Lara Trubowitz (Newark: University of Delaware Press, 2008), 63–80.

42. Arendt, *The Origins of Totalitarianism*, 272.

role in the awakening of Jewish national consciousness in Europe. Those who fought for recognition as a national minority as well as those who went further and argued that Jews should have a nation-state of their own were working under the same assumption, namely that the totality of the nation-state system ruled out the possibility of not integrating into it in one of those two ways.[43] However, since, as Arendt notes, "the first *Heimatlose* or *apatrides*, as they were created by the Peace Treaties, were for the most part Jews who ... were unable or unwilling to place themselves under the new minority protection of their homelands,"[44] the problem of stateless people in Europe and "the Jewish problem" quickly became synonymous.[45] Utilizing a broader historical lens, Arendt's analysis differs from Roth's eyewitness reports, yet both ultimately make a similar observation. For Arendt as for Roth, Jewish refugees in the interwar period, a population consisting predominantly of Eastern European Jews immigrating westward, came to be identified as a superfluous exception, unsettling a compulsively integrative mechanism.

While Arendt's analysis concludes with a kind of realist pessimism about the prospects of collective existence outside the nation-state system, Roth's writings see in the *Ostjude* a possibility, albeit a highly romanticized one, of its disruption. Arendt and Roth wrote, of course, at different historical moments. Arendt's relation to the Jewish state remained critical, yet her post–World War II perspective nevertheless compelled her to critique what she saw as a Jewish withdrawal from political life.[46] For Roth, writing in 1927,

---

43. As Arendt indicates, the erection of a Jewish state, however, did not solve the refugee problem but merely transposed it onto the local Arab population. See Arendt, *Origins of Totalitarianism*, 290.

44. Arendt, *Origins of Totalitarianism*, 289.

45. It should be rightly noted that in her analysis, Arendt overlooks other groups, including Roma, the Basque, Flemings, Slovenes, and others who did not have a state of their own at the time. See further Staudenmaier, "Hannah Arendt's Analysis of Antisemitism," 170.

46. See Hannah Arendt, introduction to *The Jew as Pariah: Jewish Identity and Politics in the Modern Age*, ed. Ron H. Feldman (New York: Grove Press, 1978), 28. The claim of an overarching Jewish reluctance to engage politically has been challenged. See, for example, David Biale, *Power and Powerlessness in Jewish History: The Jewish Tradition and the Myth of Passivity* (New York: Schocken, 1986).

this withdrawal was still a viable and even idealized form of resistance to integrative drives like that of the nation-state and was therefore itself of a certain political value.

According to Roth, the Jews who insisted on a struggle for self-determination either as a Jewish nation in Palestine or as a Jewish national minority in Europe were betraying one of their most distinguishing traits. Those who took up the "European battle cry of national autonomy," in presenting their entitlement to national rights, renounced the possibility of becoming "a far bigger thing altogether" in his view.[47] The author accused proponents of a Jewish state in Palestine of reproducing the same problematic Western ideals. This led Roth to position himself against the idea of a Jewish nation in the modern sense and against a Jewish state since, in his eyes, such projects were inevitably tainted:

> At any rate, it would be difficult for [Jewish people] to become a nation with a completely new, un-European physiognomy. The European mark of Cain won't wash off. It is surely better to be a nation than to be maltreated by one. But it's a painful necessity all the same. Where's the pride for the Jew, who disarmed long ago, in proving once more that he is capable of squad drill! Because the world isn't made up of "nations" and fatherlands. . . . Given all the millennial grief of the Jews, they still had one consolation: the fact that they *didn't* have a fatherland. If there can ever be such a thing as a just history, surely the Jews will be given great credit for holding on to their common sense in not having had a fatherland at a time when the whole world has launched itself into patriotic madness.[48]

For Roth, Eastern European Jews, who had "no home anywhere, but [whose] graves may be found in every cemetery,"[49] served as an example of an ethical alternative to national sovereignty. This group of individuals and its incompatibility with existing Western social and political structures helped Roth articulate his own opposition to the ideals of nation and state, even when those were presented by Zionism as inherently Jewish values: "Zionism and nationhood are by their nature Western European ideals, even if

---

47. Roth, *The Wandering Jews*, 17.
48. Roth, *The Wandering Jews*, 19–20.
49. Roth, *The Wandering Jews*, 11.

what they aspire towards may not be. Only in the East [*Nur im Orient*] do people live who are unconcerned with their 'nationality,' in the Western European sense. They speak several languages, are themselves the product of several generations of mixed marriages, and fatherland for them is whichever country happens to conscript them."[50]

Roth's resistance to Zionism was not simply a pacifist rejection of Jewish militarism. Zionism meant succumbing to the all-integrative impulse that was driving what he called the West. Roth's highly romanticized view can and should itself be critiqued for its tendency at times to essentialize Eastern Jews in a way that served Roth's own critique of the nation-state. His idea of the Orient or the East is similarly problematic, as it seems to encompass Eastern Jews and Muslim Armenians while failing to venture much further east beyond Europe's border with Russia.[51] It is also not out of place to challenge Roth's strategic decision to withhold the category of indigeneity specifically from Jewish people while allocating it to others in order to use this group as an idealized example of withdrawal from the pervasive model of the nation-state. While he acknowledges that the Jewish people may have indeed originated in Palestine, he does not accept this as a viable reason for their return: "The Jew has a right to Palestine, not because he once came from there but because no other country will have him."[52]

To follow Roth's vision, then, one should adopt his 1927 perspective, where the "Jewish question," while indeed acute, has not yet acquired its fully catastrophic proportions, and where singling Jewish people out for their capacity to represent a model for withdrawal could still hold the positive potential of enabling us to think outside dialectical systems. From this perspective, Roth's critique offers a valuable lesson. His opposition amounts to resisting the containment of the exception—the superfluous potential he saw reflected in the condition of Jewish refugees—by an integrative system that claimed to encompass all.

---

50. Roth, *The Wandering Jews*, 15.
51. See Roth, *The Wandering Jews*, 15.
52. Roth, *The Wandering Jews*, 18.

Being Superfluous, the Exception, and the Miracle

The unworldly figure of the *Ostjude* Mendel Singer in the novel *Hiob* is a literary embodiment of the same idealized position of Eastern European Jews that Roth described in *Juden auf Wanderschaft*. The novel follows Mendel as he immigrates to America from the town of Zuchnow located in the territories of czarist Russia. Like many immigrants before him and many more after, Mendel is not searching for a new fatherland. Russia was no fatherland to him and America will not be one either. Mendel immigrates in the hope of escaping the looming threat of assimilation, both social and political. The danger of losing his two older sons to the czar's army and his daughter to Cossack lust mobilizes Mendel to move to a new country where his position as "other" could hopefully be maintained. His ambivalence toward his new American home, expressed chiefly through a recurring wish to return to Zuchnow and search for his abandoned son, stresses that he belongs neither in the East nor in the West. As *Hiob* shows us, even after residing for several generations in czarist Russia, Eastern Jews like Mendel had no link to the land:

> Fremd war ihnen die Erde, auf der sie standen, feindlich der Wald, der ihnen entgegenstarrte, gehässig das Kläffen der Hunde, deren mißtrauisches Gehör sie geweckt hatten, und vertraut nur, der Mond, der heute in dieser Welt geboren wurde wie im Lande der Väter, und der Herr, der überall wachte, daheim und in der Verbannung.
>
> [The earth on which they stood was alien to them; the forest stared back at them with enmity; the barking of the dogs, whose suspicious ears they had awakened, was full of malice. They felt confidence only in the moon, born today in this world as it had been in the land of their fathers, and in the Lord, who watched over all, at home and in exile.][53]

America presented itself as a provisional solution to Mendel's troubles in Zuchnow. Despite the promise that it held, the journey to the new world was not happily undertaken. Even before

---

53. Roth, *Werke 5*, 43–44; Joseph Roth, *Job: The Story of a Simple Man*, trans. Dorothy Thompson (New York: Viking, 1931), 87. Translation altered.

knowing the fate that awaited him there—the death of his son and wife, his daughter's illness—Mendel anticipated that the new "fatherland" would be no different than the old one. The streets of the Lower East Side do not change him much; he wanders around them in his traditional garb, stubbornly refuses to blend in, and wonders: "Was gehen mich diese Leute an? . . . Was geht mich ganz Amerika an? Mein sohn, meine Frau, meine Tochter. . . . Bin ich noch Mendel Singer? Ist das noch meine Familie? Bin ich noch Mendel Singer? Wo ist mein Sohn Menuchim?" (What are these people to me? . . . What is all of America to me? My son, my wife, my daughter. . . . Am I still Mendel Singer? Is this still my family? Am I still Mendel Singer? Where is my son Menuchim?")[54] The first part of the novel concludes by conveying Mendel's feeling of alienation in his new "homeland."

> Es war ihm als wäre er aus sich selbst herausgestoßen worden, von sich selbst getrennt, würde er fortan leben müssen. Es war ihm, als hätte er sich selbst in Zuchnow zurückgelassen, in der Nähe Menuchims. Und während es um seine Lippen lächelte und während es seinen Kopf schüttelte, begann sein Herz langsam zu vereisen, es pochte wie ein metallener Schlegel gegen kaltes Glas. Schon war er einsam, Mendel Singer: Schon war er in Amerika . . .
>
> [It was as though he had been cast out of himself, separated from himself, and doomed to live on. It was as though he had left himself behind, in Zuchnow, near Menuchim. And while his lips smiled, and his head nodded, his heart began slowly to freeze. It pounded like a metal drumstick against cold glass. Already he was alone, Mendel Singer. Already he was in America . . .][55]

Smiling and nodding are merely outward signs that cannot truly mask the fact that Mendel is unable to fit into America. Half of him remains in Zuchnow with the abandoned Menuchim.

The second part of the novel seems to open on a different note, with the declaration that Mendel "nach einigen Monaten in New York zu Hause war. Ja er war beinahe heimisch in Amerika!" (In a few months he was quite at home in New York. Yes, he was almost

---

54. Roth, *Werke 5*, 75; Roth, *Job*, 151. Translation altered.
55. Roth, *Werke 5*, 75; Roth, *Job*, 151.

a native in America!)⁵⁶ But the ironic tone of the subsequent lines makes the reader doubt the sincerity of the previous statement:

> Er wusste bereits, daß old chap auf Amerikanisch Vater hieß und old fool Mutter, oder umgekehrt. Er kannte ein paar Geschäftsleute aus der Bowery, mit denen sein Sohn verkehrte, die Essex Street, in der er wohnte, und die Houston Street, in der das Kaufhaus seines Sohnes lag, seines Sohnes Sam. Er wußte, daß Sam bereits ein American boy war, daß man good bye sagte, how do you do und please, wenn man ein feiner Mann war. . . . Zwischen zwölf und zwei muß man Lunch essen und zwischen sechs und acht ein Dinner. Dieser Zeiten achtet Mendel nicht. Er ißt um drei Uhr nachmittags und um zehn Uhr abends, wie zu Hause, obwohl eigentlich zu Hause Tag ist, wenn er sich zum Nachtmahl setzt, oder auch früher Morgen, wer kann es wissen. All right heißt einverstanden, und statt ja! Sagt man yes!

> [He already knew that "old chap" meant father in American and "old fool" mother, or maybe the other way around. He knew a few tradesmen from the Bowery who came to see his son; he knew Essex Street, where he lived, and Houston Street, where his son's place of business was, his son Sam. He knew that Sam was already an "American boy"; that, if one was a refined gentleman, one said "Good-bye" and "How-do-you-do," and "Please." . . . Between twelve and two one eats "lunch"; between six and eight "dinner." Mendel did not observe these hours. He ate at three in the afternoon, and at ten at night, as at home, although, to be sure, it must still be daylight at home when he sat down to his evening meal, or even perhaps early morning. Who knows. "All right" meant "I agree"; and instead of "Ja!" one said "yes!"]⁵⁷

Mendel's integration in America is only superficial; it has barely progressed beyond the outward smiles and nods he displayed when he first arrived in New York. His knowledge of the city consists of only a couple of streets, where he lives and where his son works. Mendel has no need to venture beyond those stations and expand his circle. His new familiarity with American rituals (lunch at noon, dinner at six, which Mendel does not bother to observe) and phrases ("old chap" means father and "old fool" mother—or maybe the opposite?) merely tells us how little of his new surroundings Mendel was truly absorbing. A few paragraphs later, when the family

---
56. Roth, *Werke 5*, 76; Roth, *Job*, 155.
57. Roth, *Werke 5*, 76–77; Roth, *Job*, 155–57. Translation altered.

celebrates the financial success of Sam's joint business venture with his American friend Mac, we learn that, barring those few detached phrases, Mendel still does not speak any English. In order to communicate with Mac, his son Sam/Schemarjah has to translate his words.

Was Mendel better off back in Russia? It certainly seems that, at least mentally, Mendel prefers to stay in Zuchnow. He still eats in the hours he used to back when he was living there, and he periodically imagines returning there to find Menuchim. But the Zuchnow he imagines is not a concrete place; it is a memory, which he associates with the one son whose integration he has not yet witnessed.[58] Back when Mendel was living in Russia, even Zuchnow was not entirely safe. It was not impervious to the long reach of the state that tried to assimilate his sons to its militaristic efforts by conscripting them. Russia provided Mendel with his first encounter with the state's bureaucratic mechanisms. The first part of the novel narrates this encounter in a scene that depicts Mendel's attempt to obtain official documents necessary for emigration.

The exchange between Mendel and the Russian state official is particularly instructive. It reveals an unbridgeable distance between the *Ostjude* and the state representative, who fails to understand the true manner in which Mendel's presence unsettles the order in the governmental waiting room:

> Manchmal rief ein Mann in blauer Uniform einen Namen aus. Alle Schläfer erwachten. Der Aufgerufene erhob sich, wankte einer Tür zu, rückte an seinem Anzug und trat durch eine der hohen zweiflügeligen Türen, die statt einer Klinke einen runden, weißen Knopf hatte. Mendel überlegte, wie er diesen Knopf behandeln würde, um die Tür aufzumachen. Er stand auf, vom langen Sitzen, eingezwängt zwischen den Menschen, taten ihm die Glieder weh. Kaum aber hatte er sich erhoben, als ein blauer Mann auf ihn zutrat. "Sidaj!" rief der blaue Mann "setz dich!" Mendel Singer fand keinen Platz mehr auf seiner Bank. Er blieb neben

---

58. Eastern Europe as a nostalgic and literary idea in German Jewish writing is discussed in the chapter "Mediating Galicia in Joseph Roth's *Job*" in Kata Gellen, "Galicia as a Literary Idea: Jewish Eastern Europe in the Writings of Joseph Roth and Soma Morgenstern" (manuscript draft). I am thankful to Kata Gellen for allowing me to consult her work in progress.

ihr stehen, drückte sich an die Wand und hatte den Wunsch, so flach zu werden wie die Mauer.

"Wartest du auf Nummer 84?" fragte der blaue Mann.

"Ja," sagte Mendel. Er war überzeugt, daß man jetzt gesonnen war, ihn endgültig hinauszuwerfen.... Aber der blaue Mann hatte nicht die Absicht, Mendel aus dem Haus zu weisen. Dem blauen Mann lag vor allem daran, daß alle Wartenden ihre Plätze behielten und daß er alle übersehen konnte. Wenn einer schon aufstand, so konnte er eine Bombe werfen.

Anarchisten verkleiden sich manchmal—dachte der Türsteher. Und er winkte Mendel zu sich heran, betastete den Juden, fragte nach den Papieren.

[Sometimes a man in a blue uniform called out a name. All the sleepers awakened. The one called rose, scrambled towards the door, pulled his clothes into order, and walked through one of the high double doors which had a round white button in the place of a latch. Mendel considered how he would handle this button in order to open the door. He stood up. His limbs ached from long sitting crowded in amongst the others. Hardly had he risen, when one of the blue uniforms approached him.

"*Sidai*" called the blue man. "Sit down, you!" Mendel Singer no longer found a place on the bench. He stood beside it, pressed himself against the wall, and wished he could become as flat as the wall.

"Are you waiting for number eighty-four?" asked the blue man.

"Yes," said Mendel. He was convinced now that they intended to throw him out.... But the blue man had no intention of throwing Mendel out. The blue man set great store by having all the waiting crowd in their places where he could observe them. If one stood up, he might be preparing to throw a bomb. Anarchists sometimes disguised themselves, thought the man at the door. And he beckoned Mendel to come to him, felt him over, asked for his papers.][59]

As he awaits his audience with the clerk, Mendel attempts to orient himself in the room. This unfamiliar setting with its strange and slumberous order and the unusual doors that he does not know how to operate all indicate to Mendel that he is out of place. Although he tries to blend in, be "as flat as the wall," he cannot but draw attention to himself as he rises for a moment to stretch his legs. This provokes the blue man, the policeman charged with keeping order in the waiting room. As he commands Mendel to sit back down,

---

59. Roth, *Werke 5*, 54; Roth, *Job*, 108–9.

the blue man is concerned with that exact act of containment, of "having all the waiting crowd in their places where he could observe them." Government order means no exceptions, all are equal in the eyes of the state and its law, and so all are equally expected to remain seated. But the blue man misinterprets Mendel's act of rising from the bench. He understands it as a gesture of engaged rebellion against the order that he represents. As far as the blue man is concerned, there can only be two options: one can either collaborate with or fight against the state. Either way, one exists in a dialectical relation to it. Mendel, however, is superfluous to this order. Neither blending in nor actively resisting, he exists entirely outside of this discursive relation. Mendel's nonrelation to the state and its integrative mechanism is that of difference as such, not difference from or than. It is a difference emancipated from the threat of integration into purportedly universal orders.

Mendel's difference, his position as superfluous or an uncontained exception, is a form of divine excess. While others participate in the order of the state by struggling against it or by fighting for it in wars, Mendel reckons only with God. The Great War that rages in Europe throughout the second part of the novel is mentioned only in passing even though Mendel loses his son Schemarjah to it. The nations' wars are of no concern to Mendel. His existence does not depend on human affairs; it is one grounded in divine punishments and miracles. For this reason, the war and its horrors do not affect him directly as they do his neighbor Lemmel, who lost his arm in the Great War, but rather indirectly, as a decree from above: "Kämpfte Lemmel gegen die Deutschen, so kämpfte Mendel gegen überirdische Gewalten.... Ohne Zweifel ein Auserkorener war Mendel Singer. Als erbarmungswürdiger Zeuge für die grausame Gewalt Jehovahs lebte er in der Mitte der andern." (If Lemmel was fighting the Germans, Mendel was fighting supernatural powers.... Undoubtedly Mendel Singer was a man marked by God. In the midst of the others, he lived as the pitiful witness of the cruel power of Jehovah.)[60]

---

60. Roth, *Werke 5*, 107; Roth, *Job*, 218–19.

Mendel is *ein Auserkorener*, an elected one, an exception prescribed from beyond all world orders.⁶¹ Roth's archaistic tone matches Mendel's unworldly existence, which is ultimately affirmed by the miraculous healing and return of his lost, disabled son Menuchim. Menuchim's return distinguishes Mendel as the receiver of miracles, events that are themselves superfluous to worldly logical procedures, indeed a disruption of "natural" processes. In this day and age, as Mendel's friends remind him, being granted miracles should not be taken for granted. For while God might be almighty, "so ist doch anzunehmen, daß er die ganz großen Wunder nicht mehr tut, weil die Welt ihrer nicht mehr wert ist." (It is probable that he no longer performs the greatest miracles, because the world is no longer worthy of them.)⁶² Most people are not entitled to great miracles nowadays, but Mendel is an exception. His *Weltfremdheit* is accordingly not limited to his incompatibility with existing political orders; it is the driving force behind his entire story's unfolding. The Singer family's first plague, the illness of the young son Menuchim, might have been prevented had Mendel not refused treatment for his son by Russian doctors. But *Hiob* commences with the recognition that Menuchim's state is divinely prescribed, and its undoing will occur in a like manner. As Mendel declares, "gesund machen kann ihn kein Doktor, wenn Gott nicht will." (No doctor can cure him if God does not will it.)⁶³

When other plagues befall the Singers and Mendel is urged by his wife Deborah to reach out to people for help, Mendel replies: "Was redest du für Dummheiten? . . . Wohin soll ich gehn? Und wen soll ich um Rat fragen? . . . Welche Hilfe erwartest du von den Menschen, wo Gott uns gestraft hat?" (What nonsense are you talking? . . . Where shall I go and whom shall I ask for advice? . . . What sort of help do you await from mankind when God has so punished

---

61. I am further grateful to Kata Gellen for her insightful comment on the relevance of this word choice over the more familiar *auserwählt*. As an *Auserwählter*, Mendel would still be associated with a group (the Jews as *die Auserwählten*, the chosen people). *Auserkorener*, on the other hand, is both archaic and defies any notion of stable group belonging.
62. Roth, *Werke 5*, 104; Roth, *Job*, 213.
63. Roth, *Werke 5*, 7; Roth, *Job*, 1.

us?)[64] Mendel is then moved to recite verses from the Bible to support his position: "Gegen den Willen des Himmels gibt es keine Gewalt. 'Von ihm donnert es und blitzt es, er wölbt sich über die ganze Erde, vor ihm kann man nicht davonlaufen'—so steht es geschrieben." (Against the will of heaven there is no power. "He is the thunder and the lightning, He arches Himself over the whole world. No man can escape Him," thus it is written.) To this Deborah replies: "Der Mensch muss sich zu helfen suchen, und Gott wird ihm helfen. So steht es geschrieben, Mendel! Immer weißt du die falschen Sätze auswendig. Viele tausend Sätze sind geschrieben worden, die überflüssigen merkst du dir alle!" (God helps those who help themselves. So it is written, Mendel! You always know the false verses by heart. Thousands of verses are written, you notice all the superfluous ones!)[65]

In this brief domestic-theological quarrel, Deborah rejects Mendel's argument with the claim that he only quotes the Bible's "superfluous" verses. Deborah's own reading of the Bible is still bound to the contained systems of human economy and politics, where superfluousness remains a mere redundancy. This perspective has no scope for events occurring without a catalyst. If a man wishes to better his situation, he must act. Every effect in the world is dialectically paired with a cause. But Mendel knows that like his quotations, divine punishments and miracles are superfluous insofar as they are arbitrary, not simply redundant. They are not a response to or a result of human action and they cannot be integrated into human orders. Just as his punishments cannot be linked to any sins committed, so too can no miracle be precipitated.

The nonlogic of the miracle has direct implications for literary form in *Hiob*. The condition of being superfluous in Roth's novel carries with it a corresponding literary-formal expression, which, together with the work's subtitle, "*Roman* eines einfachen Mannes," pushes back against the tradition of the German-language novel.[66]

---

64. Roth, *Werke* 5, 24; Roth, *Job*, 47.
65. Roth, *Werke* 5, 26; Roth, *Job*, 51. Translation altered.
66. This allusion is lost in the English translation, which substitutes "story" for novel (*Roman*).

To the latter's underlying movement of development and organic integration,[67] *Hiob* offers an alternative movement of displacement. This movement is manifest not only in the displacement of its protagonist from the Pale of Settlement bordering Russia and Eastern Europe to the streets of New York's Lower East Side but also, and on a more profound level, in the transition from one occurrence to another in Roth's novel. Events in *Hiob* are not the organic product of human decisions, deeds, or sentiments. Rather, they are—like the series of calamities and miracles that visit Mendel—assembled one on top of the other; they succeed one another in a notably arbitrary fashion. Even their final resolution, the miraculous return of the healed Menuchim, is indiscriminately imposed on them (Menuchim happens to show up at the Passover Seder dinner like the prophet Elijah) and leaves no clear conclusion: Will Mendel and Menuchim return to Eastern Europe together? Will they find a doctor who could cure Mirjam? Will the oldest son Jonas ever be reunited with his father? All of this is left undetermined at the end of the novel.

Mendel's movement from one circumstance to the next, from punishment to punishment to miracle, is itself a movement of displacement occurring abruptly and arbitrarily rather than emerging organically out of a coherent development. In *Hiob*, distinguishing between a miracle and a coincidence is merely a question of perspective. Occurrences could unfold either haphazardly or as a product of divine intervention, but from a human perspective—and no text demonstrates this better than the Book of Job upon which Roth's novel is based—their unfolding is arbitrary. Neither Roth's "simple man" nor any other human figure controls the course of *Hiob* since, as we are told, the disasters that befall Mendel can in no way be linked to any of his deeds. Their accumulation suggests a kind of additive structure that defies any notion of organic development. If another calamity were to be added or one were to be

---

67. See for example Franco Moretti, *The Way of the World: The Bildungsroman in European Culture* (New York: Verso, 2000), 17.

subtracted from this series of events in *Hiob*, the principle underlying its movement would not be altered.[68]

Despite the constant reference to miracles, legends, and biblical stories, Roth's *Hiob* demonstrates a particularly progressive approach to the tradition of the German-language novel. As Georg Lukács indicates in *The Theory of the Novel*, the novelistic program of organic integration had already been thwarted in the nineteenth century.[69] Lukács's study of the loss of totality and integration in the novel was itself a response to the First World War. It acknowledged the fragmentary state of a world shattered by unspeakable horrors and found in the novel a corresponding aesthetic response. Nevertheless, the study's argument about the forfeited integrative principle of the novel was involuntarily a gesture of preservation. The failure of integration in Lukács's study—especially if we follow its historico-philosophical outlook—could only be measured against an integrative ideal projected to have been previously attainable. As such, nonintegration still appeared to Lukács as a loss, absence, or indeed a failure even in 1920, the year his study appeared as a book in Berlin.[70] Roth's *Hiob*, however, is not a novel that laments a lost harmony in a kind of second disillusionment after the war. It does not respond to a "crisis" of fragmentation. Its relation to the tradition of the novel can itself be described as superfluous, a nonrelation. With its own miracle-based, additive structure it relinquishes both nostalgia and resistance to this principle of integration.

For Roth, this relinquishment was linked to the ceding of similarly integrative forms of collective identity, first and foremost among them nationalism and nation-states. By positioning the unworldly Mendel as superfluous to both the nation-state and the program of

---

68. Furthermore, the exceptional nature of the miracle, dictating Mendel's own position as an exception, contrasts with Georg Lukács's stipulation that the protagonist of the novel be an individual only insofar as he is an exemplary representative of the whole: See Georg Lukács, *The Theory of the Novel*, trans. Anna Bostock (Cambridge, MA: MIT Press, 1999), 134.
69. Lukács, *The Theory of the Novel*, 112.
70. Georg Lukács, *Die Theorie des Romans* (Berlin: Paul Cassirer, 1920).

the German-language novel, Roth reveals the intertwined aesthetic and political stakes of integrative ideals that continued to prevail well into the twentieth century.

Indeed, at first glance, the novel's focus on the "story of a simple man" seems to stand out in relation to Roth's other works whose political engagement is easier to recognize. Yet *Hiob*'s social and political critiques are in fact equally poignant. The political withdrawal of the novel, just like that of its protagonist Mendel, is itself a strong commentary on the problems generated by integrative systems that cannot tolerate uncontained exceptions. By juxtaposing Roth's reports on Eastern European Jewish immigrants and refugees in the interwar period with Arendt's analysis of the same historical conditions, we can identify the compulsion toward integration as the guiding principle of the nation-state system. Furthermore, we can see how the rising numbers of refugees and stateless people after the war exposed a paradox at the foundation of this system. Despite this system's claim to be all-encompassing—its assumption that all human beings should belong to a certain nation and therefore could be integrated into one nation-state if not another—exceptions to this system were continuously being created.

For Arendt, the condition of uncontained exceptions came to be synonymous with the "Jewish problem" during the interwar period. And similarly, for Roth, being superfluous to such systems was reflected notably in the position of Eastern European Jewish immigrants. In Roth's eyes, this condition offered a challenge to such integrative models. It was the same condition of being superfluous that he continued to explore in his novel *Hiob* through the figure of Mendel, the exception who was chosen to receive divine punishments and an exceptional miracle. Mendel's superfluousness denotes a position of difference. Yet this difference is not perceived as a particularity, which can itself only be understood against a universality, an integrated, broader whole that gives it meaning. Mendel's difference is emancipated from any relation to systems of integration. It is difference conceived on its own terms. This is the shape that Jewish difference takes in Roth's work: difference inspired by the condition of *Ostjuden*, unintegrated immigrants and refugees, whose arrival in the

West was unsettling to many who still deemed integration a valid ideal, including assimilated German-speaking Jews. Yet, as the next chapter will show, even those assimilated Jews could not escape the condition of being superfluous. Their exceptional condition emanated directly from their assimilation.

5

INORGANIC QUOTATIONS

Revisiting Assimilation with Eric Zeisl's Hiob

With numerous parallels in the biographies and work of Joseph Roth and the Viennese-born composer Eric Zeisl (1905–1959), it is no surprise that many of the themes surrounding Roth's *Hiob* continue to play an important role in Zeisl's operatic rendition of the novel. The opera *Hiob* offers an opportunity to reflect further on the condition of being superfluous and the notion of the uncontained exception, which allow us to think of Jewish difference without subsuming it under an overarching integration paradigm. Zeisl began to work on the opera in Paris in 1939 after fleeing Vienna the previous year. Although Paris provided refuge for both Austrian exiles, author and composer never met in person. Roth passed away shortly before Zeisl became acquainted with his novel. Work on the opera *Hiob* accompanied Zeisl to the United States, to which he immigrated in that same year and where most of the music was composed after 1945. The post-Holocaust perspective of the opera *Hiob* calls for a shift in our understanding of the condition of being superfluous. For Roth, superfluousness was a category inspired by the situation of Eastern European Jewish immigrants, which, in 1930, he could still idealize as a unique form of existence. For Zeisl and his contemporaries, however, it was difficult, when faced with the catastrophic events of the interim, to escape the painful recognition that superfluousness applied not just to Eastern Jews but equally well to assimilated German-speaking Jews.

This recognition also shaped the post-Holocaust reexamination of antisemitism and Jewish assimilation by Hannah Arendt, whose work continues to guide the analysis in this chapter. By linking the early stages of Jewish emancipation to a paradoxical notion of the exception, whereby being integrated was contingent upon remaining exceptional, Arendt provides us with a starting point for a reflection on how the linked categories of exception and superfluousness operated in the process of Jewish assimilation in Central Europe, and moreover, how Jewish assimilation was likewise tied to an emancipated notion of difference.

The topic of assimilation stands at the center of the opera *Hiob*. Zeisl's own compositional practice allows us to revisit this term, which has attracted extensive scholarly criticism precisely because of its perceived erasure of difference. The assumption behind such criticism, and its preference for alternative terms like "acculturation" or "minority subculture," is that assimilation implies the outright elimination of Jewish particularity. This chapter will offer another perspective on assimilation according to which difference occupies a central role, yet not in the form of particularity and its relation to universality. This alternative perspective grows out of Zeisl's own compositional practice, which lends itself to comparisons with another assimilated Austrian composer, Gustav Mahler. Through a comparison with Mahler, Zeisl's compositional practice emerges as quotational.[1] The music of both composers is saturated with an eclectic array of musical quotations, be they from folk

---

1. I borrow the term "quotational practice" from Patrick Greaney's study of quotation in montage art practices. See Patrick Greaney, *Quotational Practices: Repeating the Future in Contemporary Art* (Minneapolis: University of Minnesota Press, 2014).

music or from other periods in the history of Western music. The quotational practices of both Mahler and Zeisl are themselves a form of musical assimilation that involves repetition, reappropriation, and recontextualization of existing materials.

Tracing the function of quotation in Zeisl's music informs this chapter's exploration of the theoretical stance of German Jewish assimilation as a form of quotation, a repetition as difference. In Zeisl's *Hiob*, the superfluous condition of quotation as a form of repetition attaches itself to the repetition that is implied in the gesture of assimilation. Highlighting the nondialectical and nonorganic attributes of both in the opera will not only point at a restoration of the term "assimilation" but also connect the phenomenon of Jewish assimilation in German-speaking society and culture with a prominent modernist aesthetic debate concerning the role of organicism and integration in artworks.

Tradition and Eclecticism in Zeisl's Music

Eric Zeisl was born in 1905 in Vienna's Leopoldstadt district to an assimilated Jewish family with Bohemian roots. The son of Sigmund and Kamilla, who were middle-class coffee shop owners, the musically precocious Erich (the *h* was dropped after his immigration to America) was only fourteen when he was granted a place at the Vienna State Academy. Among his teachers were the Austrian composers Richard Stöhr, Joseph Marx, and Hugo Kauder, whose conservative resistance to the atonal trends of the time permeated their student's work. Under their influence, Zeisl developed a rich tonal compositional style that was firmly grounded in traditional forms. The numerous accolades and awards he won, including a state prize for a setting of the Requiem Mass in 1934, indicated a promising future for the young composer. But Zeisl was struggling to obtain a permanent position and publication contracts, as his music was already banned in Germany. Fleeing Vienna on the night of November 9, 1938, he first found temporary refuge in Paris and later immigrated to the United States. An opportunity to work in the film industry as an (uncredited) composer drew him from New York to

Southern California. Zeisl was soon disillusioned by what he called "the sunny blue grave" of Hollywood.[2] He finally found a teaching position at Los Angeles City College, where he taught until his untimely death at the age of fifty-three.[3]

Zeisl's Parisian and American periods, though they in many ways hampered his development as a composer, facilitated numerous fruitful interactions with other émigré artists and intellectuals.[4] In California, Zeisl belonged to an illustrious milieu that included figures like Erich Wolfgang Korngold, Igor Stravinsky, Hanns Eisler, Mario Castelnuovo-Tedesco, Alma Mahler-Werfel, and Arnold Schoenberg, who would later become the father of Zeisl's son-in-law. Along with a lifelong friendship with the composer Darius Milhaud, the Parisian sojourn gave Zeisl the opportunity to encounter Roth's *Hiob*. As a tribute to the author who died in Paris in May 1939, members of the Reinhardt Ensemble decided to produce a staged version of Roth's novel at the Théâtre Pigalle. Zeisl was invited to contribute incidental music for the play. The performance took place in July 1939, accompanied by three short musical pieces: a prelude, a Cossack dance, and "Menuhim's Song," all of which later served as the basis for Zeisl's opera.[5] Zeisl undoubtedly felt an affinity with Roth's modern Job as well as with the author himself, much of whose background and fate he shared. He quickly obtained the rights to compose a full opera based on Roth's novel and enlisted his former Viennese friend Hans Kafka as a librettist.

---

2. See catalogue for the exhibition "Endstation Schein-Heiligenstadt: Eric Zeisls Flucht nach Hollywood/Vienna California: Eric Zeisl's Musical Exile in Hollywood," Jewish Museum of Vienna (November 2005–May 2006), curated by Michael Haas, Werner Hanak, and Karin Wagner (Wien: Jüdisches Museum, 2005).

3. There are two published biographies on Eric Zeisl: Malcolm S. Cole and Barbara Barclay, *Armseelchen: The Life and Music of Eric Zeisl* (Westport, CT: Greenwood Press, 1984); and Karin Wagner, *Fremd bin ich ausgezogen: Eric Zeisl-Biographie* (Wien: Czernin, 2005).

4. On the problems of constructing tragic historical narratives of exiles, see Michael Beckerman, "Jezek, Zeisl, Améry, and the Exile in the Middle," in *Music and Displacement: Diasporas, Mobilities, and Dislocations in Europe and Beyond*, ed. Erik Levi and Florian Scheding (Lanham, MD: Scarecrow Press, 2010).

5. The operatic rendition of *Hiob* uses different spellings of some of the characters' names, which will be preserved in this chapter.

The original plan was to complete the libretto by February 1940 and have a full score by August 1941. However, the expanding war prevented both librettist and composer from completing their work as intended. Kafka managed to finish the first act shortly after escaping to New York but abandoned the project shortly thereafter and did not return to it until 1957. The finished libretto is divided into four acts: the first two correspond to part 1 of Roth's novel and take place in Zuchnow; the third and fourth acts take place in America and match part 2 of the novel. The libretto follows Roth's work with some adjustments, such as the condensation of certain scenes to facilitate a sequence of action onstage and the omission of some secondary characters and the renaming of others.

Due to the gap between the writing of the first act and the remainder of the libretto, Zeisl was only able to complete the music for the second act in January 1959. He died the following month, leaving the opera in a condition similar to Schoenberg's *Moses und Aron*, with only two acts set to music.[6] As his biographer Malcolm Cole notes, it is unclear whether Zeisl intended to use Kafka's libretto unaltered.[7] Since there is no clear indication as to Zeisl's intention for the composition of the third and possibly fourth acts, the present deliberations concentrate only on those first two acts that Zeisl did compose. Taken as it is, Zeisl's opera has a slightly different focus from Roth's novel. It is not so much the suffering of the righteous that is at its center—many of Mendel Singer's disasters, including his great miracle, occur in the second part of the novel, consisting in Kafka's libretto of the two acts that Zeisl did not compose—but rather the question of assimilation, which already looms above the heads of Mendel's children in Zuchnow.

Roth's novel and Zeisl's opera seem to occupy a similar position within the oeuvre of their respective creators. Just as critics tend to set Roth's *Hiob* apart as a retreat into the idiosyncratic, traditional

---

6. See also Michael Beckerman, "Job, Zeisl, and the Suffering of the Ordinary," *Music & Politics* 5, no. 2 (2011).

7. On the title page of his manuscript, for example, Zeisl wrote *Hiob: Oper in drei Akten*, which indicates that he might have been planning to condense the two remaining acts into one. See further Malcolm S. Cole, "Eric Zeisl's Hiob: The Story of an Unsung Opera," *The Opera Quarterly* 9, no. 1 (1992): 52–76.

Figure 5.1. First page of act 2, scene 1 ("Kossakenchor und Tanz") from the manuscript of *Hiob*. Image credit: Courtesy of the Eric Zeisl Papers at UCLA Special Collections. Reproduced with permission of Barbara Zeisl Schoenberg.

world of East European Jewry, Zeisl appears to have discovered a "Hebraic" compositional idiom in his opera *Hiob*, which sets the work apart from the composer's earlier Viennese works.[8] Zeisl's early compositions are cast in a predominantly Austro-German style demonstrated in the approximately one hundred Lieder he composed before leaving Vienna.[9] Although Zeisl produced an impressive number of instrumental works throughout his career, including solo, chamber, and orchestral pieces, he favored dramatic, textually based music. The reported stylistic transition his work underwent pertains also to the texts he chose for his compositions. The early period includes Lieder to texts by Christian Morgenstern, Richard Dehmel, Rainer Maria Rilke, Goethe, and Nietzsche, in addition to dramatic works like the ballet *Pierrot in der Flasche* (Pierrot in the Bottle, 1929), which reworks Gustav Meyrink's short story *Der Mann auf der Flasche* (*The Man on the Bottle*, 1913), and the opera *Leonce und Lena* (1937) based on Georg Büchner's play. The interest in biblical texts that commenced with *Hiob* prevailed in later works like the *Four Songs for Wordless Chorus* (1948, subtitled "Songs for the Daughter of Jephthah") and the ballets *Naboth's Vineyard* (1953) and *Jacob and Rachel* (1954). The 1934 Catholic Requiem Mass finds its counterpart in the *Requiem Ebraico* from 1945, a setting of the Hebrew text of Psalms 92 that Zeisl composed in memory of family members murdered by the Nazis.

Responding to a radio interviewer's question about the first time Jewish music was introduced into his work, Zeisl recalled: "I believe it was in Paris when I was commissioned to set music to Joseph Roth's book on Job. The story of the persecuted Jew who escaped from Poland [sic] to America suggested in itself an outspoken Jewish music."[10] Zeisl's answer explicitly designates his opera "Jewish." Yet this confession notwithstanding, a discussion of

---

8. Cole uses the term "Hebraic" to indicate Zeisl's combination of musical materials from "Central and Eastern Europe," which are often identified as Jewish music. See Cole, "Eric Zeisl's Hiob," 61; and Cole and Barclay, *Armseelchen*, 40, 92.

9. For the most comprehensive audio catalogue of Zeisl's works, including recordings of many of his Lieder, see http://www.zeisl.com/catalogue/songs.htm.

10. Interview with Anneliese Landau on the Los Angeles radio station KFWB. Cited in Cole and Barclay, *Armseelchen*, 40.

"Jewish" or "Hebraic" music in *Hiob* must be pursued with some caution. Beyond the evident textual themes of the opera, it is difficult to identify what distinguishes Zeisl's music as unequivocally Jewish.

Jewish music scholarship emphasizes the lack of a clear consensus on what defines Jewish music. The category has historically ranged from essentialist views that any music composed by a Jew is considered Jewish music to a demand that the music exhibit formal and semantic Jewish signs (though without much clarification as to what those might be).[11] Within the broader field of Jewish studies, Jewish music has increasingly attracted scholarly attention. Yet its study always considers a broad and complex contextual framework that includes elements such as social and cultural aspects and performance practices, where the "Jewish" element is less ambiguously located.[12] In the case of Zeisl's *Hiob*, the Jewish aspect is gleaned from the broader historical circumstances of the composition as well as the subject matter of Roth's novel. But the question remains whether one can identify anything unequivocally Jewish in Zeisl's composition.[13]

In *Hiob* and the works that followed it, Zeisl began to incorporate modal harmonies and themes with increasing frequency. The modes appearing most commonly in his work, the Dorian, Phrygian, and minor with augmented second, are found in a number of Eastern European Jewish musical practices, but these practices never developed independently and were in fact the product of an interaction with the music of coterritorial, non-Jewish milieux.[14] Moreover, as

---

11. See for example Max Brod, *Die Musik Israels* (Kassel: Bärenreiter Verlag, 1976), as well as Hanoch Avenary, "Jüdische Musik," in *Die Musik in Geschichte und Gegenwart. Allgemeine Enzyklopädie der Musik*, vol. 4, no. 2, ed. Ludwig Finscher (Kassel-Stuttgart-Weimar: Bärenreiter-Metzler, 1996): 1511–69.

12. See Edwin Seroussi, "Music: The Jew of Jewish Studies," *Jewish Studies* 46 (2009): 3–84.

13. For a broader discussion of the problem of Jewish music in Zeisl's work, see Karin Wagner, ed., *Es grüsst Dich Erichisrael: Briefe von und an Eric Zeisl* (Wien: Czernin Verlag, 2008), 55–58.

14. See Seroussi, "Music," 34. Direct quotations of biblical cantillation, inspired by the research of one of Zeisl's colleagues, Solomon Rosowsky, are found in Zeisl's cello sonata (1951), dedicated to Gregor Piatigorsky, but those are otherwise

Cole remarks, treating the opera *Hiob* as a clear transition point from a purportedly stable "Austro-German" style to a "Hebraic" one overlooks the numerous "Slavic" or "Hebraic" musical allusions that appeared in Zeisl's earlier Viennese works, as well as the fact that the composer continued to work in a general Austro-German musical idiom even in his later "Hebraic" period.[15]

More productive than the search for concrete elements of "Jewish music" in *Hiob* is an examination of Zeisl's seemingly conservative approach to composition. It is not only the so-called discovery of Jewish themes that Zeisl's opera and Roth's novel have in common; both composer and author also share an ostensible adherence to traditional aesthetic forms, which sets their work apart from that of their more avant-garde contemporaries. Roth's referencing of archaic forms like the *Legende* complemented the general nostalgia for the monarchic period that characterized his later works. Zeisl's adherence to traditional tonal forms likewise separates him from the musical vanguard—the atonal innovations of the Second Viennese School—and particularly the work of his relative, Arnold Schoenberg. Instead of developing new methods for composition, Zeisl reaches back to the nineteenth century and beyond to locate the formal principles of his music.

The heavy use of reminiscence motifs in *Hiob* and subsequent dramatic works evoke the Wagnerian leitmotif practice in a way that leads Cole to refer to *Hiob* as a "Hebraic music drama."[16] Next to such neo-Romantic allusions, Zeisl regularly employs baroque formal procedures in his composition. The passacaglia, ritornello, and fugue, musical forms prevalent in the seventeenth and eighteenth centuries, allow him to sustain longer pieces like the ballet *Naboth's Vineyard* and the *Sonata Barocca* for piano (1949), whose last movement consists of an elaborate prelude and fugue.[17] Additionally, the frequent use of parallel open fifths creates archaistic moments in his works by

---

rare. See also Solomon Rosowsky, *The Cantillation of the Bible* (New York: Reconstructionist Press, 1957).

15. Cole and Barclay, *Armseelchen*, 94.

16. Cole, "Eric Zeisl's Hiob," 61. The casting of Mendel Singer as a Heldentenor in Zeisl's score is another Wagnerian reference.

17. See further Cole and Barclay, *Armseelchen*, 162, 205.

evoking the sound of early Western polyphony.[18] This combination of various compositional forms, all referencing different periods in the history of Western music, distinguishes Zeisl's eclectic style.

Compared to the "number structure" of Zeisl's earlier dramatic works, the multisectional arrangement of *Hiob* seems to flow more smoothly. Each act is divided into a series of musical-poetic complexes that join to create a clear dramatic arc. However, a look at the overture alone is enough to reveal a compositional eclecticism that rules out any organic unity. The opening measures of the overture introduce the opera's two main themes or leitmotifs. The first is a heroic one in D minor, which appears throughout the opera in relation to salvation and miracles (mm. 1–5 in figure 5.2). The second, more chromatic one is associated with suffering (mm. 6–7 in figure 5.2). Onto the diatonic arpeggios that open the first theme Zeisl grafts a pronounced ending in the form of a descending augmented second (C♯ to B♭ in m. 3), which contrasts with the diatonic movement that preceded it. The hybrid nature of the first theme announces the general tone of the opera, which pastes together various musical idioms as a kind of musical chimera.

Following an exposition of the two themes, the overture continues with a fugue that expands and develops the second theme, bringing it to a climactic conclusion. The fugal elaboration of the chromatic second theme results in a strident, dissonant contrapuntal texture that dictates the nature of additional fugal sections later in the opera. Contrapuntal techniques such as the canon or the fugue are dominant in Zeisl's opera. Some of them, like the children's fugue opening the first act, are composed in a neoclassical polyphonic style while others, like the canon sung by Mendel and Deborah in the fourth complex of the first act, apply Western contrapuntal techniques to a melismatic cantillation theme.

The stylistic variety in *Hiob* also includes modal allusions to Slavic and Eastern European musical practices, as one can find in

---

18. Parallel or consecutive fifths are progressions in which an interval of a perfect fifth follows another perfect fifth between the same musical parts. Though common in early polyphony and preserved in some folk musical practices, parallel fifths were forbidden in species counterpoint instructions because they did not support the independence of individual parts.

Figure 5.2. Zeisl, *Hiob*, Overture, piano and violin reduction (mm. 1–7).

the Cossack dance that opens the second act. The Cossack dance, whose first measures recur throughout the opera and serve as another reminiscence motif, operates as a double reference. It points at once to Slavic and Eastern European folk musical practices as well as to the nineteenth-century tradition of quoting such practices as part of a general nationalist trend in Western art music (see figure 5.3).[19]

This diversity demonstrates Zeisl's ability to assimilate a wide range of compositional procedures. His opera, however, does not favor any one style over another. It references Eastern European, Slavic, and Jewish-liturgical musical practices alongside traditional Austro-German or Western classical musical forms without committing

---

19. See further Timothy J. Cooley, "Folk Music in Eastern Europe," in *The Cambridge History of World Music*, ed. Philip Bohlman (Cambridge: Cambridge University Press, 2013), 352–70.

Figure 5.3. Zeisl, *Hiob*, act 2, scene 1, "Cossack Chorus and Dance" (piano reduction).

to any one of them in particular. In this equality between musical references lies the progressive nature of Zeisl's music. Although Zeisl's adherence to tonal music seems outdated, his opera—much like Roth's novel—is only outwardly conservative. Without needing to resort to any of the innovations of new music, Zeisl's work manages to be progressive simply in the way it references "old music."

The versatility of his musical language mediates the appearance of each practice he references. By refusing to emphasize one practice over others, Zeisl's musical eclecticism renders the appearance of each reference a moment of quotation: a musical utterance that is simultaneously endorsed and kept at a distance. The quotational style of the opera *Hiob* dictates the fragmentary nature of the work much more than the fact of its incomplete composition. Comprised of discrete moments of quotation, the opera assumes the manner of a musical patchwork or a montage of sorts. It thereby approximates the literary source of its libretto even more. Like the additive structure of Roth's novel, a nonorganic assembly of divine punishments and miracles, Zeisl's opera patches together an array of musical practices whose diversity testifies to the absence of organic integration.

The absence of organic integration in Zeisl's music provides another important perspective on the condition of being superfluous and its implications for unsettling and emancipating the notion of Jewish difference. Zeisl's opera does this by calling on us to explore the role of difference in the case of assimilated Jews. Assimilation, as the opera *Hiob* helps us to recognize, is itself a superfluous condition that exceeds rather than confirms integration. By understanding the inorganic assembly of various musical practices in *Hiob* as moments of quotation, the opera's formal and compositional facets connect to its thematic focus on assimilation. The distance created by the appearance of each moment of musical quotation in *Hiob* foregrounds the recognition that every compositional practice employed in the opera is in fact acquired, or rather, assimilated, as there is no single "authentic" mode of musical expression. Yet musical quotation in *Hiob* not only invites a theoretical deliberation on the link between quotation and assimilation, it also instructs us on the relevance of such a theoretical consideration of assimilation for modernist aesthetics.

Assimilation and the Exception

The fraught term "assimilation" engenders numerous interpretations today, and its earlier iterations have been equally ambiguous. The diverse language used to designate the integration of German-speaking Jews in the eighteenth and nineteenth centuries included words such as *Annäherung* (approximation), *Anpassung* (adaptation), and *Amalgamierung* (amalgamation).[20] This terminological plurality did not add clarity to the nature of what was denoted, and opinions were divided over the kind of Jewish difference such an integration was expected to retain. Some scholars note a tension between certain liberal, non-Jewish figures and other, Jewish proponents of assimilation. While the first group understood assimilation

---

20. See David Sorkin, "Emancipation and Assimilation: Two Concepts and Their Application to German-Jewish History," *Leo Baeck Institute Yearbook* 35, no. 1 (1990): 17–33, 19.

to mean the ultimate disappearance of Judaism through conversion, the second linked assimilation with additional terms like *Veredelung* (refinement), *Verbesserung* (amelioration), and above all *Bildung*.[21] Thereby, this group hoped to achieve a certain balance between a *Deutschtum* that would grant it social and political equality and a *Judentum* that would allow it to preserve the distinct collective identity of a subculture.[22] Despite the tension between them, both approaches theorized assimilation as a tension between two opposing poles: *Deutschtum* on the one side and *Judentum* on the other. The closer one got to a complete disappearance of distinct Jewish attributes, the more "German" one became.

Growing awareness of the inadequacy of such understandings of the term assimilation underpinned the scholarly wish to supplement or replace it altogether.[23] As Scott Spector observes, the model of assimilation as a movement along a linear spectrum from "total German identification" to "total Jewish identification" was as deficient as it was restrictive.[24] Alternatives to this model include regarding assimilation in dialectical terms, a perspective guided by the sense that one cannot easily distinguish between spontaneous and acquired cultural components.[25] Diversity among the Jewish population became pertinent as well as the internal relations between *West-* and *Ostjuden* and their role in depicting the complex intertwinement of assimilation and dissimilation.[26] Self-assertion and active participation in

---

21. Part of the discussion on the incompletion of Jewish assimilation addresses the fact that assimilation has from the beginning been restricted to a specific class, the bourgeoisie. See Jacob Katz, "German Culture and the Jews," in *The Jewish Responses to German Culture: From the Enlightenment to the Second World War*, ed. Jehuda Reinharz and Walter Schatzberg (Hanover, NH: University Press of New England, 1985), 85–99.

22. David Sorkin, *The Transformation of German Jewry 1780–1840* (New York: Oxford University Press, 1987).

23. See, for example, Sorkin, "Emancipation and Assimilation," 30.

24. See Spector, *Modernism without Jews? German-Jewish Subjects and Histories*; Scott Spector, "Forget Assimilation: Introducing Subjectivity to German-Jewish history," *Jewish History* 20, no. 3 (2006): 349–36.

25. See, for example, Amos Funkenstein, "The Dialectics of Assimilation," *Jewish Social Studies* 1, no. 2 (1995): 1–14.

26. See Shulamit Volkov, "The Dynamics of Dissimilation: *Ostjuden* and German Jews," in *The Jewish Response to German Culture*. The term "dissimilation"

the "dominant" culture began to occupy a central position in the study of assimilation alongside an acknowledgment that the term had consequences reaching far beyond the cultural sphere, into politics, economics, religion, and affect.[27]

Although the term was thoroughly complicated in the course of such debates, a delicate interaction between what Shulamit Volkov called *Verschmelzung* and *Eigenart*, integration and exceptionality, remained a constant principle guiding discussions on assimilation through numerous transformations.[28] This interaction kept Jewish *Eigenart*, Jewish exceptionality or difference, irrevocably tied to an integrative concept. More specifically, within the bounds of such an approach to assimilation, the exception—*Eigenart*, or difference—stood in direct opposition to *Verschmelzung*, the dissolution of difference. Admittedly, the notion of the Jew as an exception was crucial in the historical circumstances that contributed to the process of assimilation in Western and Central Europe. Yet a careful look at those same circumstances reveals that exceptionality operated there in a manner far from unequivocal. To demonstrate this, we should turn again to the gradual involvement of Jewish people in the European project of the modern state.

Zygmunt Bauman's *Modernity and Ambivalence* is unambiguously clear about the homogenizing stakes of the modern state and its specific implication for the German Jewish emancipation project.[29] As Bauman stresses, the demand for assimilation that was placed on German-speaking Jews was inseparable from the requirement that the

---

was coined by Franz Rosenzweig in a diary entry from April 3, 1922. See Franz Rosenzweig, *Der Mensch und sein Werk: Gesammelte Schriften I, Briefe und Tagebücher*, vol. 2, *1918–1929*, ed. Rachel Rosenzweig and Edith Rosenzweig-Scheinmann (The Hague: Martinus Nijhoff, 1979), 770. See also Jonathan Skolnik, *Jewish Pasts, German Fictions: History, Memory, and Minority Culture in Germany, 1824–1955* (Stanford, CA: Stanford University Press, 2014), 7–9.

27. See, for example, Sabine Sander, "Between Acculturation and Self-Assertion: Individualization in the German-Jewish Context of the German Empire and the Weimar Republic and Its Contribution to the Development of Modern Sociology," *Religion* 45, no. 3 (2015): 429–50; and Katja Garloff, *Mixed Feelings: Tropes of Love in German-Jewish Culture* (Ithaca, NY: Cornell University Press, 2016).

28. Volkov, "The Dynamics of Dissimilation," 196.

29. See Bauman, *Modernity and Ambivalence*, 85, 102.

state ensure equality and uniformity among its subjects. The modern state's intolerance of exceptions is itself the subject of Bauman's critique, which considers the Enlightenment's demand to subsume and ultimately eliminate Jewish collective exceptionality as leading directly to the later physical destruction of European Jews. Volkov, who weighs Bauman's critique of modernity's drive toward homogeneity against Arendt's remarks on the same topic of Jewish assimilation and the European nation-state, notes that in contrast to Bauman, Arendt's critique focused on Jewish refusal to assimilate rather than on the universalist principle of the modern state.[30]

While Arendt does indeed consider Jewish reluctance to relinquish collective exceptionality, her critique offers a far more nuanced understanding of the status of Jewish exceptionality than Volkov's comparison suggests. Arendt's analysis reveals a paradoxical notion of the exception shaped by the problematic role that privilege played in this developing relation between Jews and the state.[31] In *The Origins of Totalitarianism*, Arendt shows how the state, as the new body politic succeeding the feudal order in the late eighteenth century, could never truly rid itself of the need to bestow privileges, despite—or, better yet, precisely because of—its promise of equality. If the state were to be truly impartial, it could not officially associate itself with any one of the classes that still comprised its population. This impartiality worked to its detriment since, in order to establish itself as an independent entity, the state nevertheless required credit, which it could not expect to obtain from the bourgeoisie, the rising property-owning class. "It was only natural," Arendt remarks, "that the Jews, with their age-old experience as moneylenders and their connections with European nobility . . . would be called on to help."[32] Wishing to remain impartial, the

---

30. Shulamit Volkov, *Germans, Jews, and Antisemites: Trials in Emancipation* (Cambridge: Cambridge University Press, 2006), 166.

31. Steven Aschheim defended Arendt for not being interested in the ordinary writing of history and emphasized that her aim was rather "to present events as mere surface phenomena, reflecting deeper subterranean currents of meaning." See Aschheim, "Arendt and the Discourse of Evil," 119. A similar view guides the present analysis of the exception.

32. Arendt, *The Origins of Totalitarianism*, 11.

state could not allow the group upon which it relied financially to fully assimilate into the rest of its class-based population. It therefore resorted to giving special privileges to individual Jews who supported it. As Arendt explains:

> Emancipation of the Jews ... as granted by the national state system in Europe during the nineteenth century, had a double origin and an ever-present equivocal meaning. On the one hand, it was due to the political and legal structure of a new body politic which could function only under the conditions of political and legal equality.... On the other hand, it was the clear result of a gradual extension of specific Jewish privileges, granted originally only to individuals, then through them to a small group of well-to-do Jews.... Thus, at the same time and in the same countries, emancipation meant equality *and* privileges, the destruction of the old Jewish community autonomy *and* the conscious preservation of the Jews as a separate group in society, the abolition of special restrictions and special rights, *and* the extension of such rights to a growing group of individuals.[33]

The state's desire to prevent the full assimilation of all Jews within society was backed by a growing Jewish understanding of emancipation not as an extension of equal rights to all but of special liberties offered to individual exceptions. Jews who secured such liberties in return for services rendered, Arendt writes, were naturally aware of the conditions that facilitated their intimate relation to the state and therefore reluctant to accept these privileges as rights deserved by all Jews. Many of Arendt's critics were provoked by what they saw as a lack of sympathy for Jews in her analyses.[34] However, Arendt's comments on Jewish reluctance to regard their exceptional status as a right deserved by all are important, for they reveal that equality for Jews was originally facilitated by the creation of privileged exceptions.

---

33. Arendt, *The Origins of Totalitarianism*, 12.
34. Comments range from Gershom Scholem's famous remark on Arendt's lack of *Ahavat Israel* (love of fellow Jews) through the controversy following the publication of *Eichmann in Jerusalem*, to more recent critiques claiming that Arendt relied primarily on antisemitic sources in her analysis in the *Origins of Totalitarianism*. See Peter Staudenmaier, "Hannah Arendt's Analysis of Antisemitism in the *Origins of Totalitarianism*: A Critical Appraisal," *Patterns of Prejudice* 46, no. 2 (2012): 154–79, 157–64.

This complicates the condition of exception in the case of Jewish emancipation, as it no longer positions exceptions and equality or uniformity as opposites. From Arendt's remarks, we also learn that the position of Jews as exceptions was acknowledged by non-Jews and Jews alike.

While the state's emancipation project nevertheless managed to maintain at least a semblance of political and legal equality, it made the societal inequality that dictated the nature of Jewish assimilation even more obvious. According to Arendt, what appeared as the mere by-product of the state's need for credit—the creation of "exceptional Jews" who were handpicked to be equal—was later bluntly declared as the essential condition for assimilation into society: "Society, confronted with political, economic, and legal equality for Jews, made it quite clear that none of its classes was prepared to grant them social equality, and that only exceptions from the Jewish people would be received. Jews who heard the strange compliment that they were exceptions, exceptional Jews, knew quite well that it was this very ambiguity—that they were Jews and yet presumably not *like* Jews—which opened the doors of society to them. If they desired this kind of intercourse, they tried, therefore, 'to be and yet not to be Jews.'"[35] Society demanded that the Jews it accepted be "cultivated," where cultivation or *Bildung* meant conforming to a non-Jewish societal standard while distinguishing oneself from "other Jews." But mere cultivation was not enough. Jews had to be *exceptionally* cultivated since their acceptance depended not on their indistinguishability from other educated non-Jews but rather on their being distinctively foreign. According to Arendt, this paradoxical conception issued from the Enlightenment's assumption of an essential difference between peoples, which was required as proof that all people are indeed human beings despite their difference. As she writes, "In the eighteenth century, this had its source in the new humanism which expressly wanted 'new specimens of humanity' (Herder), intercourse with whom would serve as an example of possible intimacy with all types of mankind. To the enlightened Berlin of Mendelssohn's time, the Jews served as living

---

35. Arendt, *The Origins of Totalitarianism*, 56.

proof that all men are human."³⁶ Thus, to gain social equality by means of admittance into cultured European society, Jews had to fashion themselves as "exceptional specimens of humanity."³⁷

Those "exceptional specimens," who first gained their alleged indistinguishable (i.e., "equal") status through financial means, were later replaced by the "culturally exceptional" Jews. Interestingly, Arendt chose the vibrant cultural atmosphere of prewar Vienna depicted in Stefan Zweig's *Die Welt von Gestern* (*The World of Yesterday*, 1941) as the basis for her critical inquiry into the place of the "genius" Jew within Austro-German culture. The cultural ideals of Jewish youth in Zweig's book captured the ambiguity of Jewish exceptionality. The goal was to become an exceptional genius, to be sure, but one who is nonetheless *just like* other geniuses: "Every Jewish youth able to rhyme passably played the young Goethe, as everyone able to draw a line was a future Rembrandt and every musical lad an irresistible Beethoven. The more cultured the parental homes of these *Wunderkinder*, the more coddled along were the imitations."³⁸ The uniqueness of these exceptions was complicated by a desire for indistinguishability and compromised by the charge of imitation.

Arendt's use of the word "imitation" is important since it captures the well-known accusation of the assimilated Jew as imitator made most notoriously in Richard Wagner's "Judaism in Music." Wagner identified Jewish assimilation as a form of repetition. The assimilated Jew, he wrote, "can only after-speak [*nachsprechen*] and after-create [*nachkünsteln*]."³⁹ What Wagner found most threatening about assimilated Jews was their ultimate indistinguishability from other Germans. It was exactly because *der gebildete Jude* (the cultivated Jew) could not be easily identified that Wagner felt compelled to argue that this form of repetition was a lesser one, *superfluous* in the most limited sense, namely as a redundancy.

---

36. Arendt, *The Origins of Totalitarianism*, 57.
37. Arendt, *The Origins of Totalitarianism*, 58.
38. Hannah Arendt, "Portrait of a Period: A Review of *The World of Yesterday: An Autobiography* by Stefan Zweig," in *The Jew as Pariah*, 116.
39. Richard Wagner, *Das Judentum in der Musik* (Leipzig: Verlagsbuchhandlung von J. J. Weber, 1869).

Arendt's observations, however, provide an interesting retort to Wagner. She by no means rejects the view of assimilation as a form of repetition. But she intertwines this repetition with a far more complex understanding of superfluousness and difference. Through her comments on the ambiguous status of the exception associated with the process of Jewish emancipation and assimilation, Arendt unsettles the oppositional relation between equality (uniformity, identity, etc.) and the exception (difference). For assimilated Jews, the exception was not the opposite of being equal but rather its prerequisite. This meant that the repetition involved in the act of Jewish assimilation—what one had to assume or do in order to be indistinguishable—was the same thing that rendered one different. If Wagner's repetition-as-identity brought him to insist on repetition's inferior status—superfluousness as redundancy—Arendt's repetition-as-difference helps us conceptualize another form of superfluousness, one that is emancipated from a simple relation to identity and thereby offers an invaluable critical potential.

Assimilation and Zeisl's *Hiob*

Zeisl's opera similarly calls on us to reflect on assimilation and its entanglement with an ambiguous notion of the exception. The opera complements Roth's notion of the exceptional, unassimilated *Ostjude* with the exceptional position of the assimilated Jew. The first act contrasts Mendel's dogged, Jewish piousness with the assimilatory desires of his children: Jonas is eager to join the czar's army, Schemariah wishes to become a worldly capitalist, and Mirjam, dreams of becoming a Cossack's bride:

> JONAS UND SCHEMARIAH: (tonlos) Wir sind genommen!
> MENDEL: (traurig) Das Unglück lässt nicht ab, von meinem Haus!
> JONAS: (fröhlich unvermittelt) Wenn der Tag kommt zur Erde
>   Der Kosak steigt zu Pferde
>   Und er jagt fort mit andern
>   Liebste Magd, lass ihn wandern.

...

SCHEMARIAH: Ich will nicht Soldat werden, ich möchte ein Kaufmann werden und die Welt sehn.
JONAS: Als Soldat siehst du genug von der Welt, besonders wenn Krieg ist! ...
MIRJAM: Ihr werdet prächtige Uniformen tragen wie Pavel und Feodor. Zu ihnen werdet ihr gehören und keine fremden Juden mehr sein.
MENDEL: Schweig! Schweig!
MIRJAM: (verzückt) Immer hab ich die Soldaten geliebt. Ich war noch klein an einem schönen Tag im Sommer, da blinkten tausend Kerzen in der russischen Kirche. Und vorm Eingang zum Altar standen reglos zwei Reihen herrlicher Kosaken. Ein Offizier feiert Hochzeit, die Orgel braust und ich träumte ich wäre die Braut.... Oh wie schön ist das Leben, fern dieser engen Gasse![40]

[JONAS AND SCHEMARIAH: (toneless) we were conscripted!
MENDEL: (sorrowful) Misfortune will not leave my house!
JONAS: (suddenly cheerful) When the day runs its course
　The Cossack mounts his horse
　And he chases off with others
　Dearest maid, see how he wanders.

...

SCHEMARIAH: I don't wish to be a soldier, I would like to become a merchant and see the world.
JONAS: As a soldier you would see enough of the world, especially when there is war! ...
MIRJAM: You will wear splendid uniforms like Pavel and Feodor. You will belong to them and will no longer be foreign Jews.
MENDEL: Silence! Silence!
MIRJAM: (ecstatic) I have always loved the soldiers. I was still young, on a beautiful summer day, when a thousand candles twinkled in the Russian church. And at the entryway to the altar stood motionless two rows of magnificent Cossacks. An officer celebrated a wedding, the organ blared, and I dreamed I was the bride.... Oh, how beautiful is life far from this narrow alley!]

---

40. Hans Kafka, *Hiob Textbuch*, act 1, complex 5, 4. Electronic copy of typescript courtesy of Barbara Zeisl Schoenberg. Reproduced with permission.

Mendel's three adult children represent different assimilatory strategies: conversion, acculturation, and intermarriage. But the full nature of assimilation is embodied by none other than the youngest son Menuhim. In Roth's novel, the resurfaced Menuhim embodies at once both identity and difference, or rather, identity as difference. He is both the transformed, cultivated musician performing around the world and the one who suggests to his father the possibility (however fantastical) of returning to Zuchnow and the life that the Singer family left behind. Even the new name that Menuhim selects for himself, Alexis Kossak, is ambiguous. Is Kossak a reference to his mother's maiden name, as Mendel speculates, or to the gentile "other," the Cossack?

Menuhim's destiny to become a musical genius reminds us that music has often been portrayed as an ideal path to assimilation.[41] At least ostensibly, its repute as an abstract universal language allowed it to bypass a linguistic specificity that would otherwise situate one irrevocably in a distinct region or heritage. This is why Menuhim does not speak; *er musiziert* (he makes music). In the opera this is made clear by the fact that Menuhim does not have a textual part, only a recurring musical theme entitled "Menuhims Lied." He could therefore be both Kossak and Cossack, but his existence will always remain miraculously exceptional, superfluous to the oppositional pairing of difference and identity. In *Juden auf Wanderschaft*, Roth recalled a conversation he once had with an Eastern European Jewish musician in Paris who perhaps served as a model for the character of Menuhim. For this musician as for his literary counterpart, none of the many doors that music had opened led to an escape from being superfluous:

> In France I was talking to a Jewish artiste from the old Russian Austrian border town of Radziwillow. He was a musical clown, and he was very successful. He was a clown by conviction, rather than by birth. He came

---

41. See Leon Botstein, "Introduction: Tragedy and Irony of Success: Locating Jews in the Musical Life of Vienna" and "Social History and the Politics of the Aesthetic: Jews and Music in Vienna 1870–1938," in *Vienna: Jews and the City of Music 1870–1938*, ed. Leon Botstein and Werner Hanak (Annandale, NY: Yeshiva University Museum and Bard College, 2004), 13–24, 43–64.

from a family of musicians. His great-grandfather, grandfather, father, and brothers had all been Jewish wedding musicians. He was the only one who had been able to go and study in the West. . . . He was accepted at a conservatory in Vienna. He began to compose his own music. He gave concerts. "But," he said, "what business has a Jew got to be making serious music for the public? I've always been a clown in this world, even if they give lectures on me and a bespectacled newspaper critic sits in the front row. Should I play Beethoven? Should I play *Kol Nidre*? . . . That evening it dawned on me that there was nothing else open to me except joining a circus. . . . I play the concertina and the harmonica and the saxophone and it pleases me that people don't know I can play Beethoven."[42]

Arendt has often stated that, in actuality, there was no great difference between what she called the Jewish pariah and parvenu. Whether one consciously decided to occupy a position outside society or otherwise endeavored to gain social acceptance, one remained superfluous, an exception.[43] Elected foreignness and the careful acquisition of the cultural and societal parlance resulted in a similar condition.

Arendt found a perfect example of a union between these two aspects in another assimilated "clown," Heinrich Heine, who "boldly introduced Yiddish expressions into the German language" and would not shy away from transforming Schiller's verse into an ode to Jewish cuisine.[44] For Arendt, Heine's ability to reproduce the German cultural vernacular without denying his difference made him "the only outstanding example of a really happy assimilation in the entire history of that process."[45] She described this reproduction as "holding up a mirror," a repetition from a position of aloofness that accounted for the "divine laughter" in his verses.[46]

---

42. Roth, *The Wandering Jews*, 86.
43. For Arendt, the problem has always been that both pariah and parvenu occupied a position outside politics. The ideal solution in her view was embodied in figures like Bernard Lazare, who attempted to politicize the pariah. See Arendt, "The Jew as Pariah" and "Herzl and Lazare," in *The Jew as Pariah*.
44. Arendt, *The Jew as Pariah*, 74. See Heine's poem *Prinzessin Sabbat*: "Schalet, schöner Götterfunken, Tochter aus Elysium! Also klänge Schillers Hochlied, Hätt' er Schalet je gekostet."
45. Arendt, *The Jew as Pariah*, 74.
46. Arendt, *The Jew as Pariah*, 72.

Heine's ability to reproduce the vernacular from a position of distance also appealed to Adorno, who was interested in the critical potential that such an act entailed.[47] Like Arendt, Adorno's view of Heine reframed the Wagnerian accusation of the imitating Jew. Rather than as evidence of the absence of an authentic mode of expression, he similarly saw in Heine's quotational gesture a kind of mirror-holding: Heine's repetition confronted society with the decline of its own procedures by reflecting those procedures back to it with a minor slant. Critical reflection necessitates difference. "Only he who is truly not in it has command over language as over an instrument,"[48] Adorno wrote of Heine, indicating that the poet's distance from a tradition he could nevertheless faithfully quote fortified his critical stance toward it.

Adorno and Arendt's reflections on Heine modify the discussion of the cultural product of the assimilated Jew, shifting the focus away from a Jewish mimesis to the critical and revolutionary possibilities that are embedded in the gesture of quotation. By doing so, the two critics neutralize the question of authorship and originality. In his short essay on Heine, Adorno did not fail to mention "the well-known anecdote according to which the youthful Heine, when asked by the elderly Goethe what he was working on, replied 'A Faust' and was thereupon ungraciously dismissed."[49] It was clear to Adorno that a "repetition" of Goethe's *Faust* implied a form of difference that could be unsettling to those who placed their stock in ideals like originality and organicism. The work of the assimilated genius confirmed that both originality and organicism assumed a troublesome significance.[50]

---

47. Theodor W. Adorno, "Heine the Wound," in *Notes to Literature*.
48. Adorno, "Heine the Wound," 82. Translation altered.
49. Adorno, "Heine the Wound," 83.
50. Assimilation's repetition merely reformulates Kant's concept of "exemplary originality," which reconciles the two contradicting demands of the genius: first that their work be unique and second that it would serve as a model for imitation by other geniuses. Immanuel Kant, *Critique of Judgement*, trans. Werner S. Pluhar (Indianapolis, IN: Hackett, 1987), 186; see also Martin Gammon, "Exemplary Originality: Kant on Genius and Imitation," *Journal of the History of Philosophy* 35, no. 4 (1997): 563–92.

Quotation, Repetition, and Difference: Gustav Mahler as a Case Study

Heine's case begins to clarify the position of Zeisl, the composer who likewise integrated "foreign" elements into a Western musical tradition he was fluent in. But to comprehend the progressive nature of Zeisl's relation to the tradition of Western art music—namely, his choice to quote outdated tonal and formal practices at a time when they had already been sidelined for newer procedures such as atonality and serialism—one should look beyond Heine to Mahler as a model. It was in his book on Mahler that Adorno elaborated on the relation between critique, quotation, and difference, which he only outlined in his earlier essay on Heine.[51]

Two things caught Adorno's attention in the music of the post-Romantic Viennese composer: the unusual adherence to a diatonic major and minor tonality when the harmonic developments of Wagner's chromaticism had already rendered it obsolete, and the frequent referencing of German literary and musical folklore. Quotation in Mahler's case, then, as it would later be in Zeisl's, meant both the seemingly conservative reproduction of so-called outdated musical practices as well as the espousal of and uncanny command over the German cultural vernacular. The more flawless the command, Adorno observed, the clearer it allowed the speaker's difference to emerge: "That Mahler was both a part of musical culture as a master saturated with its language, and yet separate from it, produces the specific atmosphere of his language. It is at once colloquial and that of a stranger. Its strangeness is heightened by the overfamiliar element, absent from compositions so deeply at one with their language that it changes dialectically with them. In Mahler the laconic and the concrete form a constellation recalling the German of Heine."[52]

---

51. Theodor W. Adorno, *Mahler: A Musical Physiognomy*, trans. Edmund Jephcott (Chicago: University of Chicago Press, 1996). Adorno makes the initial comparison between Heine and Mahler in "Heine the Wound."

52. Adorno, *Mahler*, 31.

Heine's introduction of journalistic colloquialism into the poetic, which incited the wrath of conservatives and avant-garde modernists alike, found its musical counterpart in Mahler's relation to the vulgar.[53] Mahler's symphonies and song cycles, as Adorno noted, "shamelessly flaunt what rang in all ears, scraps of melody from great music, shallow popular songs, street ballads, hits."[54] The vulgar in Mahler's music was a quoted *Bodenständigkeit* (rootedness), an adoption of autochthonous elements that went beyond a simple incorporation of the popular into "high art." In the same vein was Mahler's choice to set music to texts like the folk poems from Arnim and Brentano's collection *Des Knaben Wunderhorn*.[55]

Rendering the autochthonous foreign was possible to a great degree thanks to the way in which Mahler constructed his quotes. In a memorial essay on the composer from 1912, Schoenberg recalled "a well-known writer on music" who designated Mahler's works "gigantic symphonic potpourris." Characteristic of Mahler's potpourri, Schoenberg explained further, was "the unpretentiousness of the formal connectives. The individual sections are simply juxtaposed, without always being connected, and without their relationships (which may also be entirely absent) being more than mere accidents in the form."[56] Mahler's quotational style had its own formal principle. Adorno would later see a revolutionary potential in this rough assembly of themes and the dismissal of "trivialized connecting material."[57] But even before Adorno, Schoenberg had grasped the straining effect that this formal principle had on the symphony, the quintessential Austro-German musical genre. The accidental structure of Mahler's symphonies, Schoenberg wrote, "is contradicted by the term 'symphonic,' which means the opposite. It means that the

---

53. Adorno briefly mentions the opposition to Heine's work by Friedrich Gundolf, a member of the George circle, as well as by Karl Kraus. See further Ulrich Plass, *Language and History in Theodor W. Adorno's Notes to Literature* (New York: Routledge, 2007), 115–52.
54. Adorno, *Mahler*, 35.
55. See also Carl Niekerk, *Reading Mahler: German Culture and Jewish Identity in Fin-de-Siècle Vienna* (Rochester, NY: Camden House, 2010).
56. Schoenberg, *Style and Idea*, 462.
57. Adorno, *Mahler*, 35.

individual sections are organic components of a living being, born of a creative impulse and conceived as a whole."[58]

Schoenberg exposed the formal paradox that was implied by the originally dismissive description of Mahler's music as "symphonic potpourri." Whereas the symphonic principle assumed the integration of all its individual components within an organic whole, the potpourri meant the opposite. In Mahler's music, however, the two existed side by side. His quotational style defied organic cohesion by forgoing transitions, yet it refused to give up the symphony altogether. On the contrary, Mahler turned the symphony into his primary musical genre only to subvert its integrative principle with the nonorganic construction of his quotations. This, in Adorno's eyes, defined the progressive nature of Mahler's work, which otherwise did "not reside in tangible innovation and advanced material."[59] Mahler's individual quotations allowed him to reference the entire formal tradition of Western tonal music as if in quotation marks. Adorno's observation that "Mahler's emancipation from sonata form was mediated by sonata" brought home the capacity of quotations to expose decay and distance "because everything is composed within quotation marks—because the music says: Once upon a time there was a sonata."[60]

Mahler's relation to tradition was that of overexertion through quotation. The distance that was generated by his quotational gesture pulled Mahler's quoted materials out of their original setting, rendering them artificial. This denaturalization of music was a deliberate strategy, something made evident by the composer's own remarks on the forced production of beautiful sound. "If I want to produce a soft, subdued sound," Mahler admitted once, "I don't give it to an instrument which produces it easily, but rather to one which can get it only with effort and under pressure—often only by forcing itself and exceeding its natural range."[61] Sonic overexertion accompanied what Adorno called an "overstretching" of tonality. Along with Mahler's position as a "foreigner [who] speaks music

---

58. Adorno, *Mahler*, 35.
59. Adorno, *Mahler*, 19.
60. Adorno, *Mahler*, 96.
61. Natalie Bauer-Lechner, *Recollections of Gustav Mahler*, trans. Dika Newlin (Cambridge: Cambridge University Press, 1980), 160.

fluently but as if with an accent,"[62] it was this that rendered his insistence on the tonal and diatonic modernist, bringing Adorno to conclude that "the hatred of Mahler, with antisemitic overtones, was not different from that of the new music."[63]

Mahler was progressive in the same manner that Zeisl would later be. Instead of new material, Mahler's modernism introduced a new relation to the old. This referencing of fragments from tradition ties his work with the avant-garde practice of montage that gained popularity primarily in the visual arts a few years later and intrigued critics like Adorno and Walter Benjamin.[64] In both Mahler's and Zeisl's cases, quotation as the reassigning of meaning and recontextualization of unaltered pieces from the past plays a key role.[65]

One way to consider Mahler's use of quotations and the unsettling effect it had on organic aesthetic models like the symphony is through the comparison that Peter Bürger draws between the quoting montage artist and Benjamin's notion of the allegorist.[66] Acknowledging that Benjamin developed the aesthetic category of the allegory while working on the literature of the Baroque, Bürger nevertheless argues that it was Benjamin's exposure to avant-garde works that facilitated these theoretical observations and their application to Baroque works.[67] Benjamin's interest in the practice of quotation was indeed extensive. It encompassed not only his *Arcades Project*, a monumental work of quotations, but also his *Trauerspiel* book whose composition, as Benjamin proudly remarked, "consists largely of quotation—the craziest mosaic technique imaginable."[68] Quotative

---

62. Adorno, *Mahler*, 32.
63. Adorno, *Mahler*, 19. Spelling altered.
64. See "Convolute N" in Walter Benjamin, *The Arcades Project*, trans. Howard Eiland and Kevin McLaughlin (Cambridge, MA: Harvard University Press, 2002); and Theodor W. Adorno, *Aesthetic Theory*, trans. Robert Hullot-Kentor (Minneapolis: University of Minnesota Press, 1997), 155.
65. See also Patrizia C. McBride, *The Chatter of the Visible* (Ann Arbor: University of Michigan Press, 2016).
66. Peter Bürger, *Theory of the Avant-Garde*, trans. Michael Shaw (Minneapolis: University of Minnesota Press, 1984), 68–73. See also Benjamin, *The Origin of the German Tragic Drama*, 174–77.
67. See Bürger, *Theory of the Avant-Garde*, 68.
68. Quoted in Hannah Arendt's introduction to Walter Benjamin, *Illuminations: Essays and Reflections*, trans. Harry Zohn (New York: Schocken, 1968), 8.

practices provided Benjamin a way to wrestle a lost potential from history's forgotten objects.

Like the allegorist in Benjamin's *Trauerspiel* book, Bürger's quoting montage artist isolates one element from a certain living totality and transports it out of its natural context, thus rendering it a fragment. The transported fragment, now no longer perceived in its original context, is depleted of its prior meaning and remains a dead object or an empty sign. By joining such fragments together, both allegorist and the montage artist assign their quotations new meaning. This, however, is arbitrary, posited meaning.

Seeing how quotational gestures complicate notions of meaning and interpretation elucidates the affinity between quotation and assimilation. This affinity is not grounded in a simple formality that deems the assimilated Jew a suitable or even an ideal quoting artist (or allegorist). Merely arguing that the assimilated person's difference renders their use of the vernacular a quotation is not enough without further insight into the nature of their difference. We gain this insight by thoroughly investigating quotation's superfluous (non)relation to meaning. Linking assimilation and quotation within such an inquiry liberates us from the need to evaluate the assimilated Jew's difference in terms of their dialectical relation to a dominant culture as a kind of authentic origin.

As an allegorical object, a quotation declares its repetitive nature while acknowledging its arbitrary and transient relation to meaning. It indicates that just as it previously appeared with one meaning, it may appear again with an altogether different meaning. As Patrick Greaney explains, quotations foreground the "repeatability of the moment of emergence of the original." They indicate "the possibility that this coming into being could have been different."[69] The recipient of quotations, becoming aware of this inexhaustible relation to meaning, is nevertheless compelled to interpret the quoted object, knowing that this task will never yield a conclusive outcome.

To hermeneutics, quotations posed a particular challenge. As Helmut Müller-Sievers observes, quotations were considered superfluous contaminants that had to be removed before the divinatory

---

69. See Greaney, *Quotational Practices*, 6.

act of interpretation was to begin.[70] In the works of Georg Büchner for example, Müller-Sievers shows how the interspersing of unacknowledged quotations undermined the scientific aspiration of hermeneutics to separate the original utterances of the author from textual "contaminants," such as quotations, that need not be interpreted.[71] Furthermore, the authorial ambivalence that accompanied quotations undermined the hermeneutic expectation of reaching a finite, conclusive meaning through interpretation. This was radicalized in works that were constructed entirely from quotations, where the previous dialectic unity between parts and whole was breached. According to Bürger, recipients who wished to grasp a meaning from these nonorganic works by way of the hermeneutic circle, hoping to understand the parts by observing the whole and vice versa, encountered instead emancipated parts whose individual meanings cannot anticipate the meaning of the work as an organic whole and, likewise, cannot be inferred from the meaning of the whole.[72]

Quotation turned interpretation from a gateway to meaning into the very vessel of difference as such. The only assurance that quotation afforded its interpreter was the knowledge that there will always be a different meaning out there.[73] Quotation's relation—or rather, nonrelation—to meaning resulted in a lack of transparency. Its promise of difference rather than concrete meaning rendered it opaque and impenetrable as a foreign body. The attempt to interpret quotations thus became an encounter with alterity.[74]

---

70. See Helmut Müller-Sievers, "On the Way to Quotation: Paul Celan's 'Meridian' Speech," *New German Critique* 91 (2004): 131–49, 137.

71. See also Helmut Müller-Sievers, *Disorientierung: Anatomie und Dichtung bei Georg Büchner* (Göttingen: Wallstein, 2003).

72. See Bürger, *Theory of the Avant-Garde*, 79–81; Greaney, *Quotational Practices*, 6.

73. Quotation allows us to get closer to discovering what Adorno called the "joy of interpretation." The pleasure derived from interpretation, Adorno explains, comes from the realization that "the phenomena always mean something different from what they simply are.... The deepest promise interpretation makes to the mind is perhaps the assurance that it gives that what exists is not the ultimate reality." See Theodor W. Adorno, *History and Freedom: Lectures 1964–1965*, trans. Rodney Livingstone (Cambridge, MA: Polity, 2010), 138.

74. See also Müller-Sievers, "On the Way to Quotation," 144–45.

Quotation provides us with a productive strategy for reconsidering assimilation. As the embodiment of difference, quotation is by no means an approximating, mimetic gesture. Eliminating the element of approximation in quotation has a direct effect on the relation between *Verschmelzung* and *Eigenart* that underlies certain conceptions of assimilation. Upon further scrutiny, the *Verschmelzung* and *Eigenart* duo—regardless of the varying degrees of agency it grants the assimilated person—confines any consideration of assimilation to a discursive relation that always evaluates the former in terms of the culture they assimilate into. To say that assimilation is always assimilation *into* means that assimilation is always bound to a dialectic between a major and minor culture. In such a relation, power may be distributed differently according to the different perspectives from which assimilation is examined, but power always remains the hinge upon which assimilation revolves. The complexities of quotation, on the other hand, help us consider assimilation outside the confines of this master-slave dialectic.

If quotation is the embodiment of difference, it is at the same time a complete loss of meaning through excess. This is what the example of Mahler, the allegorist, reveals. Mahler eliminates the meaning that previously inhabited his quotations when they were still presented in their initial context.[75] This is also what separates Mahler's quotational practice from the practice of musical parody, since the latter indicates work on musical materials that preserves some degree of the material's earlier meaning. The absence, in music, of punctuation such as quotation marks allows Mahler's quotations to plant the suspicion that everything in his music is quoted. And indeed, through Adorno's analysis, we realize that Mahler's quotations are not simply localized moments. They amount to the quotation of an entire tradition. It is an overarching gesture that precludes evaluating his music against an original since the original has already forfeited its meaning. In this way, Mahler's quotation becomes superfluous, yet

---

75. The fact that meaning in music is not equal to meaning in language, something that can be and has been argued extensively, does not affect the applicability of the theoretical discussion on quotation to music in general and Mahler's music in particular. In Mahler's music, displaced meaning ranges from expressing Austro-German national sentiments to an aspiration toward organic aesthetic ideals.

not in relation to a still stable and integrated body of meaning. Its superfluousness is rather an emancipated form of excess.

The relinquishment of meaning defines Mahler as an assimilated Jew sui generis and liberates him from a discursive relation with a major Austro-German culture. In this capacity, Mahler is just as superfluous as Roth's *Ostjude*. Their condition resembles what Jacques Derrida, reading Georges Bataille, defined as sovereignty, a condition that evades the dialectic of lordship and servility. In Derrida's analysis, this Hegelian dialectic is characterized as a contained economy consisting of the "conservation, circulation and reproduction of meaning."[76] Sovereignty, a concept that, as Derrida stresses, is not equivalent to lordship, is defined as uncontained excess in terms of its nonrelation to meaning. It exceeds the hermetic condition that assigns meaning to any discursive confrontation (between master and slave, major and minor, or, in our case, distinct "Austro-German" and "Jewish" positions). Thus, as a quoting assimilated Jew, Mahler evades the discussion of German Jewish (or Austrian Jewish) *identity*. The nonidentity of his quotations calls into question the integrity of any context against which they are considered.

Adorno's observation that the hatred of Mahler's quotational practice had "antisemitic overtones" can be linked to earlier antisemitic accusations of the inorganic nature of Jewish expression. Wagner had already attacked Jewish musicians who "hurl together the diverse forms and styles of every age and every master," and in whose work one finds "packed side by side ... the formal idiosyncrasies of all the schools, in motliest chaos."[77] Wagner's vitriol, like the later hatred of Mahler's music, betrayed an anxiety born of the growing awareness and simultaneous refusal to accept that organic integrity was becoming an increasingly untenable aesthetic, social, and political value. Figures like Wagner preferred to conceive of a fragmentary and assembled form of expression that was essentially Jewish and contrast it with an essentially organic, well-integrated German

---

76. Jacques Derrida, "From Restricted to General Economy. A Hegelian without Reserve," in *Writing and Difference*, trans. Alan Bass (Chicago: University of Chicago Press, 1978), 256.
77. Wagner, *Das Judentum in der Musik*, 11.

expression. But quotations, as we have just seen, were not simple contaminants that needed to be removed from an organic whole. They rather exposed cracks in the integrity of this presumed "whole," revealing it to be equally constructed. Like quotation, assimilation could reveal the false promise of integration and its homogeneous telos.

Jewish Difference, Integration, and "Bad" Counterpoint

Naturally, any comparison between Mahler and Zeisl must account for the historical gap that separated the two composers. Between Mahler's death in 1911 and the completion of *Hiob*'s second act in 1959 stand two world wars that leave no doubt of the difference in circumstances under which Mahler's and Zeisl's works were conceived. Yet I would argue that the historical gap yields an intensification of circumstances rather than a complete modification. Like the majority of Zeisl's compositions, the opera *Hiob* was written in exile in Paris and the United States. Outside Vienna, Zeisl's use of the Austro-German musical idiom therefore acquired the status of a double quotation.[78] Musical developments in interwar Vienna, led primarily by the Second Viennese School, amplified the outdatedness of Zeisl's tonal language. This outdatedness is not diminished by the observation that other composers—in Zeisl's immediate vicinity, another well-known example would be Korngold—also declined the path to atonality. For in historical accounts of the so-called progression of Western art music, tonal composers like Zeisl and Korngold still appear in the shadow of figures like Schoenberg and Eisler. Regardless of whether one considers this a historical injustice or not, this is the result of accounts, which strive to present a history of musical forms as a narrative of linear progress.[79]

---

78. The period that Mahler spent in New York conducting the Metropolitan Opera and the New York Philharmonic between 1908 and 1911 is also worth noting here.

79. In this context, Adorno's critique of the view of history as progress, inspired by Walter Benjamin, can be linked to his critique of Schoenberg's musical "progress" in Adorno's *Philosophy of New Music*.

The absence of any substantial symphonic pieces in Zeisl's oeuvre is another formal aspect that distinguishes his work from Mahler's.[80] Zeisl's shunning of the symphonic genre was construed by critics as a technical inadequacy, a composer's "struggle with the casting of large forms."[81] Yet it is exactly this failure to produce a major symphony in the tradition of the great Viennese composers who preceded him that allows us to trace a line of succession between Mahler and Zeisl. Zeisl's work acknowledges Mahler's exhaustion of the symphonic genre. Prominent among the progressive elements of Zeisl's music is precisely the admission that grand symphonic narratives had lost their former stature thanks to Mahler. In adhering to shorter forms, Zeisl was responding to what Karen Painter called "the collapse of grand systems into fragmentary insights," a phenomenon that reached all arts in the twentieth century, including music.[82] According to Painter, references to the symphony after Mahler were always nostalgic or, more precisely, an attempt to revive a genre in decline.

Mahler's exhaustive quotation of the symphony caused Zeisl to fall back onto even earlier formal musical procedures in his own works. Like his contemporary, Schoenberg, Zeisl availed himself of the adhesive capacities of contrapuntal techniques. For Schoenberg, contrapuntal techniques served as the pervasive foundation for an altogether new, atonal method of composition with the aim of achieving cohesion throughout entire pieces. The appearance of contrapuntal techniques in the context of Zeisl's tonal language was more localized. In *Hiob*, short fugal interludes operate primarily as discrete connectors between scenic complexes. This renders their occurrence separate from the rest of the music. Even where they do not function as proper connectors, their distinct appearance is contrasted with the otherwise homophonic style of the opera. This articulation foregrounds these fugal interludes as quotational moments.

---

80. Aside from Zeisl's Piano Concerto (1951), other orchestral works are divided into shorter forms such as suites and programmatic pieces. See Cole and Barclay, *Armseelchen*, 370.

81. Cole and Barclay, *Armseelchen*, 91.

82. Karen Painter, *Symphonic Aspirations: German Music and Politics, 1900–1945* (Cambridge, MA: Harvard University Press, 2007), 4.

In the opening scene of *Hiob*'s first act, a fugal interruption voicing Deborah's complaint about poverty and daily hardships suspends the homophonic texture that accompanied her husband's preceding soliloquy. Mendel's musings on theodicy, mediated through quotations from the Book of Job and interspersed with reflections on his children, transitions quickly into an agitated fugato on Deborah's cry, "Die Karotten verringern sich, die Kartoffeln erfrieren, die Eier werden hohl, die Suppe wässrig, die Karpfen schmal, die Hechte kurz, die Gänse hart."[83] (The carrots diminish, the potatoes freeze, the eggs become hollow, the soup watery, the carps meager, the pikes short, the geese hard.) *Hiob*'s fugal interludes are restless and often express implicit or explicit anxieties. Deborah's second fugal interjection in the same scene gives musical form to apprehensions about the drafting of her two older sons into the czar's army. "Glaubst du Mendel, dass man sie genommen hat?" (Do you believe, Mendel, that they have been recruited?) she asks nervously. Mendel joins her as the fugato spirals further: "Warum soll man sie nicht genommen haben? Jonas ist stark wie ein Bär und Schemariah ist flink wie ein Wiesel."[84] (Why wouldn't they be drafted? Jonas is strong as a bear and Schemariah is swift as a weasel.)

Deborah and Mendel's contrapuntal anxiety is not so much the fear of losing both sons to war as it is the fear of losing them to a foreign culture. Put plainly, it is an anxiety of assimilation. In Roth's novel, Mendel's worst visions involve harrowing images of his sons dressed in uniform, consuming pork and wielding bayonets. His notion of assimilation involves both the violation of traditional taboos concerning food and garb as well as the active participation in asserting a country's political sovereignty through military service. A close connection between contrapuntal techniques and assimilation anxiety is maintained in the closing scene of the second act, which, being the final act composed, serves de facto as the opera's finale. While Mendel could not prevent his son Jonas from enlisting, he is determined to prevent his daughter's fraternizing with the Cossack soldiers. The opera's final complex has Mendel frantically

---

83. Kafka, *Hiob Textbuch*, 2.
84. Kafka, *Hiob Textbuch*, 3.

searching for Mirjam, who is hiding with her Cossack lover. It concludes with a grand fugue for orchestra, soloists, and a double chorus. Its disorienting 5/4 metered theme, appearing first in the strings, is quickly picked up by the chorus and coupled with the line "Den Juden fehlt ein Mädel, den Kosaken fehlt ein Mann!" (The Jews are missing a girl; the Cossacks are missing a man!)

The opera *Hiob* is not the first to pair contrapuntal writing with apprehensions about assimilation. In the early twentieth century, the critical discourse on "bad" counterpoint was steeped in reverse metaphors about failed Jewish assimilation. As a compositional technique, counterpoint demanded a delicate balance between harmonic interdependence and rhythmic independence of different melodic lines. Its main principle was the mastery of variance through integration. What the symphony set as its goal on the level of musical form—namely, the integration of musical themes into a coherent and unified narrative—was to be achieved on the level of technique with the contrapuntal synthesis of rhythmically varied voices. In the German musical tradition, counterpoint occupied a practically sacred position from Bach through the late Beethoven to Brahms and Max Reger. Its association with musical giants of German music combined with its reputation as an austere, mathematical art endowed counterpoint with a unique kind of authority. Its task of achieving mastery over variance exceeded the status of an aesthetic principle and approached that of a scientific pursuit on the one hand, giving counterpoint an air of objectivity. On the other hand, there was no doubt that the mastery that counterpoint involved was considered the venerable achievement of German music, the conquest of variance as a sacred national feat.

As Painter shows, in the wake of early twentieth-century formal and harmonic developments, most notable among them the decline of the symphony, counterpoint remained one of the last strongholds of stability and orientation. After all, even modernist iconoclasts like Schoenberg were proponents of (what they considered) good counterpoint. An offence against "good" counterpoint principles was naturally taken to have implications beyond the musical work. At stake in the discourse on good and bad counterpoint was society's ability to integrate foreign elements. When counterpoint was judged unsuccessful in its prescribed mission, its failure was immediately projected onto the precarious integration of the most discussed minority in the Austro-German landscape at that time: Jews. Bad counterpoint, where voices are "too independent" and appear "one *on top* of the other" rather than "*against* another" came to be recognized as "Jewish," regardless of the actual background of its composer.[85]

Public anxieties about the violation of counterpoint rules did not only respond to a growing awareness of what Adorno called "the chaotic, unorganized sound, the unregulated, fortuitous simultaneity of the 'world.'"[86] According to Painter, work in the emerging field of musicology—and particularly the writings of one of its pioneers, Guido Adler—augmented contrapuntal anxieties by suggesting potential non-Western origins to polyphony. In 1908, Adler published his study *Über Heterophonie* (On heterophony), which traced a link between the polyphonic writing of Western art music and the "exotic and folkloristic" heterophonic practices that were still present in Siamese, Japanese, and Javanese music.[87] The distinction that Adler himself drew between heterophony and polyphony was an attempt to distinguish the venerated German practice of counterpoint, or "polyphony," from "heterophony," the "primitive" music of non-Western cultures. Heterophony, Adler explained, was "polyphony without rules, with cohesion being left largely to chance."[88]

Studies like Adler's placed additional weight on the rules of counterpoint. Good counterpoint was no longer just a source of stability and assurance for a society disoriented by the collapse of its former values. It now also became the last line of defense that kept the revered polyphonic tradition of Western art music, and specifically Austro-German music, away from the clutches of the Orient.

---

85. See Karen Painter, "Contested Counterpoint: 'Jewish' Appropriation and Polyphonic Liberation," *Archiv für Musikwissenschaft* 58, no. 3 (2001): 201–30, 210.

86. Adorno, *Mahler*, 112.

87. Adler bases his study on earlier work done in the field. The term heterophony became part of the (ethno)musicological discussion in 1901 through the work of Carl Stumpf. See Carl Stumpf, "Tonsystem und Musik der Siamesen," in *Beiträge zur Akustik und zur Musikwissenschaft*, vol. 3 (Leipzig, 1901).

88. Guido Adler, *Heterophony*, cited in Donald Mitchell, *Gustav Mahler: Songs and Symphonies of Life and Death* (Woodbridge, UK: Boydell Press, 2002), 628.

Violation of counterpoint rules, including polyphonic writing that defied counterpoint's spirit of coordination and control by allowing voices excessive independence, were inevitably met with chastising remarks referencing Germany's and Austria's local "Orientals." The most immediate targets were Eastern European Jews, and the complexity of the discourse is further apparent in remarks made by assimilated Jewish music critics who joined others in pairing the practice of bad counterpoint with the unassimilated *Ostjude*.[89]

But anxieties about errant counterpoint were also expressed in a stereotypical language frequently used to describe assimilated Jews. The discourse articulated just how precarious the attainment of social integration was even for that group. Bad counterpoint in the music of Schoenberg, for example, was decried as urban and artificial.[90] Mahler's counterpoint was deemed intellectual and unemotional; in the absence of inspiration, one could find only "combinations."[91]

Critique of bad counterpoint, Painter shows, was expressed primarily in terms of excess. The excessive liberation and abundance of voices were condemned along with other excessive elements of bad counterpoint such as orchestration and rhythmic complexity. This contrapuntal excess was paired with a vocabulary denoting the excessive nature of Jews, that is, with depictions of Jewish *over*productivity and excessive rationality.[92] Contrapuntal excess was threatening due to the potentially unregulated and limitlessly additive structure it implied, where voices stack one "on top" of the other instead of being set organically against each other. Here, too, superfluousness compromised organic integration. But the reason that anxieties concerning the precariousness of social integration found expression in the discourse on counterpoint was the overwhelmingly unmediated effect that counterpoint had on the listening subject, as Painter observes:

---

89. Painter, "Contested Counterpoint," 222.
90. Painter, "Contested Counterpoint," 205.
91. Painter, "Contested Counterpoint," 207.
92. Painter, "Contested Counterpoint," 218. In contemporaneous works like Otto Weininger's *Geschlecht und Charakter*, Jewish overproductivity is also linked to excessive sexuality. See also Christine Achinger, "Allegories of Destruction: 'Woman' and 'the Jew' in Otto Weininger's *Sex and Character*," *The Germanic Review: Literature, Culture, Theory* 88, no. 2 (2013): 121–49.

"Hearing counterpoint entailed being *in* the music . . . in effect being surrounded by the voices. . . . Counterpoint allowed no safe distance from the composition."[93] Excessive counterpoint did not merely reflect social and political anxieties about failed integration from a figurative distance; it provided the most immediate and visceral experience of a phenomenon whose broad scope could otherwise be perceived only in abstract terms.

With its dense orchestration and rhythmic complexity, *Hiob*'s closing fugue re-creates that same unmediated disorientation. While the opera does not exhibit tonal innovation, its use of timbre, register, and meter has as great—if not greater—an effect on its audience. Odd meters and rhythmic patterns like those of the closing fugue have the capacity to bewilder a listener who attempts to retain an integrated overview of the fugue and a clear mental image of the theme and its various occurrences. Zeisl achieves this by presenting a metrically even theme in the uneven 5/4 meter. This discrepancy causes the theme to appear on a different beat each time and acquire different accents that alter its profile on each entry. Fragments of themes distributed between the orchestra, soloists, and chorus make it even more difficult to perceive clear entries (see figure 5.4).

Zeisl's fugal finale adds yet another voice *on top* of the discourse on counterpoint and integration. It inverts the assimilation anxieties that were associated with counterpoint, those that expressed doubt about the ability of assimilated Jews to truly eliminate any trace of difference and integrate seamlessly into an otherwise "homogeneous" German-speaking society and culture. Mendel's cry "Lieber hätt ich sie tot gesehen!" (I'd rather see her dead!), uttered upon the discovery of Mirjam and her Cossack lover Mikhail, dismisses the principle of integration altogether by giving expression to Mendel's own assimilation anxiety, the fear of total integration as subsumption of difference. Zeisl's counterpoint thus ceases to be "bad." It proposes instead that the unintegrated fugue is not deficient but rather more faithful to what Mahler himself recognized as the true chaotic polyphony of the world, a pandemonium of themes coming

---

93. Painter, "Contested Counterpoint," 203.

Figure 5.4. Zeisl, *Hiob*, from act 2—final complex (fugue).

from "quite different directions" and "different from each other in rhythm and melodic character."[94]

The inorganic nature of Zeisl's quotational practice is also present in his contrapuntal writing. Like his quotations, his counterpoint is superfluous, excessive. Here, again, being superfluous has nothing to do with inferior redundancies and everything to do with the refutation of organicism and integration as teleological, comprehensive ideals. Thus, in Zeisl's unintegrated counterpoint, difference is emancipated as there is no longer a need to understand it against integration.

The main thesis of Adorno's *Mahler* pertains to the disintegrating notion of an organic "we," which Mahler's music makes visible. Difference in the composer's work is "the ferment of a particular that is not absorbed into the general," as Adorno put it.[95] Adorno knew that music, as all other arts, cannot be contemplated independently of social processes, and that in fact the critic is able to locate in music a more distilled version of such developments. That society would then project its anxieties back onto a musical discourse, as it did in relation to counterpoint, is only an extension of

---

94. Bauer-Lechner, *Recollections of Gustav Mahler*, 162.
95. Adorno, *Mahler*, 26.

these reciprocal relations with music. But the displacement of sociopolitical anxieties onto the realm of musical aesthetics points at a further, more substantial displacement: that of a society growing painfully aware of its nonorganic makeup and choosing to displace the condition of being superfluous onto one of its subgroups in order to retain an illusion of integrity for itself.[96]

In the Austro-German tradition, investment in a notion of organicism had directed aesthetic discussions since the eighteenth century. Political upheavals and a growing national consciousness in the following century reinforced this investment by entangling it with a complementary organic notion of the people. Wagner's vision of the *Volk* as an organic community was not all that remote from the German idealist search for transcendent unity in artworks, or from accolades like those bestowed on Johann Sebastian Bach in 1802 by the protomusicologist J. N. Forkel, who commended the German master on the perfect integration of single parts into the great whole in his music.[97] The stakes were raised at the close of the nineteenth century with the unification of Germany and the promise of national cohesion that it held. Any indication that such organic unity could not in fact be sustained either on a social or on a political level was anxiously suppressed. But it is actually with Germany's neighbor to the south that such anxieties attained their most radical expression, for nowhere was dedication to an organic integration of parts into the whole greater than in the land that produced the tradition of Viennese Classicism.

Early Viennese modernism had to contend with a persistent gnawing at this principle on both aesthetic and sociopolitical fronts. It is worth noting that some of the most progressive modernists were those who, when confronted with the alarming decline of this integrative principle, felt compelled to defend and uphold it. Their anxiety deemed everything superfluous a crime against the hallowed integrity of the work. Before the First World War, this was manifest in

---

96. See also the discussion of the Jew as society's "symptom" in Slavoj Žižek, *The Sublime Object of Ideology* (New York: Verso, 1989).

97. Johann Nikolaus Forkel, "On Johann Sebastian Bach's Life, Genius, and Works," in *The Bach Reader*, ed. Hans T. David and Arthur Mendel (New York: Norton, 1999), 352–53.

the denouncement of ornament by figures like Karl Kraus and Adolf Loos. Kraus's caustic satire of figurative language joined essays like "Die Überflüssigen" (The Superfluous, 1908) and "Ornament und Verbrechen" ("Ornament and Crime," 1913) by Loos, which stressed the redundancy of ornaments on utilitarian objects.[98] Importantly, Loos makes full use of organic metaphors in "Ornament and Crime" to illustrate the natural process of growth that culture has undergone to exceed the need for ornaments. As he writes, "Since ornament is no longer organically linked with our culture, it is also no longer the expression of our culture."[99] Essays like Max Nordau's *Entartung* (*Degeneration*, 1892), which greatly influenced Loos, condemned the tendency toward excess in the decorative *Jugendstil* and likewise voiced intolerance toward artworks that did not exhibit a healthy balance between parts and whole. Nordau had even targeted "excessive" polyphony in his writings: "In the orchestra a vigorous polyphony must summon the attention in several directions at once; particular instruments, or groups of instruments, must address the listener simultaneously without heeding each other, till he gets as nervously excited as the man who vainly endeavors to understand what is being said in the jangle of a dozen voices."[100]

Aesthetic superfluousness was also threatening after World War I. Heinrich Schenker's method of musical analysis is one important example of an endeavor to validate works according to a principle of organic integration in the interwar Viennese musical landscape. Ultimately, the goal of Schenkerian analysis consists in showing graphically how all details of a composition are integrated by performing some function in subordination to a generative, organic total structure. Schenker's analysis is firmly grounded in the tonal

---

98. See also Gilbert J. Carr, "The 'Habsburg Myth,' Ornament and Metaphor: Adolf Loos, Karl Kraus, and Robert Musil," *Austrian Studies* 15 (2007): 65–79; and Christopher Long, "The Origin and Context of Adolf Loos's 'Ornament and Crime,'" *Journal of the Society of Architectural Historians* 68, no. 2 (2009): 200–223.

99. Adolf Loos, "Ornament and Crime," in *Programs and Manifestoes on 20th-Century Architecture*, ed. Ulrich Conrads, trans. Michael Bullock (London: Lund Humphries, 1970), 22. Even the strict separation between art and utility that is the product of Loos's polemic implies an attempt to preserve a sense of integrity in art by preventing it from spilling over into other areas.

100. Max Nordau, *Degeneration* (New York: D. Appleton, 1895), 12–13.

system. Yet even the bitter dispute between this conservative music theorist and his atonal Viennese counterpart Schoenberg could not obscure the fact that both were united when it came to the importance of organicism in musical works, though they may have taken different paths to arrive at that point.[101] Nor could this dispute deny that the integrity that Schenker ascribed to tonal works was in some ways perpetuated in Schoenberg's twelve-tone composition method, which, at least theoretically, left no room for loose ends.[102]

Considered in a broader historical context (and admitting that the examples mentioned here are but a fraction of the entire phenomenon), it is unsurprising that analytical theories like Schenker's and Schoenberg's, which advocate so vehemently for organic integration, emerged at a time when the validity of what they defended was called into question by the growing visibility of superfluousness in both art and society. And just as commitment to this principle was not limited to one aesthetic camp, it was also not limited to any particular social or political camp. That assimilated Jews like Schenker and Schoenberg would search for organicism in musical works is proof that a sense of dread in the face of excess and superfluousness permeated all parts of society and carried with it even those who, in other discourses, were accused of threatening what they themselves believed to be defending.

These are the realities that Roth's novel and Zeisl's opera invoke, the former by literary means, the latter in music. Both works expose the interconnections between the emerging superfluous social and political status of assimilated and unassimilated Jews, the anxieties that their status generated in a society and a culture so deeply invested in aesthetic and political notions of remainderless integration, and the concomitant decline of grand aesthetic forms that served as a model for such principles. Roth's essay series *Juden auf*

---

101. See Carl Dahlhaus, "Schoenberg and Schenker," *Proceedings of the Royal Musical Association* 100 (1973–1974): 209–15; and Gianmario Borio, "Schenker versus Schoenberg versus Schenker: The Difficulties of a Reconciliation," *Journal of the Royal Music Association* 126 (2001): 250–74.

102. On the relation between Schoenberg's *Harmonielehre* and Loos's "Ornament und Verbrechen," see Holly Watkins, "Schoenberg's Interior Designs," *Journal of the American Musicological Society* 61 (2008): 152–54.

Wanderschaft and novel *Hiob* appeared at a time when discussions of Jews as superfluous was approaching a critical point. Zeisl's opera, whose composition process began in 1939 and continued until the composer's untimely death in 1959, is steeped in this history, which it takes with it to another continent and a new period after 1945.

Asking whether similar conditions and values accompanied the work on *Hiob* in the United States exceeds the scope of this chapter. The opening scene of the third, uncomposed act of Kafka's libretto depicts New York as home to a vibrant, versatile immigrant community, a stark contrast to Zuchnow. But since Zeisl never composed it, there is no telling what he might have made of Kafka's depiction. The 1950s saw the growing popularity of movements like New Criticism in American literary theory, as well as the unprecedented success of Schenkerian analysis among American music theorists, which even thirty years later brought musicologists like Ruth A. Solie and Joseph Kerman to wonder about the persistence of organic integration as a validating criterion for musical works in American academia.[103] It seems that, at least aesthetically, such values were held in high regard also in Zeisl's adopted homeland.

---

103. Ruth A. Solie, "The Living Work: Organicism and Musical Analysis," *19th-Century Music* 4, no. 2 (1980): 147–56; and Joseph Kerman, "How We Got into Analysis, and How to Get Out," *Critical Inquiry* 7, no. 2 (1980): 311–31.

Afterword

Identity and Difference beyond Dialectics

The "return to the Bible" marks a crucial step in studies about the formation of Jewish modernity. In *The Hebrew Bible Reborn*, for example, Yaacov Shavit and Mordechai Eran locate the origins of Jewish European modernity in the Reform movement of *Haskalah*, which emerged alongside many of the modern developments in German Bible criticism during the eighteenth and nineteenth centuries. For Shavit and Eran, the return to the Bible within the *Haskalah* movement was a "prerequisite for the modernization of Judaism" as well as for "the national revival of the Jewish people," which the authors regard as the direct outcome of the discourse of Jewish identity that the movement instigated.[1] The narrative that Shavit and Eran put forth casts Jewish modern readings of the Bible as a vehicle for expressing a distinct modern Jewish culture. The Bible

---

1. Yaacov Shavit and Mordechai Eran, *The Hebrew Bible Reborn: From Holy Scripture to the Book of Books*, trans. Chaya Naor (Berlin: De Gruyter, 2007), 1.

made it possible to articulate a modern Jewish identity that simultaneously preserved a link to Jewish tradition while releasing its adherents from the restrictions of rabbinical literature and thereby announcing itself as "secular."

Gershon Shaked surveys the outcomes of this development in Jewish literature. His book *The New Tradition* outlines the formation of the modern Hebrew literary canon at the close of the nineteenth and the beginning of the twentieth centuries in very similar terms. Shaked identifies the roots of the "new tradition," which heralded the advent of national Hebrew literature, in what he terms the "return of the Bible as a major source of inspiration and as the intertextual mastertext" among members of the *Haskalah* movement in Germany.[2] This new "secularized" approach to the Bible, he explains, paved the way for the Bible's later role as the "cultural foundation of the Zionist movement, providing the ultimate proof of the historical independence of the Jewish people and the compelling rationale for its return to Eretz Israel."[3] As Shaked further elaborates, secularized readings of the Bible, originating in the Germany of the previous centuries, served the Zionist educational system in presenting its own secularized national and cultural program. This account of the development of a national Hebrew literary corpus based on "secularized," cultural readings of the Bible finds a counterpart in Assaf Shelleg's study of biblical tropes in Israeli art music, which voiced, according to Shelleg, a territorialized Zionist view in the state's formative years.[4]

The linear trajectory from German *Haskalah* and its cultural readings of the Bible to the formation of a national Jewish culture and identity in the twentieth century tells one story about the implications of the modern return to the Bible. This teleological narrative preserves the discourse of identity and its reliance on a more rigid conception of Jewish difference while also promoting a linear view of secularization as an uncomplicated, unidirectional movement toward a modernity emancipated from religious residues. The

---

2. Gershon Shaked, *The New Tradition: Essays on Modern Hebrew Literature* (Cincinnati: Hebrew Union College, 2006), 2.
3. Shaked, *The New Tradition*, 2.
4. See Shelleg, *Theological Stains*, 2.

aim of this book was to locate another trajectory resulting from the same modern readings of the Bible, one that does not culminate in a territorialized notion of identity but rather proceeds to critique it. The ambivalent nature of the biblical discourse, however, prevents this critique from standing in direct opposition to its object.

The Bible discourse serves neither a deterritorialized nor a territorialized view insofar as they are associated with mutually exclusive minority and majority positions. Even within the so-called territorialized rhetoric of Israeli art music, as Shelleg deftly shows, the use of biblical tropes eventually worked concomitantly to uphold *and* undermine the narrative of Jewish and Hebrew territorial sovereignty. The same use of biblical subject matter by Israeli composers, as Shelleg additionally shows, also exposed the latent theological strands that persisted within Zionism despite its self-presentation as a secular movement. Thus, alongside its defiance of categorization—its rejection of the unequivocal delineation between the territorialized and deterritorialized positions—the use of biblical subject matter also undermined the so-called linearity of the process of secularization as it applied to modern biblical readings. Rather than confirming a simple transition from "religious" to "secular" readings, modern biblical references confounded these two categories as well. In this, the bible discourse and its artistic applications offered a concentrated image of the problem of modernity and categorization.

The problem of modernity, as Zygmunt Bauman famously argued, is entwined with that of categorization and ambiguous difference, be it between the "old" and the "new," the "religious" and the "secular," the "universal" and the "particular," the "major" and the "minor," or the "territorialized" and the "deterritorialized." According to Bauman, while modernity has striven toward unambiguous classification as a way of establishing order through the operation of inclusion and exclusion, it could not help but create further ambivalence. "Modern consciousness," Bauman notes, "is the suspicion or awareness of the inconclusiveness of extant order; a consciousness prompted and moved by the premonition of inadequacy, nay non-viability, of the order-designing, ambivalence-eliminating project."[5] The fate of

---

5. See Bauman, *Modernity and Ambivalence*, 9.

Jewish difference within this modern predicament is significant to Bauman's project. It receives direct consideration through the "case study" of assimilation and German-speaking Jews.[6]

To unsettle Jewish difference is to become aware of the indissoluble entwinement between categorization and ambivalence that Bauman sees as defining modernity. Jewish difference, like modernity itself, moves constantly back and forth between the drive to establish differentiated categories and their inevitable dissolution through ambivalence. This also pertains to the study of the Bible's modern afterlife and its role in shaping conceptions of Jewish difference and identity. The two trajectories of the Bible discourse, the one outlined by scholars like Shaked and Shelleg and the one outlined in this book, should not be regarded as opposing alternatives but rather as two sides of the same coin. Only by tracing moments where the so-called minor assumes major traits and, inversely, where the major is revealed in its becoming-minor is it possible to address the questions of Jewish difference and identity without uncritically succumbing to the drive toward rigid and systematic categorization.

In her book *The Translated Jew*, Leslie Morris confronts this drive with her challenge to the stability and delineation of the "German" and the "Jewish."[7] By removing the hyphen from the term "German-Jewish," Morris seeks to counter the rigid purity that the hyphen, as a kind of border, paradoxically bestows upon the categories on both its sides. Instead, she emphasizes their permeability and translatability. Morris's project shows the capaciousness and mutability of the term "German Jewish" by liberating it from established "German-Jewish" genealogies and allowing it to include cultural phenomena that would otherwise not fit the more rigid, hyphenated term. She thus strives to eliminate the stagnant major-minor relation that has long served scholars in their definition of the German Jewish condition. She likewise challenges the boundaries of a fixed German Jewish canon. Her suggestion that "German writing is always already 'Jewish'"[8] seems

---

6. See Bauman, *Modernity and Ambivalence*, 102.
7. Leslie Morris, *The Translated Jew: German Jewish Culture outside the Margins* (Evanston, IL: Northwestern University Press, 2018).
8. Morris, *The Translated Jew*, 198.

radical precisely because it requires that we relinquish the most foundational categories that have hitherto guided most accounts of the relation between German Jews and other Germans. Even discussions that emphasize the essential role that Jews played in the formation of German society and culture are bound to a conception of Jewish participation from a minor position defined strictly through its relation to a dominant culture.

Claims like "the German is always already Jewish" are anti-Hegelian; their unpalatability demonstrates the difficulty of breaking out of contained systems that subsume all questions of identity and difference within the master-slave dialectic. Ironically, it was Hegel's own antisemitic understanding of Jews as "unproductive" and therefore alienated from work that disqualified them from inclusion in (or rather, subsumption under) his dialectic insofar as it consisted of the mutual recognition (and concomitant self-recognition) based on the labor of one of its sides.[9] This could be another explanation for Hegel's exclusion of Jews from his world-historical system. Interestingly, as Michael Steinberg observes, there were two things that were left outside of Hegel's system: Jews and music.[10]

In their own attempt to get out of the Hegelian dialectical bind, Gilles Deleuze and Félix Guattari explore the concept of "minor literature" and its deterritorializing potential.[11] The deterritorialization of minor literature, as they write, is that of its language, which no longer operates as an organ of sense-making. The language of Kafka in Deleuze and Guattari's example moves away from the signifier, away from metaphor: "We are no longer in the situation of an ordinary, rich language where the word dog, for example, would directly designate an animal and would apply metaphorically to other things (so that one could say 'like a dog'). . . . Kafka deliberately kills all metaphor, all symbolism, all signification. . . . There is no longer any proper sense or figurative sense, but only a distribution

---

9. In this context, see also Werner Hamacher, "Working through Working," translated by Matthew T. Hartman, *Modernism/modernity* 3, no. 1 (1996): 23–56.
10. Steinberg, *Judaism Musical and Unmusical*, 222.
11. Gilles Deleuze and Félix Guattari, *Kafka: Towards a Minor Literature*, trans. Dana Polan (Minneapolis: University of Minnesota Press, 1986).

of states that is part of the range of the word."¹² For Deleuze and Guattari, Kafka's deterritorialized language defies the play of identity that is embedded in the process of representation and signification (x is x because it exists in a stable relation to y, itself defined as *not x*).

Nonsignification is nonidentity, or rather a critique of identity. This is the musicality that the two thinkers see in Kafka's minor literature, a musicality that several years earlier in *A Thousand Plateaus* offered the authors "lines of flight" out of the systematic tradition of Western philosophy. As they wrote there, "Music has always sent out lines of flight, like so many 'transformational multiplicities,' even overturning the very codes that structure or arborify it; that is why musical form, right down to its ruptures and proliferations, is comparable to a weed, a rhizome."¹³ Music does not confront the monolith of identity from the outside. Its critique of identity comes from within, from a place of participation in the mechanisms of representation and identity, a participation that is ultimately subversive. It mines at the foundations of such concepts and thereby undermines them.¹⁴

Deleuze and Guattari have been critiqued for presenting a restrictive notion of the minor. As Chana Kronfeld argues, by stipulating that minor literature be written in the major language, Deleuze and Guattari replicate the majoritarian nature of the very thing they wished to dismantle with their notion of the minor.¹⁵ For Kronfeld, it was important to open the term to include other modes of opposition to hegemony that remain excluded, in her view, from Deleuze and Guattari's theoretical reflections. Yet although she states her project's mission is to "call into question the simple opposition of minor and major literature and expose the fuzziness of the distinction

---

12. Deleuze and Guattari, *Kafka*, 22.
13. Gilles Deleuze and Félix Guattari, *A Thousand Plateaus: Capitalism and Schizophrenia*, trans. Brian Massumi (Minneapolis: University of Minnesota Press, 1987), 11–12. See also Ben-Horin, *Reading the Voices*, 57.
14. The French *littérature mineure* is a wordplay on the dual meaning of the word *mineur*—both minor and miner.
15. Chana Kronfeld, *On the Margins of Modernism: Decentering Literary Dynamics* (Berkeley: University of California Press, 1996).

between a deterritorialized and a reterritorialized language,"[16] Kronfeld remains dedicated to the recovery of an oppositional tradition, which she indeed expands but nonetheless still understands *against* a stable category of majority.

Such criticism of Deleuze and Guattari fails to account for the broader nondialectical impetus of their philosophical project, which also sustains their idea of minor literature. For Deleuze and Guattari, the categories of major and minor exist, but only so that they can repeatedly consolidate, explode, and disintegrate into one another. As they elaborate in the introductory chapter to *A Thousand Plateaus*, deterritorialized or nomad thinking, similar to the rhizome, flows in and out of territorialized and reterritorialized thought. "Every rhizome contains lines of segmentarity according to which it is stratified, territorialized, organized, signified, attributed, etc., as well as lines of deterritorialization down which it constantly flees.... How could movements of deterritorialization and processes of reterritorialization not be relative, always connected, caught up in one another?"[17]

Deleuze and Guattari's elaboration of deterritorialization inspired the term "unsettling" in this book. To deterritorialize and to unsettle is to make sure that even the so-called minor will not remain bound to a fixed position of marginality. If the minor is invariably defined by its oppositionality, it does nothing to unsettle the very thing it claims to oppose. The patterns of difference that this book has traced did not constitute moments of opposition or dialectical negotiation with an uncomplicated majority. For authors like Joseph Roth, Jewish difference presented a line of flight from the synthesizing mechanism of the (nation-) state. Mendel Singer, the protagonist of Roth's novel, did not oppose the state apparatus from an entrenched diasporic position. He was superfluous to it, an exception that could not be contained by one side of a struggle. I found that the nondialectical condition of being superfluous offered a productive way to think about difference in this book, not only because it presented a form of existence that is excessive to—and indeed exceeds—dialectical struggles with mechanisms like the state but also since it allowed me

---

16. Kronfeld, *On the Margins of Modernism*, 13.
17. Deleuze and Guattari, *A Thousand Plateaus*, 9–10.

Identity and Difference beyond Dialectics 255

to contemplate a different form of assimilation into so-called major cultures. By conceiving the act of assimilation as a form of quotation, notably, as a repetition of a certain cultural behavior and its modes of expression from an "aloof position," to quote Hannah Arendt,[18] we see how assimilation can dismantle the majority position of the quoted culture. Rather than confirm it as the telos of a process of integration (a target that can be either rejected or adopted to varying degrees, but still always engaged with dialectically), the idea of Jewish assimilation as repetition—an action that renders itself superfluous in this way—was able to wrench out the originary, organic, rooted status of the so-called major German culture.

Through assimilation understood as repetition or quotation, a difference between the minor position of the Jewish assimilant and the major position of the German only existed insofar as it was ambiguously volatile and emancipated from a relation of oppositionality. This is the emancipated notion of difference that Theodor Adorno encountered in the assimilated Gustav Mahler, the same difference that I also found in the assimilated Austrian-born composer Eric Zeisl and his opera *Hiob*.

The works of Arnold Schoenberg, Paul Ben-Haim, and Rudolf Borchardt offered other strategies to unsettle Jewish difference from dialectical binds. In Schoenberg's *Moses und Aron*, oppositional difference was unsettled by the radical heterogeneity that characterized Schoenberg's unstable image of the people. Understanding the people as constantly mutable, the composer came to contemplate some of the questions that have perturbed political theorists for centuries, at their center the problem of representation as that of reducing an irreducible collective to a stable sign. The people, as Schoenberg recognized, could not be reduced to the fixed concept of the general will; heterogeneity could not be substituted for the homogeneous, stable identity of a representative without admitting that the process involved a certain corruption. Read against the specific historical circumstances that surrounded Schoenberg's confrontation with the problem of representation in the 1930s, his observations about the

---

18. See Hannah Arendt, *The Jew as Pariah*, 72, as well as the discussion of Arendt's view of assimilation in chapter 5.

heterogeneity of the people link directly to the question of difference between Germans Jews and other Germans. Since neither group could be conceived as a stable homogeneous body, the issue of their oppositional difference was neutralized.

The ambiguity of Jewish difference as it pertained to various approaches to biblical language and translation in the twentieth century found expression in the work of Borchardt, arguably one of the most ambiguous figures in the poetic landscape of his time. The subversive nature of Borchardt's poetry, his theories of Creative Restoration and translation and their relation to his idea of the German nation, relied exactly on his presentation of commonly understood Jewish attributes as unequivocally German. "German," for Borchardt, was a title firmly grounded in cultural Protestantism. The broader debate about Bible translation that Borchardt and his narrative poem *Das Buch Joram* participated in continued to show the difficulty in assigning distinctly Jewish and German approaches to cultural Bible translations in the twentieth century.

While Borchardt tried to situate his own creative restoration of Luther's biblical German in opposition to what he saw as the Jewish Bible of Martin Buber and Franz Rosenzweig, critical reception grouped both works together when it considered the role of biblical language in modernism. Borchardt's polemic engagement with Buber's and Rosenzweig's philosophy of translation revealed multiple moments of role reversal, whereby a Jewish approach to language and translation aimed to supersede an existing German Protestant one rather than oppose it or offer an alternative from the margins. Claiming to supersede a Protestant position that regarded itself as the supersession of Judaism was a tactic that sought to reverse the relations between the two. For Rosenzweig, a new German Bible translation meant the supersession of Luther's Bible not only for Jews but for all Germans. And although Borchardt believed his own project opposed Buber's and Rosenzweig's work, he similarly sought not merely to preserve but to transcend Luther's Bible and offer it a "correction" of sorts, which his reception predominantly deemed Jewish.

This same ambiguous role reversal between the German-speaking Protestant and Jewish positions was also at the center of Ben-Haim's oratorical rendering of Borchardt's poem. By evoking the specific musical-dramatic form of the oratorio, together with Bach's passions as the genre's exemplary model in the German tradition, the oratorio *Joram* continued to offer commentary on the aesthetic entwinement of the Protestant and Jewish communities. It prompted a reflection on the oratorio's history of confounding the collective identities of Christians and Jews in Germany while calling on its audience to consider the formal-aesthetic potential of the open work that the oratorio offered.

The oratorical "opening" of the work—an action that reflected the condition of post-Reformation modernity both aesthetically and philosophically and thereby designated the oratorio a preeminently modern form—promoted the view of modern artworks as unstable and incomplete. This had a bearing on the notion of Jewish difference and the undeniable aesthetic stakes it acquired after Wagner. Wagner rigidified Jewish difference by linking his aesthetically constituted notion of the German people with a notion of a complete and total artwork and by imagining this total image against a Jewish foil. But if Wagner's idea of a total work sought to fix the German and Jewish positions in their opposition, the oratorio *Joram* neutralized this opposition by eroding the boundaries of the work and exposing both the work and the notion of the community that accompanied it in their fragmentariness and interminability.

Such moments of shifting and interchanging positions make it difficult to assign one side an unequivocal dominant role and another an equally unambiguous marginal role. We can understand this kind of subversion as quintessentially modernist. As Kronfeld observed, modernism was characterized by its effort to deterritorialize dominant major enunciations. This meant dismantling the major status of certain cultural modes of expression, but also the supremacy of canonical works. The contradiction that Kronfeld sought to critique was exactly the formation of a so-called modernist canon, a canon for a movement that aimed to abolish the canonical status as such.

The selections of works discussed in this book followed the same recognition that a modernist subversion of the major-minor relation cannot be limited to works that reception designated canonically modernist.[19] These were considered alongside works that in other contexts would be deemed epigonic or marginal.[20] From a theoretical perspective, perhaps no modernist aesthetic discussion referenced in this book demonstrates the issue better than the one that engaged Adorno, Benjamin, and, later, Lacoue-Labarthe concerning the persistence of the notion of "great works" in the twentieth century. Schoenberg's *Moses und Aron*, arguably the most canonically modernist work discussed here, is itself a contradiction: a "great work" that is nothing but a fragment. This same work presented a substantial challenge to someone like Adorno, who knew how problematic it was to still talk about "great works" in the twentieth century (because of the idolatrous substance that Wagner poured into this concept and because it overlooked the fragmented condition of life in modernity and in the twentieth century in particular) and was nevertheless still compelled to designate Schoenberg's opera a great work, as Lacoue-Labarthe observed. For Benjamin, too, the idea of a work's "truth content" indicated a lingering indebtedness to the notion of great works. But perhaps his view was the most modernist of them all (although, ironically, it was salvaged from German Romanticism). In Benjamin's writings from the 1920s, the notion of greatness migrates away from values that are intrinsic to the work and toward a critical capacity that is to be found only partially in the work itself, and partially in subsequent criticisms that sustain the work's ever-shifting afterlife.

A final word about the scope of the understanding of Jewish difference in this book. My object was to articulate modes of unsettled and uncontained difference, which I found by examining the relation between the German and Jewish positions in a certain historical period within specific geographical and cultural coordinates. I am wary of designating this mode of difference inherently or exclusively Jewish by proposing that it exceeds the historical, political, geographical, and cultural coordinates I set for this book.[21] This

---

19. See also Kita, *Jewish Difference and the Arts in Vienna*, xxii.
20. See also Kronfeld, *On the Margins of Modernism*, 227.
21. This would require separate studies of each case. Leslie Morris, for example, argues for a similar notion of difference in the German Jewish condition

mode of unsettled difference crystallized through the Jewish condition in a particular time and place. But in tracing its complexities, one must be cautious not to reify it again by rendering it unproblematically and ahistorically "Jewish." The "Jewish" aspect of such difference—like the musicality that Steinberg attributed to it—suffers itself from "an anxiety of articulation,"[22] namely, from a desire to "project a version of itself and at the same time embody its opposite," as Caroline Kita pithily put it.[23] In other words, just as music cannot articulate a critique of representation and identity from a place of fixed oppositionality but rather partakes in the same representational practices it critiques, so does Jewishness not remain exclusively Jewish in fixed opposition to non-Jewishness. If we strive to understand Jewish difference in this way, we realize that studying it is a plea to continue looking for similar modes of unsettled difference beyond Judaism.

---

post-1945. At the same time, she contrasts this deterritorialized difference to what she regards as the established German Jewish condition before 1945.
 22. See Steinberg, *Judaism Musical and Unmusical*, 223–28.
 23. Kita, *Jewish Difference and the Arts in Vienna*, xxviii.

Bibliography

Primary Sources

Adorno, Theodor W. *Aesthetic Theory*. Translated by Robert Hullot-Kentor. Minneapolis: University of Minnesota Press, 1997.
Adorno, Theodor W. *History and Freedom: Lectures 1964–1965*. Translated by Rodney Livingstone. Cambridge, MA: Polity, 2010.
Adorno, Theodor W. *In Search of Wagner*. Translated by Rodney Livingstone. New York: Verso, 2005.
Adorno, Theodor W. *Mahler: A Musical Physiognomy*. Translated by Edmund Jephcott. Chicago: University of Chicago Press, 1996.
Adorno, Theodor W. *Minima Moralia: Reflections from Damaged Life*. New York: Verso, 2005.
Adorno, Theodor W. *Notes to Literature*. Edited by Rolf Tiedemann. Translated by Shierry Weber Nicholsen. New York: Columbia University Press, 2019.
Adorno, Theodor W. *Philosophy of New Music*. Translated by Robert Hullot-Kentor. Minneapolis: University of Minnesota Press, 2006.
Adorno, Theodor W. *Quasi una Fantasia: Essays on Modern Music*. Translated by Rodney Livingstone. New York Verso, 2002.

Adorno, Theodor W. *Towards a Theory of Musical Reproduction*. Edited by Henri Lonitz. Translated by Wieland Hoban. Cambridge, UK: Polity Press, 2006.
Arendt, Hannah. *The Jew as Pariah: Jewish Identity and Politics in the Modern Age*. Edited by Ron H. Feldman. New York: Grove Press, 1978.
Arendt, Hannah. *The Origins of Totalitarianism*. New York: Harcourt, 1994.
Benjamin, Walter. *The Arcades Project*. Translated by Howard Eiland and Kevin McLaughlin. Cambridge, MA: Harvard University Press, 2002.
Benjamin, Walter. *Gesammelte Schriften III/1: Kritiken und Rezensionen*. Frankfurt am Main: Suhrkamp, 1980.
Benjamin, Walter. *Illuminations: Essays and Reflections*. Translated by Harry Zohn. New York: Schocken, 1968.
Benjamin, Walter. *Origin of the German Tragic Drama*. Translated by John Osborne. New York: Verso, 2009.
Benjamin, Walter. *Selected Writings I: 1913–1926*. Edited by Marcus Bullock and Michael W. Jennings. Cambridge MA: Harvard University Press, 2004.
Borchardt, Rudolf. *Ausgewählte Gedichte: Auswahl und Einleitung von Theodor W. Adorno*. Frankfurt am Main: Suhrkamp, 1968.
Borchardt, Rudolf. *Das Buch Joram*. Leipzig: Insel Verlag, 1907.
Borchardt, Rudolf. *Der Deutsche in der Landschaft besorgt von Rudolf Borchardt*. München: Bremer Presse, 1927.
Borchardt, Rudolf. *Gesammelte Briefe I*. Edited by Gerhard Schuster and Hans Zimmermann. München: Carl Hanser, 1994.
Borchardt, Rudolf. *Gesammelte Werke in Einzelbänden*. Edited by Marie Luise Borchardt. Stuttgart: Klett-Cotta, 2004.
Borchardt, Rudolf. *Handlungen und Abhandlungen*. Berlin-Grunewald: Horen, 1928.
Buber, Martin, and Franz Rosenzweig. *Scripture and Translation*. Translated by Lawrence Rosenwald and Everett Fox. Bloomington: Indiana University Press, 1994.
Devrient, Eduard. *Meine Erinnerungen an Felix Mendelssohn-Bartholdy und seine Briefe an mich*. Leipzig: Verlagsbuchhandlung Weber, 1872.
Dohm, Christian Wilhelm. *Ueber die buergerliche Verbesserung der Juden*. Berlin: Nicolai, 1783.
Forkel, Johann Nikolaus. "On Johann Sebastian Bach's Life, Genius, and Works." In *The Bach Reader*, edited by Hans T. David and Arthur Mendel, 352–53. New York: Norton, 1999.
Freud, Sigmund. *Moses and Monotheism: Three Essays*. Translated by James Starchey. London: Hogarth, 1974.
Haas, Willy. "Der Fall Rudolf Borchardt." In *Juden in der deutschen Literatur: Essays über zeitgenössische Schriftsteller*. Edited by Gustav Krojanker. Berlin: Weltverlag, 1922.
Hegel, Georg Friedrich. *Gesammelte Werke, Frühere Schriften I*. Edited by Friedhelm Nicolin and Gisela Schüler. Hamburg: Felix Meiner, 2014.

Bibliography   263

Hegel, Georg Friedrich. "The Spirit of Christianity and Its Fate." In *Early Theological Writings*. Translated by T. M. Knox. Chicago: Chicago University Press, 1948.
Heine, Heinrich. *The Harz Journey and Selected Prose*. Translated by Ritchie Robertson. London: Penguin, 1993.
Hobbes, Thomas. *Leviathan*. Edited by Richard Tuck. Cambridge: Cambridge University Press, 1991.
Hume, David. *A Treatise of Human Nature*. Edited by L. A. Shelby-Bigge. Oxford: Clarendon, 1968.
Kant, Immanuel. *Critique of Judgement*. Translated by Werner S. Pluhar. Indianapolis, IN: Hackett, 1987.
Kant, Immanuel. *Werke in 12 Bänden*. Edited by W. Weisched. Frankfurt: Suhrkamp, 1964.
Kracauer, Siegfried. *The Mass Ornament*. Translated by Thomas Y. Levin. Cambridge, MA: Harvard University Press, 1995.
Lessing, Gotthold Ephraim. *Werke in acht Bänden*. Edited by Herbert Göpfert. München: Hanser, 1979.
Lessing, Theodor. *Jüdischer Selbsthaß*. Berlin: Jüdischer Verlag, 1930.
Loos, Adolf. "Ornament and Crime." In *Programs and Manifestoes on 20th-Century Architecture*. Edited by Ulrich Conrads. Translated by Michael Bullock. London: Lund Humphries, 1970.
Mann, Thomas. *Das Gesetz*. Stockholm: Berman-Fischer Verlag, 1944.
Mattheson, Johann. *Der vollkommene Capellmeister*. 1739. Reprinted and translated by Ernest C. Harris. Ann Arbor: University of Michigan Research Press, 1981.
Nietzsche, Friedrich. *The Basic Writings of Nietzsche*. Translated by Walter Kaufmann. New York: Modern Library, 2000.
Nietzsche, Friedrich. *Briefe 1*. Edited by Giorgio Colli and Mazzino Montinari. Berlin: De Gruyter, 1977.
Nordau, Max. *Degeneration*. New York: D. Appleton, 1895.
Rosenzweig, Franz. *Der Mensch und sein Werk: Gesammelte Schriften I, Briefe und Tagebücher II: 1918–1929*. Edited by Rachel Rosenzweig and Edith Rosenzweig-Scheinmann. The Hague: Martinus Nijhoff, 1979.
Rosenzweig, Franz. "Die Schrift und das Wort: zur neuen Bibelübersetzung." In *Kleinere Schriften*. Berlin: Schocken, 1937.
Roth, Joseph. *The Collected Stories of Joseph Roth*. Translated by Michael Hofmann. New York: Norton, 2002.
Roth, Joseph. *Job: The Story of a Simple Man*. Translated by Dorothy Thompson. New York: Viking, 1931.
Roth, Joseph. *A Life in Letters*. Translated and edited by Michael Hofmann. New York: Norton, 2012.
Roth, Joseph. *The Wandering Jews*. Translated by Michael Hofmann. New York: Norton, 2001.
Roth, Joseph. *Werke*. Edited by Fritz Hackert and Klaus Westermann. Köln: Kiepenheuer & Witsch, 1991.

Roth, Joseph. *The White Cities: Reports from France 1925–39*. Translated by Michael Hofmann. London: Granta, 2005.
Rousseau, Jean-Jacques. *The Basic Political Writing*. Translated by Donald A. Cress. Indianapolis, IN: Hackett, 1987.
Schmitt, Carl. *Constitutional Theory*. Translated by Jeffrey Seitzer. Durham, NC: Duke University Press, 2008.
Schmitt, Carl. *The Crisis of Parliamentary Democracy*. Translated by Ellen Kennedy. Cambridge, MA: MIT Press, 1988.
Schmitt, Carl. *Legalität und Legitimität*. Berlin: Duncker und Humblot, 1932.
Schmitt, Carl. *Political Theology*. Translated by George Schwab. Chicago: Chicago University Press, 2005.
Schoenberg, Arnold. "Jeder junge Jude." *Journal of the Arnold Schoenberg Institute* 17, no. 1–2 (1994): 452–55.
Schoenberg, Arnold. *Moses und Aron Oper in drei Akten: Textbuch*. Mainz: Schott, 1957.
Schoenberg, Arnold. *Style and Idea: Selected Writings*. Edited by Leonard Stein. Translated by Leo Black. Berkeley: University of California Press, 1984.
Schoenberg, Arnold. *Theory of Harmony*. Translated by Roy E. Carter. Berkeley: University of California Press, 1983.
Scholem, Gershom. *On Jews and Judaism in Crisis*. Philadelphia: Paul Dry Books, 2012.
Scholem, Gershom. *The Messianic Idea in Judaism*. New York: Schocken, 1971.
Smith, Adam. *Theory of Moral Sentiments*. Edited by Knut Haakonssen. Cambridge: Cambridge University Press, 2002.
Stumpf, Carl. "Tonsystem und Musik der Siamesen." In *Beiträge zur Akustik und zur Musikwissenschaft*. Vol. 3. Leipzig, 1901.
Wagner, Richard. *Prose Works*. Vol. 4, *Art and Politics*. Translated by William Ashton Ellis. London: Paul, Trench, Trübner, 1895.
Wagner, Richard. *Das Judentum in der Musik*. Leipzig: Verlagsbuchhandlung von J. J. Weber, 1869.

Secondary Literature

Achinger, Christine. "Allegories of Destruction: 'Woman' and 'the Jew' in Otto Weininger's *Sex and Character*." *The Germanic Review: Literature, Culture, Theory* 88, no. 2 (2013): 121–49.
Albright, Daniel. "Butchering Moses." *The Opera Quarterly* 23, no. 4 (2007): 441–54.
Almog, Yael. *Secularism and Hermeneutics*. Philadelphia: University of Pennsylvania Press, 2019.
Applegate, Celia. *Bach in Berlin: Nation and Culture in Mendelssohn's Revival of the St. Matthew Passion*. Ithaca, NY: Cornell University Press, 2005.

Arndt, Erwin, and Gisela Brandt. *Luther und die deutsche Sprache.* Leipzig: VEB Bibliographisches Institut, 1983.
Aschheim, Steven E. "Nazism Culture, and the Origins of Totalitarianism: Hannah Arendt and the Discourse of Evil." *New German Critique* 70 (1997): 117–39.
Assmann, Jan. "Die Mosaische Unterscheidung in Arnold Schönbergs *Moses und Aron.*" *Musik und Ästhetik* 33 (2005): 5–29.
Assmann, Jan. *Moses the Egyptian: The Memory of Egypt in Western Monotheism.* Cambridge, MA: Harvard University Press, 1997.
Assmann, Jan. *The Price of Monotheism.* Translated by Robert Savage. Stanford, CA: Stanford University Press, 2010.
Auner, Joseph. *A Schoenberg Reader: Documents of a Life.* New Haven, CT: Yale University Press, 2003.
Avenary, Hannoch. "Jüdische Musik." In *Die Musik in Geschichte und Gegenwart. Allgemeine Enzyklopädie der Musik*, vol. 4, no. 2. Edited by Ludwig Finscher, 1511–69. Kassel-Stuttgart-Weimar: Bärenreiter-Metzler, 1996.
Badiou, Alain. *Five Lessons on Wagner.* London: Verso, 2010.
Barnard, Frederick M. *Herder on Nationality, Humanity, and History.* Montreal: McGill University Press, 2003.
Bauer-Lechner, Natalie. *Recollections of Gustav Mahler.* Translated by Dika Newlin. Cambridge: Cambridge University Press, 1980.
Bauman, Zygmunt. "The Fate of Humanity in the Post-Trinitarian World." *Journal of Human Rights* 1, no. 3 (2002): 283–303.
Bauman, Zygmunt. *Modernity and Ambivalence.* Cambridge, UK: Polity Press, 1991.
Beckerman, Michael. "Jezek, Zeisl, Améry, and the Exile in the Middle." In *Music and Displacement: Diasporas, Mobilities, and Dislocations in Europe and Beyond.* Edited by Erik Levi and Florian Scheding. Lanham, MD: Scarecrow Press, 2010.
Beckerman, Michael. "Job, Zeisl, and the suffering of the Ordinary." *Music & Politics* 5, no. 2 (2011).
Benhabib, Seyla, and Raluca Eddon. "From Antisemitism to 'the Right to Have Rights': The Jewish Roots of Hannah Arendt's Cosmopolitanism." In *Antisemitism and Philosemitism in the Twentieth and Twenty-First Centuries: Representing Jews, Jewishness, and Modern Culture*, edited by Phyllis Lassner and Lara Trubowitz, 63–80. Newark: University of Delaware Press, 2008.
Ben-Horin, Michal. *Reading the Voices: Musical Poetics between German and Hebrew.* Jerusalem: Bialik Publishing, 2022.
Bernauer, Markus. "Das Zentrum der Poesie: Rudolf Borchardts Garten Idee." In *Rudolf Borchardt und seine Zeitgenossen.* Edited by Ernst Osterkamp. Berlin: De Gruyter, 1997.
Berry, Mark. *After Wagner: Histories of Modernist Music Drama from Parsifal to Nono.* Woodbridge, UK: Boydell Press, 2014.

Berry, Mark. "Arnold Schoenberg's Biblical Way: From 'Die Jakobsleiter' to 'Moses und Aron.'" *Music and Letters* 89, no. 1 (2008): 84–108.
Besch, Werner. *Luther und die deutsche Sprache: 500 Jahre deutsche Sprachgeschichte im Lichte der neueren Forschung*. Berlin: Erich Schmitt, 2014.
Biale, David. *Power and Powerlessness in Jewish History: The Jewish Tradition and the Myth of Passivity*. New York: Schocken, 1986.
Blumenberg, Hans. *Arbeit am Mythos*. Frankfurt am Main: Suhrkamp, 1979.
Borio, Gianmario. "Schenker versus Schoenberg versus Schenker: The Difficulties of a Reconciliation." *Journal of the Royal Music Association* 126 (2001): 250–74.
Botstein, Leon, and Werner Hanak, eds. *Vienna: Jews and the City of Music 1870–1938*. Annandale, NY: Yeshiva University Museum and Bard College, 2004.
Brah, Avtar. *Cartographies of Diaspora: Contesting Identities*. New York: Routledge, 1996.
Britt, Brian. "The Romantic Roots of the Debate on the Buber-Rosenzweig Bible." *Prooftexts* 20, no. 3 (2000): 262–89.
Brod, Max. *Die Musik Israels*. Kassel: Bärenreiter Verlag, 1976.
Bronsen, David. "Austrian versus Jew: The Torn Identity of Joseph Roth." *Leo Baeck Institute Year Book* 18 (1973): 220–26.
Bronsen, David. *Joseph Roth: Eine Biographie*. Köln: Kiepenheuer & Witsch, 1974.
Bronsen, David. "Der Jude auf der Suche nach dem Vaterland: Joseph Roths Verhältnis zur habsburgischen Monarchie." *Wiener Tagebuch* 8 (1979).
Bürger, Peter. *Theory of the Avant-Gard*. Translated by Michael Shaw. Minneapolis: University of Minnesota Press, 1984.
Butler, Geoffrey P. "'It's the Bitterness That Counts': Joseph Roth's 'Most Jewish' Novel Rediscovered." *German Life and Letters* 41, no. 3 (1988): 227–34.
Butt, John. *Bach's Dialog with Modernity: Perspectives on the Passions*. Cambridge: Cambridge University Press, 2010.
Butt, John. "Bach's Vocal Scoring: What Can It Mean?" *Early Music* 26 (1998): 99–107.
Canovan, Margaret. *The Political Thought of Hannah Arendt*. New York: Harcourt, 1974.
Carr, Gilbert J. "The 'Habsburg Myth,' Ornament and Metaphor: Adolf Loos, Karl Kraus, and Robert Musil." *Austrian Studies* 15 (2007): 65–79.
Clifford, James. "Diasporas." *Cultural Anthropology* 9, no. 3 (1994): 302–38.
Cohen, Yehuda. *The Heirs of the Psalmists*. Tel-Aviv: Am-Oved, 1990.
Cole, Malcolm S. "Eric Zeisl's Hiob: The Story of an Unsung Opera." *The Opera Quarterly* 9, no. 1 (1992): 52–76.
Cole, Malcolm S., and Barbara Barclay. *Armseelchen: The Life and Music of Eric Zeisl*. Westport, CT: Greenwood Press, 1984.
Cooley, Timothy J. "Folk Music in Eastern Europe." In *The Cambridge History of World Music*, edited by Philip Bohlman, 352–70. Cambridge: Cambridge University Press, 2013.

Dahlhaus, Carl. "Schoenberg and Schenker." *Proceedings of the Royal Musical Association* 100 (1973–1974): 209–15.
Deleuze, Gilles, and Félix Guattari. *Kafka: Towards a Minor Literature*. Translated by Dana Polan. Minneapolis: University of Minnesota Press, 1986.
Deleuze, Gilles, and Félix Guattari. *A Thousand Plateaus: Capitalism and Schizophrenia*. Translated by Brian Massumi. Minneapolis: University of Minnesota Press, 1987.
de Man, Paul. "Political Allegory in Rousseau." *Critical Inquiry* 2, no. 4 (1976): 649–75.
Derrida, Jacques. *Acts of Literature*. Edited by Derek Attridge. New York: Routledge, 1992.
Derrida, Jacques. *Acts of Religion*. Edited by Gil Anidjar. New York: Routledge 2002.
Derrida, Jacques. "What Is a 'Relevant' Translation?" Translated by Lawrence Venuti. *Critical Inquiry* 27, no. 2 (2001): 174–200.
Derrida, Jacques. *Writing and Difference*. Translated by Alan Bass. Chicago: University of Chicago Press, 1978.
Dewitz, Hans-Georg. *Dante Deutsch: Studien zu Rudolf Borchardts Übertragung der Divina Comedia*. Göppingen: Verlag Alfred Kümmerle, 1971.
Ferber, Ilit, and Paula Schwebel, eds. *Lament in Jewish Thought: Philosophical, Theological, and Literary Perspectives*. Berlin: De Gruyter, 2014.
Fraiman, Sarah. "Joseph Roth: Dichter des Offenen." *Bulletin des Leo Baeck Instituts* 76 (1987): 35–50.
Friedlander, Eli. "On the Musical Gathering of Echoes of the Voice: Walter Benjamin on Opera and the Trauerspiel." *The Opera Quarterly* 21, no. 4 (2005): 631–46.
Friedländer, Saul. *Nazi Germany and the Jews: Volume 1: The Years of Persecution*. New York: Harper, 1997.
Funkenstein, Amos. "The Dialectics of Assimilation." *Jewish Social Studies* 1, no. 2 (1995): 1–14.
Gammon, Martin. "Exemplary Originality: Kant on Genius and Imitation." *Journal of the History of Philosophy* 35, no. 4 (1997): 563–92.
Garloff, Katja. *Mixed Feelings: Tropes of Love in German-Jewish Culture*. Ithaca, NY: Cornell University Press, 2016.
Geck, Martin. *Johann Sebastian Bach: Life and Work*. Translated by John Hargraves. Orlando, FL: Harcourt, 2006.
Geck, Martin. *Die Wiederentdeckung der Matthäuspassion im 19. Jahrhundert*. Regensburg: Gustav Bosse Verlag, 1967.
Gillman, Abigail. *A History of German-Jewish Bible Translation*. Chicago: University of Chicago Press, 2018.
Glatzer, Nahum, and Paul Mendes-Flohr, eds. *The Letters of Martin Buber*. Translated by Richard Winston, Clara Winston, and Harry Zohn. New York: Schocken, 1991.
Goetschel, Willi. *Heine and Critical Theory*. New York: Bloomsbury, 2019.

Goetschel, Willi. *Spinoza's Modernity: Mendelssohn, Lessing, and Heine.* Madison: University of Wisconsin Press, 2004.
Goldstein, Bluma. "Schoenberg's Moses und Aron: A Vanishing Biblical Nation." In *Political and Religious Ideas in the Works of Arnold Schoenberg*, edited by Charlotte M. Cross and Russell A. Berman, 159–92. New York: Garland, 2000.
Graetz, Daniela. "Ästhetische Selbstmächtigung im Namen der Nation: Rudolf Borchardt als Nationalpädagoge und Anthologe." In *Die Souveränität der Literatur: Zum Totalitären der Klassischen Moderne 1900–1933.* Edited by Uwe Hebekus and Ingo Stöckmann. München: Wilhelm Fink, 2008.
Greaney, Patrick. *Quotational Practices: Repeating the Future in Contemporary Art.* Minneapolis: University of Minnesota Press, 2014.
Grout, Donald J., and Hermine Weigel Williams. *A Short History of Opera.* New York: Columbia University Press, 2003.
Gurkiewicz, Liran. "Paul Ben-Haim: The Oratorio *Joram* and the Jewish Identity of the Composer." *Min-Ad* 11 (2013): 106–29.
HaCohen, Ruth. "Between Noise and Harmony: The Oratorical Moment in the Musical Entanglement between Jews and Christians." *Critical Inquiry* 32, no. 2 (2006): 250–77.
HaCohen, Ruth. *The Music Libel against the Jews.* New Haven, CT: Yale University Press, 2011.
Heizmann, Jürgen. *Joseph Roth und die Ästhetik der neuen Sachlichkeit.* Heidelberg: Mattes, 1990.
Herf, Jeffrey. *Reactionary Modernism: Technology, Culture, and Politics in Weimar and the Third Reich.* Cambridge: Cambridge University Press, 1984.
Herzog, Andreas. "'Der Segen des ewigen Juden': Zur 'jüdischen Identität' Joseph Roths." In *Habsburger Aporien? Geisteshaltungen und Lebenskonzepte in der multinationalen Literatur der Habsburger Monarchie.* Edited by Eva Reichmann. Bielefeld: Aisthesis, 1998.
Hess, Jonathan. *Germans, Jews, and the Claims of Modernity.* New Haven, CT: Yale University Press, 2002.
Hirshberg, Jehoash. *Paul Ben-Haim: His Life and Work.* Tel-Aviv: Israel Music Institute, 2010.
Holl, Ute. *The Moses Complex: Freud, Schoenberg, Straub/Huillet.* Translated by Michael Turnbull. Zurich: Diaphanes, 2017.
Hummel, Hildegard. *Rudolf Borchardt: Interpretationen zu seiner Lyrik.* Frankfurt am Main: Peter Lang, 1983.
Ilany, Ofri. *In Search of the Hebrew People: Bible and Nation in the German Enlightenment.* Bloomington: Indiana University Press: 2018.
Jay, Martin. *Permanent Exiles: Essays on the Intellectual Migration from Germany to America.* New York: Columbia University Press, 1985.
Jones, Richard D. P. *The Creative Development of Johann Sebastian Bach.* Vol. 2, *1717–1750.* Oxford: Oxford University Press, 2013.
Kaufmann, Kai. *Rudolf Borchardt und "der Untergang der deutschen Nation": Selbstinszenierung als Geschichtskonstruktion im essayistischen Werk.* Tübingen: Niemeyer, 2003.

Kerman, Joseph. "How We Got into Analysis and How to Get Out." *Critical inquiry* 7, no. 2 (1980): 311–31.
Kesten, Hermann. "Joseph Roth." *Wort in der Zeit* 9 (1959).
Kissler, Alexander. *"Wo bin ich den behaust?" Rudolf Borchardt und der Erfindung des Ichs*. Göttingen: Wallstein, 2003.
Kita, Caroline A. *Jewish Difference and the Arts in Vienna: Composing Compassion in Music and Biblical Theater*. Bloomington: Indiana University Press, 2019.
Knödler, Stefan. *Rudolf Borchardt Anthologien*. Berlin: De Gruyter, 2010.
Koss, Juliet. *Modernism after Wagner*. Minneapolis: University of Minnesota Press, 2009.
Kraft, Werner. *Rudolf Borchardt: Welt aus Poesie und Geschichte*. Hamburg: Claassen, 1961.
Kronfeld, Chana. *On the Margins of Modernism: Decentering Literary Dynamics*. Berkeley: University of California Press, 1996.
Lacoue-Labarthe, Philippe. "The Caesura of Religion." In *Opera through Other Eyes*. Edited by David J. Levin. Stanford, CA: Stanford University Press, 1993.
Lacoue-Labarthe, Philippe. *Musica Ficta: Figures of Wagner*. Translated by Felicia McCarren. Stanford, CA: Stanford University Press, 1994.
Lazar, Moshe. "The Biblical Way." *Journal of the Arnold Schoenberg Institute* 17 (1994): 162–330.
Lazaroms, Ilse Josepha. *The Grace of Misery: Joseph Roth and the Politics of Exile, 1919–1939*. Boston: Brill, 2013.
Leonard, Miriam. *Tragic Modernities*. Cambridge, MA: Harvard University Press, 2015.
Lewin, David. "Moses und Aron: Some General Remarks and Analytic Notes for Act 1, Scene 1." *Perspectives of New Music* 6, no. 1 (1967): 1–17.
Long, Christopher. "The Origin and Context of Adolf Loos's 'Ornament and Crime.'" *Journal of the Society of Architectural Historians* 68, no. 2 (2009): 200–223.
Lukács, Georg. *Die Theorie des Romans*. Berlin: Paul Cassirer, 1920.
Lukács, Georg. *The Theory of the Novel*. Translated by Anna Bostock. Cambridge, MA: MIT Press, 1999.
MacDonald, Malcolm. *Schoenberg*. 2nd ed. Oxford: Oxford University Press, 2008.
Mack, Michael. *German Idealism and the Jew*. Chicago: Chicago University Press, 2003.
Mäckelmann, Michael. *Arnold Schönberg und das Judentum: Der Komponist und sein religiöses, nationales und politisches Selbstverständnis nach 1921*. Hamburg: K. D. Wagner, 1984.
Magris, Claudio. *Der Habsburgische Mythos in der österreichischen Literatur*. Salzburg: Otto Müller Verlag, 1966.
Marissen, Michael. *Bach and God*. Oxford: Oxford University Press, 2016.

Martinec, Thomas. "The Boundaries of 'Mitleidsdramaturgie': Some Clarifications Concerning Lessing's Concept of Mitleid." *The Modern Language Review* 101, no. 3 (2006): 743–58.
Matz, Wolfgang. *Eine Kugel im Leibe: Walter Benjamin und Rudolf Borchardt: Judentum und deutsche Poesie.* Göttingen: Wallstein, 2011.
McBride, Patrizia C. *The Chatter of the Visible.* Ann Arbor: University of Michigan Press, 2016.
Melamed, Daniel R. *Hearing Bach's Passions.* Oxford: Oxford University Press, 2005.
Michaud, Eric. *The Cult of Art in Nazi Germany.* Translated by Janet Lloyd. Stanford, CA: Stanford University Press, 2004.
Miller, Malcolm. "Munich: Ben-Haim's *Joram*." *Tempo* 63 (2009): 52–53.
Mishra, Sudesh. *Diaspora Criticism.* Edinburgh: Edinburgh University Press, 2006.
Mitchell, Donald. *Gustav Mahler: Songs and Symphonies of Life and Death.* Woodbridge, UK: Boydell Press, 2002.
Moore, G. F. "The Vulgate Chapters and Numbered Verses in the Hebrew Bible." *Journal of Biblical Literature* 12, no.1 (1893): 73–78.
Morazzoni, Anna Maria, ed. *Arnold Schoenberg: Stile herrschen, Gedanke siegen: Ausgewählte Schriften.* Mainz: Schott 2007.
Moretti, Franco. *The Way of the World: The Bildungsroman in European Culture.* New York: Verso, 2000.
Móricz, Klára. *Jewish Identities: Nationalism, Racism, and Utopianism in Twentieth-Century Music.* Berkeley: University of California Press, 2008.
Morris, Leslie. *The Translated Jew: German Jewish Culture outside the Margins.* Evanston, IL: Northwestern University Press, 2018.
Moyn, Samuel. "German Jewry and the Question of Identity Historiography and Theory." *The Leo Baeck Institute Yearbook* 41, no. 1 (1994): 291–308.
Müller-Sievers, Helmut. *Disorientierung: Anatomie und Dichtung bei Georg Büchner.* Göttingen: Wallstein, 2003.
Müller-Sievers, Helmut. "On the Way to Quotation: Paul Celan's 'Meridian' Speech." *New German Critique* 91 (2004): 131–49.
Neumann, Markus. *Die "englische Komponente."* Göttingen: Vandenhoeck & Ruprecht, 2007.
Neumann, Werner. *Handbuch der Kantaten Johann Sebastian Bachs.* Wiesbaden: Breitkopf und Härtel, 1966.
Niekerk, Carl. *Reading Mahler: German Culture and Jewish Identity in Fin-de-Siècle Vienna.* Rochester, NY: Camden House, 2010.
Osterkamp, Ernst. "Näherungen: Rudolf Borchardt im Werk Walter Benjamins." *Germanisch-Romanische Monatsschrift* 31, no. 2 (1981): 203–33.
Painter, Karen. "Contested Counterpoint: 'Jewish' Appropriation and Polyphonic Liberation." *Archiv für Musikwissenschaft* 58, no. 3 (2001): 201–30.
Painter, Karen. *Symphonic Aspirations: German Music and Politics, 1900–1945.* Cambridge, MA: Harvard University Press, 2007.

Piloiu, Rares G. "The Paradoxes of Left Socialism in Interwar Austria: Joseph Roth and Austro-Marxism." *Modern Austrian Literature* 40, no. 3 (2007): 21–41.
Plass, Ulrich. *Language and History in Theodor W. Adorno's Notes to Literature*. New York: Routledge, 2007.
Reinharz, Jehuda, and Walter Schatzberg, eds. *The Jewish Responses to German Culture*. Hanover, NH: University Press of New England, 1985.
Ringer, Alexander. *Arnold Schoenberg: The Composer as Jew*. Oxford: Clarendon 1993.
Ringer, Alexander. "Schoenberg and the Concept of Law." In *Bericht über den 1. Kongress der Internationalen Schönberg-Gesellschaft Wien 4.–9. Juni 1974*, edited by Rudolf Stephan, 165–72. Wien: Verlag Elisabeth Lafite, 1978.
Robertson, Ritchie. "Roth's *Hiob* and the Traditions of Ghetto Fiction." In *Co-Existent Contradiction: Joseph Roth in Retrospect*, edited by Helen Chambers, 185–200. Riverside, CA: Ariadne, 1991.
Rosenfeld, Sidney. *Understanding Joseph Roth*. Columbia: University of South Carolina Press, 2001.
Rosenthal, Michael A. "Art and the Politics of the Desert: German Exiles in California and the Biblical *Bilderverbot*." *New German Critique* 118, no. 40 (2013): 43–64.
Rosowsky, Solomon. *The Cantillations of the Bible*. New York: Reconstructionist Press, 1957.
Ross, Alex. *Wagnerism: Art and Politics in the Shadow of Music*. New York: Farrar, Straus and Giroux, 2020.
Sander, Sabine. "Between Acculturation and Self-Assertion: Individualization in the German-Jewish Context of the German Empire and the Weimar Republic and Its Contribution to the Development of Modern Sociology." *Religion* 45, no. 3 (2015): 429–50.
Schmidt, Matthias. "Vor dem Gesetz: Zur religiösen Dimension eines musikalischen Begriffs bei Schönberg." In *Arnold Schoenberg und sein Gott, Bericht zum Symposium 26.–29. Juni 2002*. Wien: Arnold Schönberg Center, 2003.
Schorske, Carl E. *Fin-de-Siècle Vienna: Politics and Culture*. New York: Knopf, 1980.
Schuster, Gerhard, ed. *Rudolf Borchardt, Martin Buber: Briefe, Dokumente, Gespräche 1907–1964*. Ebersberg: Rudolf Borchardt-Gesellschaft, 1991.
Schutjer, Karin. *Goethe and Judaism: The Troubled Inheritance of Modern Literature*. Evanston, IL: Northwestern University Press, 2015.
Seidman, Naomi. *Faithful Renderings: Jewish-Christian Difference and the Politics of Translation*. Chicago: University of Chicago Press, 2006.
Seroussi, Edwin. "Music: The Jew of Jewish Studies." *Jewish Studies* 46 (2009): 3–84.
Seter, Ronit. "Hirshberg's *Ben-Haim*: Three Decades Later." *Min-Ad: Israel Studies in Musicology Online* 9 (2010): 97–113.

Shaked, Gershon. *The New Tradition: Essays on Modern Hebrew Literature.* Cincinnati: Hebrew Union College, 2006.

Shavit, Yaacov, and Mordechai Eran. *The Hebrew Bible Reborn: From Holy Scripture to the Book of Books.* Translated by Chaya Naor. Berlin: De Gruyter, 2007.

Sheehan, Jonathan. *The Enlightenment Bible: Translation, Scholarship, Culture.* Princeton, NJ: Princeton University Press, 2005.

Shelleg, Assaf. *Theological Stains: Art Music and the Zionist Project.* Oxford: Oxford University Press, 2020.

Sieg, Werner. *Zwischen Anarchismus und Fiktion: Eine Untersuchung zum Werk von Joseph Roth.* Bonn: Bouvier, 1974.

Silverman, Lisa. "Rethinking Jews, Antisemitism, and Jewish Difference in Postwar Germany." In *The Future of the German-Jewish Past: Memory and the Question of Antisemitism*, edited by Gideon Reuveni and Diana Franklin, 135–45. West Lafayette, IN: Purdue University Press, 2021.

Skolnik, Jonathan. *Jewish Pasts, German Fictions: History, Memory, and Minority Culture in Germany, 1824–1955.* Stanford, CA: Stanford University Press, 2014.

Smith, Anthony D. *Chosen Peoples: Sacred Sources of National Identity.* Oxford: Oxford University Press, 2003.

Smith, Matthew W. *The Total Work of Art: From Bayreuth to Cyberspace.* New York: Routledge, 2007.

Smither, Howard E. *A History of the Oratorio.* 4 vols. Chapel Hill: University of North Carolina Press, 1977.

Solie, Ruth A. "The Living Work: Organicism and Musical Analysis." *19th-Century Music* 4, no. 2 (1980): 147–56.

Sorkin, David. "Emancipation and Assimilation: Two Concepts and Their Application to German-Jewish History." *Leo Baeck Institute Yearbook* 35, no. 1 (1990): 17–33.

Sorkin, David. *The Transformation of German Jewry 1780–1840.* New York: Oxford University Press, 1987.

Spector, Scott. "Forget Assimilation: Introducing Subjectivity to German-Jewish History." *Jewish History* 20, no. 3 (2006): 349–61.

Spector, Scott. *Modernism without Jews? German-Jewish Subjects and Histories.* Bloomington: Indiana University Press, 2017.

Sprengel, Peter. *Rudolf Borchardt, der Herr der Worte: Eine Biographie.* München: C. H. Beck, 2015.

Stadlen, Peter. "Schoenberg's Speech-Song." *Music and Letters* 62, no. 1 (1981): 1–11.

Staudenmaier, Peter. "Hannah Arendt's Analysis of Antisemitism in the *Origins of Totalitarianism*: A Critical Analysis." *Patterns of Prejudice* 46, no. 2 (2012): 154–79.

Steinberg, Michael P. *Judaism Musical and Unmusical.* Chicago: University of Chicago Press, 2007.

Steinberg, Michael P. *Listening to Reason: Culture, Subjectivity and Nineteenth-Century Music*. Princeton, NJ: Princeton University Press, 2004.
Steiner, George. *The Death of Tragedy*. New York: Alfred Knopf, 1963.
Stern, Guy. "Job as Alter Ego: The Bible, Ancient Jewish Discourse, and Exile Literature." *The German Quarterly* 63, no. 2 (1990): 199–210.
Szondi, Peter. *An Essay on the Tragic*. Translated by Paul Fleming. Stanford, CA: Stanford University Press, 2002.
Taubes, Jacob. *The Political Theology of Paul*. Edited by Aleida Assmann, Jan Assmann, and Wolf-Daniel Hartwich. Translated by Dana Hollander. Stanford, CA: Stanford University Press, 2008.
Taubes, Jacob. *To Carl Schmitt*. New York: Columbia University Press, 2013.
Todd, R. Larry. *Mendelssohn: A Life in Music*. Oxford: Oxford University Press, 2003.
Tonkin, Kati. *Joseph Roth's March into History: From the Early Novels to Radetzkymarsch and Die Kapuzinergruft*. Rochester, NY: Camden House, 2008.
Vogl, Joseph. *On Tarrying*. Translated by Helmut Müller-Sievers. Calcutta: Seagull Books, 2011.
Volkov, Shulamit. *Germans, Jews, and Antisemites: Trials in Emancipation*. Cambridge: Cambridge University Press, 2006.
Wagner, Karin, ed. *Es grüsst dich Erichisrael: Briefe von und an Eric Zeisl*. Wien: Czernin Verlag, 2008.
Wagner, Karin. *Fremd bin ich ausgezogen, Eric Zeisl-Biographie*. Wien: Czernin, 2005.
Wahrman, Dror. *The Making of the Modern Self: Identity and Culture in Eighteenth-Century England*. New Haven, CT: Yale University Press, 2004.
Watkins, Holly. "Schoenberg's Interior Designs." *Journal of the American Musicological Society* 61 (2008): 152–54.
Weber, Samuel. "In the Name of the Law." *Cardozo Law Review* 11 (1990): 1515–38.
Weber, Samuel. *Theatricality as Medium*. New York: Fordham University Press, 2004.
Weissberg, Liliane. "Juden oder Hebräer? Religiöse und politische Bekehrung bei Herder." In *Johann Gottfried Herder: Geschichte und Kultur*. Edited by Martin Bollacher. Würzburg: Königshausen & Neumann, 1994.
White, Pamela C. *Schoenberg and the God-Idea: The Opera Moses und Aron*. Ann Arbor: University of Michigan Research Press, 1985.
Wistrich, Robert S. *The Jews of Vienna in the Age of Franz Joseph*. Oxford: Oxford University Press, 1990.
Wollney, Peter. "Sara Levy and the Making of Musical Taste in Berlin." *The Musical Quarterly* 77, no. 4 (1993): 651–88.
Yerushalmi, Yosef Hayim. *Assimilation and Racial Anti-Semitism: The Iberian and German Models, Leo Baeck Memorial Lecture*. New York: Leo Baeck Institute, 1982.

Yerushalmi, Yosef Hayim. *Freud's Moses: Judaism Terminable and Interminable.* New Haven, CT: Yale University Press, 1991.

Yerushalmi, Yosef Hayim. "The Moses of Freud and the Moses of Schoenberg: On Words, Idolatry, and Psychoanalysis." *The Psychoanalytic Study of the Child* 47, no. 1 (1992): 1–20.

Yovel, Yirmiyahu. *Dark Riddle: Hegel, Nietzsche, and the Jews.* Cambridge, UK: Polity Press, 1998.

Žižek, Slavoj. *The Sublime Object of Ideology.* New York: Verso, 1989.

Index

Adler, Guido, 240
Adorno, Theodor W., 5, 7, 23, 27, 28, 166, 176, 240, 258; Borchardt and, 38, 47, 51–53, 74; Heine and, 227; on the "joy of interpretation," 233n73; Mahler and, 228–31, 234, 243, 255; Schoenberg and, 120–22, 134–35, 153–56, 164, 171, 236n79; Wagner and, 25, 121, 153, 228, 258
Aleichem, Sholem, 179
Almog, Yael, 15
antisemitism, 28, 47, 77; Arendt on, 187n39, 205; Mahler and, 231, 235; Roth on, 185–86; Schoenberg and, 123–24. *See also* Wagner, Richard: Judaism and
Arendt, Hannah, 33, 170–71, 176, 186–89, 202, 255; on Heine, 226–28; on Jewish exceptionality, 219–23. *See also under* antisemitism; superfluousness
Aristotle, 22–23
Aschheim, Steven, 186n39, 219n31
assimilation, 33–34, 38, 44, 184, 188, 192, 203, 216–23, 240–41, 251, 255; other German terms for, 216, 217, 218, 234; quotation and, 232, 234–36, 255; in Zeisl, 205–6, 208, 223–27, 238–39, 242, 246. *See also* Jewish integration
Assmann, Jan, 120, 138, 139, 141n54, 142
Augustine, 141
Auserkorener and *Auserwälter* terms, 198n61

Bach, Johann Sebastian, 31, 79, 86–87, 90, 93–110, 116, 239, 244, 257

Bauman, Zygmunt, 187, 218–19, 250–51
Beer-Hofmann, Richard, 27
Beethoven, Ludwig van, 222, 226, 239
Ben-Haim, Paul: background of, 76–77; Borchardt and, 78–79, 108–9, 114; *Joram*, 4, 7, 30, 31, 76–81, 90, 98, 108–18, 256–57
Ben-Horin, Michal, 21n39
Benjamin, Walter, 7, 18, 27, 28, 52, 134, 231, 236n79, 258; on allegory, 231–32; on art criticism, 80–81, 82n9, 154; on Borchardt, 50; on translation, 29–30, 57, 80, 81; on *Trauerspiel*, 31, 79–80, 82–90, 104, 117, 231–32
Bible, German translations and interpretations of, 3–4, 8–9, 11–17, 27–31, 44, 70–75, 182–83, 199; Book of Job in, 35, 65, 180, 182, 200, 238; Decalogue in, 140, 142; modern "return to the Bible," 182, 248–51. *See also* Borchardt, Rudolf; Buber, Martin; law; Luther, Martin; representation (and image making)
Blumenberg, Hans, 4n3, 142
Bodmer, Martin, 60
Boes, Tobias, 139n49
Borchardt, Rudolf: background and views of, 38–39, 41–42, 44–49, 58–59, 77; Creative Restoration project of, 30, 39–40, 53–54, 57, 71, 75, 256; *Das Buch Joram*, 4, 16–17, 30–31, 35–48, 53–59, 65–68, 74–75, 76, 77–78, 108, 118, 256; *Der Deutsche in der Landschaft*, 50; *Jugendgedichte*, 115; translations by, 39, 54–60, 81
Boulez, Pierre, 122n7
Brecht, Bertolt, 27
Britt, Brian, 72n86
Buber, Martin: Bible translation by (with Franz Rosenzweig), 16, 27, 31, 59–65, 68–75, 256; Borchardt and, 46–47, 69, 73
Büchner, Georg, 210, 233

Bürger, Peter, 231–32, 233
Butt, John, 101–2

Castelnuovo-Tedesco, Mario, 207
Chamberlain, Houston Stewart, 28
Christianity, 13, 14, 19, 29, 42, 45, 83, 136–37, 140–41
Cole, Malcolm, 208, 212
collective artwork, 6–7, 23, 25, 121–22, 153
"complete" artwork concept, 20, 24, 36, 30, 84–85, 117
counterpoint, discourse on, 239–42
Cube, Johann, 182

Dante Alighieri, Borchardt's translation of, 39, 40, 54–60
Dehmel, Richard, 210
Deleuze, Gilles: and Félix Guattari, 252–54
de Man, Paul, 149, 158
democracy and representation: critiques of, 126–30
Derrida, Jacques, 136, 148–49, 235
Dewitz, Hans-Georg, 57n56
diaspora, 5, 48–49, 254
Dohm, Christian Wilhelm von, 136
Droysen, Johann Gustav, 94

Eisler, Hanns, 27, 91, 207, 236, 236
Enlightenment values, 11, 12, 14, 134, 183, 221; Judaism and, 13, 136–37, 180–81, 219

Feuchtwanger, Lion, 27
Forkel, J. N., 244
Forst-Battaglia, Otto, 174
Franzos, Karl Emil, 179
Freud, Sigmund, 32, 123, 137, 142; *Moses and Monotheism*, 138–39, 140; *Totem and Taboo*, 149
Freytag, Gustav, 170

Gellen, Kata, 195n58, 198n61
German and Jewish difference, 1–4, 6–7, 14–17, 22, 27–28, 34, 74, 164–65, 168–69, 217, 248–52,

258–59; Borchardt on, 31, 39, 51, 256; Freud on, 139; Heine on, 7–11, 34; law and, 136–38; oratorios and, 95–98, 117; in Roth, 183, 202–3, in Zeisl, 204, 216
"German Jewish identity" term, 1–2, 5, 32, 34
Goetschel, Willi, 7, 10n15
Goethe, Johann Wolfgang von, 210, 222, 227
Goll, Yvan, 180
Greaney, Patrick, 232
"great artwork" concept, 3, 4, 24, 121, 153, 258. *See also* Wagner, Richard, *Gesamtkunstwerk*
Greek tragedy, 6, 17–23, 25, 82–83, 88–90, 93, 121
Grynäus, Simon, 182

Haas, Willy, 47–50, 52–53
HaCohen, Ruth, 90, 95, 98, 100
Handel, George Frederic, 91, 93, 95, 96
Haskalah movement, 248–49
Hecht, Georg, 46
Hegel, Georg Wilhelm Friedrich, 7, 8n10, 9–11, 24, 28, 136–37, 252; on Greek tragedy, 18–19, 20, 22, 142
Heine, Heinrich, 7–11, 15, 34, 226–29
Herder, Johann Gottfried, 13–14, 16, 61–63, 72, 221
Hess, Jonathan, 12–15
heterogeneity, 32, 34, 129, 130, 158, 168, 255–56
Hiob (novel). *See* Roth, Joseph
Hiob (opera). *See* Zeisl, Eric
Hirshberg, Jehoash, 78n5
Historie (Lutheran music form), 92
Hitler, Adolf, 25n47, 126
Hobbes, Thomas, 32, 129, 131, 152–53, 159
Hofmann, Michael, 169–70, 178n21
Hofmiller, Josef, 53
Holl, Ute, 143–44
homogeneity, 12, 24, 33, 129, 130, 153, 164, 168, 184, 219, 242, 255–56
Hume, David, 181

idealist philosophy, 7, 9, 17, 18, 19, 28, 136, 244
Ilany, Ofri, 13–14

Jewish difference. *See* German and Jewish difference
Jewish exceptionality, 205, 218–23, 225
Jewish integration, 13, 21, 33–34, 136, 241; in Roth, 169, 171, 186, 188, 191–92, 201–3; in Zeisl, 205. *See also* assimilation; *Ostjuden*
Jewishness and music, 4–6, 211–12, 240–41, 259
"Jewish question," 4n3, 45, 46, 191
Jabotinsky, Vladimir Ze'ev, 126

Kafka, Hans, 207–8, 247
Kafka, Franz, 136, 252–53
Kant, Immanuel, 7, 136, 227n50
Kauder, Hugo, 206
Kerman, Joseph, 247
Kesten, Hermann, 172
Kita, Caroline A., 27n54, 259
Klopstock, Friedrich Gottlieb, 92
Korngold, Erich Wolfgang, 207, 236
Kracauer, Siegfried, 27, 70–75
Kraft, Walter, 46, 47
Kraus, Karl, 245
Kronfeld, Chana, 253–54, 257
Kulturnation concept, 36, 75

Lacoue-Labarthe, Philippe, 23–24, 26, 142, 153–55, 156, 164, 166, 258
law, 130–41, 145, 147–53, 158, 160, 161; Mosaic law, 16, 32, 123, 125, 131, 136–41, 150, 152, 158, 164–65. *See also* representation
Lazaroms, Ilsa Josepha, 179n24
Leonard, Miriam, 18
Lessing, Gotthold Ephraim, 181–82
Lessing, Theodor, 47
Loos, Adolf, 245
Löwith, Karl, 4n3
Lukács, Georg, 201

Luther, Martin, 8–9, 11, 16, 37n6, 62–63, 73, 83–84; Borchardt and, 30–31, 35–41, 44, 53–56, 58, 59–60, 63, 65, 68, 88n24, 256; Krakauer on, 72; Nietzsche and, 95
Lutheranism, 82, 83–84, 90, 117

Mahler, Gustav, 33, 205–6, 228–31, 234–37, 241, 242–43
Mahler-Werfel, Alma, 207
Maimonides, 142
Mann, Thomas, 27, 32, 123, 128, 139–40, 149–50
Marx, Joseph, 206
Mendelssohn, Felix, 94, 96–97
Mendelssohn, Moses, 14–15, 68n78, 137, 221
Michaelis, Johann David, 13, 15, 136, 137
Mattheson, Johann, 91n32
Meyrink, Gustav, 210
Michaud, Eric, 25
Milhaud, Darius, 207
"minor literature" concept, 252–54
Mitleid (sympathy), 95, 181–83
modern Hebrew literature, 249
modernism, 3–4, 120, 206, 216, 256; Benjamin and, 82–83; Bible and, 15–16, 29; canon and, 257–58; critique of representation and, 129–30; Jewish difference and, 28; Mahler and, 231; "modern" and, 26–27; montage, 231, 232; novel and, 32, 200–203; opera and, 25; Schoenberg and, 120, 239; Vienna and, 244–45
modernity, 3–7, 12, 15, 18, 153, 257–58; assimilation and, 218–19; Bauman on, 250–51; Benjamin and, 88, 117; Bible and, 248–49; Borchardt and, 53–54, 63, 75; Heine on, 9–11; Krakauer on, 70; nation-state model and, 187; oratorio genre and, 82, 86, 90, 116–17, 257
Morgenstern, Christian, 210
Morris, Leslie, 251–52, 258n21
"Mosaic Distinction," 138, 165–66

Moses und Aron (film version), 142
Müller-Sievers, Helmut, 232–33

nation-state system, 169, 170–71, 176–77, 183–91, 201–2, 254; Arendt on, 219–21
New Objectivity movement, 173, 177
Nietzsche, Friedrich, 18, 21, 23, 88–89, 102n60; Wagner and, 89n26, 94–95, 145n65; Zeisl and, 210
Nordau, Max, 245

opera: Benjamin on, 104; history and characteristics of, 6, 20–21, 23, 88–90, 92, 106–7, 142, 164; Nietzsche on, 89, 94; *Querelle des Bouffons* and, 145n65
oratorio: history and characteristics of, 7, 31, 78–80, 82, 86, 90–98, 104, 116–18, 257
organicism, 20, 22, 121, 153, 177, 200–201, 215–16, 230, 235–36, 243–47
Orientalism and Judaism, 3, 13, 40, 41, 44, 48, 63, 125, 240–41
Ostjuden (Eastern Jews), 169, 171, 183, 184, 185–86, 189–91, 195, 195, 202–3, 217, 223, 235, 241

Painter, Karen, 237, 239–40
Paul (apostle), 140–41
Peretz, Isaac Leib, 179
Picander (Christian Friedrich Henrici), 100–101, 105
Plato, 39, 57, 131

quotational practices, 33–34, 205, 228–36. *See also under* Zeisl, Eric

Raabe, Wilhelm, 170
Racine, Jean, 93
Rand, Florens Christian, 83
Reger, Max, 239
Reformation, 8, 79–80; chorales and, 95; modernity and, 104, 257; theater and, 82–88

representation (and image-making), 4–5, 32, 100, 120, 122, 123, 127, 129–30, 145, 147, 152, 158–64, 168, 253, 255, 259; biblical ban against, 119–20, 139, 141
Rosenzweig, Franz, 27, 61, 63, 72, 83, 218n26. *See also under* Buber, Martin
Rilke, Rainer Maria, 210
Roth, Joseph, 27, 167, 169–78; *Die Büste des Kaisers*, 173–75; *Hiob*, 4, 17, 30, 32–33, 167–69, 177–83, 192–203, 208, 215, 225, 238, 246–47, 254; *Juden auf Wanderschaft*, 183–86, 189–92, 225–26, 246–47; *Legende vom heiligen Trinker*, 177–78, 212; other novels, 171–73, 179, 183; Zeisl and, 204, 207–8, 212, 223. *See also Ostjuden*; *and under* superfluousness
Rousseau, Jean-Jacques, 32, 88, 129, 145, 147–48, 149, 152, 159, 161, 162

Sachs, Nelly, 180
Second Viennese School, 212, 236
Seidman, Naomi, 29, 72–73
Sellars, Peter, 99–100
Seter, Ronit, 77
Schenker, Heinrich, 245–46, 247
Schlegel, August, 40, 48
Schlegel, Friedrich, 48
Schiller, Friedrich, 21, 226
Schmitt, Carl, 4n3, 32, 127–30, 164, 168
Schoenberg, Arnold, 7, 27, 28, 32, 171, 236, 246; *Der biblische Weg*, 125; counterpoint in, 237, 239, 241; on democracy, 126–30, 147; *Gurre-Lieder*, 144; *Die Jakobsleiter*, 134; Jewish concerns of, 123–26, 168; on Mahler, 229–30; *Moses und Aaron*, 4, 6–7, 16, 25, 30, 31–32, 119–23, 125, 129–32, 135, 137–38, 141–66, 168, 255, 258; *Pierrot lunaire*, 144; *Sprechstimme* in, 144–46, 163; twelve-tone method of, 16, 32, 122, 123, 132–35, 142–43, 246; writings, 132–33, 135, 168; Zeisl and, 207, 208, 212. *See also* Adorno, Theodor A.; law: Mosaic law
Schoenberg, Gertrud, 157
Scholem, Gershom, 27, 36, 47, 71, 74, 220n34
Schriftsprache (literary language): and *Schrifttum* (literature), 37n6, 56, 63–64, 69, 73
Schütz, Heinrich, 93
Shaked, Gershon, 249, 251
Shakespeare, William, 40, 82
Shavit, Yaacov: and Mordechai Eran, 248
Sheehan, Jonathan, 12
Shellleg, Assaf, 249, 250, 251
"shtetl literature," 179
Smith, Adam, 181
Smither, Howard, 91
Solie, Ruth A., 247
Sophocles, 19
sovereignty: Derrida on, 235
Spector, Scott, 1, 217
Steinberg, Michael, 4–6, 252, 259
Steiner, George, 18
Stern, Guy, 180
Stöhr, Richard, 206
Stravinsky, Igor, 207
superfluousness: aesthetic, 245–46; in Arendt, 33, 170, 186, 189, 223; in Roth, 33, 169–71, 186, 189, 191, 197, 199–203, 205, 254; in Zeisel, 33, 164, 204–5, 206, 216, 225–26, 243
Swinburne, Algernon Charles, 39
Szondi, Peter, 18–19

Taubes, Jacob, 32, 123, 128n17, 137–38, 140–41
Trauerspiel. *See under* Benjamin, Walter

universalism, 7, 15, 17, 18, 19, 27, 179–80, 182–83, 219
"unsettling" term, 254, 258–59

Volkov, Shulamit, 218, 219

Wagner, Richard, 3, 6–7, 17–25, 31–32, 71, 81–82, 88, 94–95, 145, 153, 164, 166, 228, 244; *Gesamtkunstwerk* concept of, 3, 20, 24, 30, 81, 117, 122, 257; *Geschichtsphilosophie* and, 25; Greek tragedy and, 19–22; Judaism and, 2, 19–23, 28, 32, 33, 222–23, 235, 257; sacred claim of, 121; Zeisl and, 212
Weber, Max, 4n3
Weber, Samuel, 83, 84, 86, 152
Weill, Kurt, 27
Weininger, Otto, 170–71, 241n92
Werfel, Franz, 27
Wetters, Kirk, 154n88

Wilamowitz-Moellendorff, Ulrich von, 58
Wolfskehl, Karl, 180

Yerushalmi, Yosef Hayim, 28n56, 139n47, 142n55
Yiddish, 179, 226

Zeisl, Eric: background of, 204, 206–7, 228; counterpoint in, 237–38, 242–43; *Hiob*, 4, 17, 25, 32–33, 167–70, 204–16, 223–25, 236–39, 242–43, 246–47, 255; musical quotation in, 33, 205–6, 214–16, 228, 231, 236, 243; other compositions by, 210, 212–13
Zionism, 124, 126, 168, 189–91, 249, 250
Zweig, Stefan, 27, 222

www.ingramcontent.com/pod-product-compliance
Lightning Source LLC
Chambersburg PA
CBHW030821230426
43667CB00008B/1320